From the Moment We Met:
The Astrology of Adult Relationships

Relationship astrology – synastry – is not just an exploration of compatibility and possibility; it calls us to honour the mystery and soul of our attachments – not for what we want them to be, but for how they truly are. *From the Moment We Met* offers a guide through the labyrinth of astrological symbols and images towards a clearer understanding and acceptance of your adult relationships.

The Family Legacy:
Astrological Imprints on Life, Love & Relationships

Images of the soul of a family are encoded into the symbols of the horoscope, therefore each individual's natal horoscope is systemic – its multidimensional symbols revealing the family system through time. *The Family Legacy* invites you to deepen your understanding of your place in the family portrait by participating with the evocative symbols embedded in your horoscope.

Vocation:
The Astrology of Career, Creativity and Calling

Your vocation is soulful; a deeply felt longing to be of service, to follow your passion and to live a meaningful life. Astrology is an ideal career counsellor, as it maps out the paths and patterns of your vocation. Using astrological symbols and images, *Vocation: the Astrology of Career, Creativity and Calling* is your guide to participating in a more fulfilling career and lifestyle.

Soul, Symbol and Imagination:
The Artistry of Astrology

Astrology is a soulful and evocative tradition that engages us in both rational and imaginal ways of knowing. Each horoscope is an invitation to consider the gods that live through us and the archetypal powers that pave our path through life. In *Soul, Symbol and Imagination*, Brian Clark shares his experiences of astrology as a profoundly therapeutic, divinatory and spiritual modality that has shaped his life.

ISBN: 978-0-9944880-8-4
Ebook: 978-1-903353-68-4

First edition published 2021 by Astro*Synthesis
PO Box 507
Launceston, Tasmania 7250
Australia
www.astrosynthesis.com.au

The author can be reached at: brian@astrosynthesis.com.au

Charts calculated using Solar Fire software
Cover Designer: Cat Keane
Proof-reader: Jane Struthers
Project Manager and Layout: Frank C. Clifford

Cover Image: The cover copies the 16th C fresco by Francesco de' Rossi
'Time as Prudence seizes Occasion by the hair', an allegorical image
that evokes the duality of time. Prudence as the embodiment of Time takes
hold of the forelock of Occasion, reminding us of the valuable and fleeting
interrelationship between temporal and soul time.

ASTROLOGICAL TIME

Cycles of the Soul:
Transits, Progressions and Returns

BRIAN CLARK

Astro*Synthesis

Acknowledgements

I am privileged to have been able to teach an ongoing developmental programme of astrology for over 35 years and shared in this astrological journey with so many students. Therefore, at the beginning I would like to express my deep appreciation to every student who has participated in our classes and seminars over these past four decades. And to the clients who have shared timely stories with me: thank you for contributing so beneficially to my understanding.

A heartfelt thank you to my mentors and colleagues who have so richly explored astrological time and motivated me to develop my own ideas and how I might present them. I fondly remember an inspirational seminar on Cycles with Alexander Ruperti in 1979 in New York City that changed the way I worked with the planets. We are blessed to have a richness of ideas and a source of wisdom amongst our astrological educators, past and present, who continue to inspire and guide us.

I would also like to express enormous appreciation to Star East Press, a division of Cite Publishing Ltd in Taipei, Taiwan who have been supportive of my work and instrumental in my writing books for students of astrology. A titanic thank you to Frank Clifford of Flare Publications in the UK whose encouragement and supervision has made the publication of my books in English possible. His support, along with Jane Struthers and Cat Keane, is deeply valued. And, as always, my heartfelt thanks to Mary Symes for her suggestions, help and red pen!

This book was completed as I was in the midst of celebrating my seventieth birthday with my dear family who have always supported my creativity. And as the book now goes into production, another solar cycle has passed and I enter my seventh Jupiter cycle and its gift of a new horizon of life.

Most importantly I thank you, the reader, for your support as well as your interest and involvement in this remarkable study of astrology.

Brian Clark, 2021

TABLE OF CONTENTS

TIME AND THE DIVINE

To everything there is a season,
and a time to every purpose under the heaven

Ecclesiastes 3:1

Phases of the Moon, the rising of Sirius, the setting of Venus, the conjunction of Jupiter and Saturn, eclipses: all heavenly timepieces that captured the imagination of our ancestors. For us here on Earth, time has always been ordered by heavenly spheres, first measured by the rotation from day to night, then chronicled by the Sun, the Moon and the planets. Time has been considered, conceived, created and charted by these planetary cycles that are intimately entwined with, and imagined as, the movements of the gods. Time has always been connected to the divine.

Telling astrological time, whether measured by lunar phases, the rising or setting of fixed stars or planetary conjunctions, is in effect divine; hence, a form of divination. Our word 'divination' conjures up many different implications, but its roots are lodged in the Latin, divinus, meaning 'of a god'. 'Divination' implies being inspired by a god, but was also used in connection with sky or heaven; therefore, the practice of astrology can essentially be considered a divinatory art. By the 14th century, 'divination' had come to commonly mean the act of foretelling the future by supernatural means.

In the early 17th century, Francis Bacon differentiated artificial from natural divination; the former was when a prediction was rationally constructed by 'signs and tokens', the latter was when a prediction arose from an internal power 'without the inducement of a sign'.[1] From our contemporary perspective, this suggests to me that there are both conscious and unconscious forces at work in divination. Although we might prefer divination to be one or the other, it is both. Its roots, like those of astrology, are embedded in the divine. But what does this mean in astrological practice?

As a divinatory art, the craft of astrology must deal with the unconscious. Divination for the modern-day astrologer is not only the intimate engagement with astrological symbols, but the willingness to participate in the fullness of their revelations. An astrological consultation journeys through the topography of archetypal divinities, and in this exploration the unconscious of both astrologer and client, the reader and listener, is stirred. Astrological time has its predictive 'signs and tokens', but it also encompasses the 'divine' voice that arises out of the unconscious inspired by the symbol.

Time, as we will explore, remains a mystery. Time is fluid, not fixed; paradoxical, not logical. Its earthly and divine duality is integral to the art of astrology. Being a *chronomantic* art, astrology is used to divine the nature of the times. *Chronomancy* is derived from the Greek *chronos* or 'time' and *mantic*, related to prophecy or divination. This is one of many words we use in English with the prefix *chrono* when referring to time. Unfortunately this prefix has come to suggest a linear or literal measure of time, as if time can be determined and prescribed. Later we will meet Father Time, christened as Chronos, the primordial god of time; but to begin our exploration, let's reflect on how astrology divines and tells time.

Astrology is astute at mapping time. Where it becomes problematic is when celestial time maps are portrayed in 'real' time, anchoring them sequentially rather than qualitatively. In this way Chronos, as the time lord, binds time to an ordered sequence. Astrology has a long association with prediction, but it becomes diminished when only perceived as a mechanistic time model. Forecasting success rests not just with techniques, but with the practitioner's mindful ability to participate with astrological symbols. Symbols are free to move through time to evoke feelings, memories, anticipation and impressions that breach linear time. Therefore, when forecasts are located in chronological time, the complexity of time is minimized, eclipsing the innate wisdom of divination that spontaneously arises from the respectful examination of astrological symbols. To concretize a symbol in the literal world is to render it lifeless and exhaust its possibilities. It no longer is able to divine, as its voice has been silenced. Working with time, whether past, present or future, our task is to constantly honour the mystery of astrological symbols that illustrate time's presence.

Each planetary movement is a metaphor for time, not just in its measurement but in its quality. The planets' continuous movement reflects the constancy of change; nothing remains fixed, yet, as astrologers we discover order and coherence in this impermanence. When planetary cycles align with archetypal images, we better understand time as a process: something happens that is not sequential, specific or permanent. Planetary divinities remind us that temporal reality is not simply a linear succession of events, but is complex and often beyond our comprehension, illuminated through participation with the divinity or, in modern terms, the unconscious.

Our reliance upon clocks to measure time maintains the illusion that time is tangible. Hourly appointments, daily rituals, monthly rent, yearly tax returns and 25-year mortgages define the modern-day parameters of our relationship with time. Because it can be defined and divided, time has become a commodity.[2] As a product it can be quantified and sold. We even have a price on what an hour of our time is worth; no wonder it is difficult to see time as something other than concrete or fixed. Time has become some-thing, when ironically it does not really exist in this way. Perhaps what exists is a complex of rules that govern time, but time itself is imperceptible. Paradoxically, even though time is invisible, it is a felt experience, fuelled by emotions.

When we liberate time from its chronological trajectory and consider its other dimensions, time becomes metaphysical. A common occurrence in crisis or under duress is the experience of a time warp: seconds feel like hours, the past may be re-lived or the future threatens the present. While the nature of time is best left to the metaphysicians and quantum physicians to probe, astrologers need to consider time and the soul to enhance participation in the fullness of the moment for ourselves and our clients. These questions about time and astrology are at the heart of this book.

Our astrological tradition has had a rich legacy of books devoted to time and timing. Therefore it will be difficult not to traverse similar territory to other authors; however, I have tried as much as possible to offer my own experience and understanding gleaned from my own practice. Many other books and Internet sites offer excellent interpretations, so I have focused more on working with, rather than interpreting, time. In my early days as an astrologer,

Robert Hand released *Planets in Transit* which soon became known as the bible to my generation of astrologers. For the first time we had a written forecast of nearly every possible transit. One Jupiter cycle later, Howard Sasportas released *The Gods of Change*, which profoundly spoke of ways to envision working with the transits of the outer planets. Since then a treasure trove of Hellenistic, Arabic, Medieval, Vedic and other time techniques have been rediscovered and brought into modern practice. Today we have a wealth of choice about the nature of time from all schools of astrological thought.

This book has been crafted out of my own consulting and educational practice. As part of our twelve-unit *Astro*Synthesis* programme, three units were devoted to Time. Unit 6 is *Cycles of Life*, Unit 8 is *Times of Life* while Unit 11 is *Cycles, Passages and Returns*. As part of the programme, workbooks and booklets on cycles, transits, secondary progressions, solar returns, planetary pairs, etc., were created and it is these sources that are the foundation stones for this book.[3] In a way I also consider this as a work in progress as I am constantly learning about astrological time through my ongoing practice and reading. But this is the nature of astrological work – it is a lifetime study and one that is ever expanding.

Time is precious. Engaging with astrology supports this axiom, as it encourages us to be more aware and to actively participate with time. It invites us to be in time with the timeless seasons of the soul.

Throughout the book I refer to soul and soul time. While there is no easy way to convey what I am suggesting by 'soul', in essence I am referring to seeing through the literal world to a more meaningful and creative way of being. I use 'soul' to engage us in the ambiguity and paradox of life experience and the mystery of time. In a world awash with facts and advice, soul returns us to our own intelligence. Horoscope symbols stimulate contemplation on living in time and inspire revelations from our inner world, our feelings and spiritual character. It is as if horoscope symbols animate time, permitting the past, the present and the future to be fluid and timeless. When I refer to soul, I am referencing the uncertainty and fragility of our outer world and invoking the mystery and depth of our inner wisdom through the symbols of astrological time. Using the word 'soul' references the mysteries of time and our fallibility to determine it.

In the first half of 2020, as the final edits were being made to the manuscript, we collectively experienced the 'uncertainty and fragility of our outer world' as the Covid-19 pandemic struck. Astrologically, the heavens illustrated the tension of the times in many ways, most notably through the social and outer planetary conjunctions. However, for us 'under the heaven', we were called not only to see the time, but to participate in its purpose.

The tables in this book refer to approximate age ranges. Some tables will include the age variants for all generations. Only Chiron and Pluto will have key ages that vary depending on their natal sign position.

PART I

TIME

Mysteries and Metaphors

You got to deep-six your wristwatch,
you got to try and understand
The time it seems to capture
is just the movement of its hands.[4]

'Walk in the Sun', The Grateful Dead

– INTRODUCTION –
THE ENIGMA OF TIME

In our third millennium CE we can measure the passing of time within milliseconds, devise precise calendars for the future and accurately date archaeological findings, yet time still remains a great mystery, inaccessible to our senses. We cannot touch, taste, see, smell or hear time; we can wonder and think about time, but it defies our sensibilities. Contemplating time in a way is a meditation on life, a record of having existed. Whether mystic or pragmatic, time is unfathomable.

An antidote to the randomness of time is the starry heavens. Stepping outside on a cloudless night, away from city lights, and looking up in the starlit darkness at the countless stars reminds us that we are overshadowed by something much larger, more infinite, timeless and certainly more intelligent. The night sky returns us to the majesty of the divine and its mysteries. Night time is different from day time and it is this shift from night to day that always brings the passage of time to mind.

Astrology sees through chronological time into mythic time, offering images and symbols to help us participate in time. The sky differentiates the passing of time through its ever-changing cycles. Long before we knew the reasons, the swelling and shrinking phases of the Moon, the disappearance and reappearance of Venus and the rising of Sirius were used as almanacs. A star's rising or setting measured successive time periods while planetary returns and conjunctions determined distinct epochs. Astrology's starry heavens embrace qualities of time through the sanctity of the planets' symmetrical cycles and the eternality of their returns, transporting us back and forth through time, mapping personal and collective moments. Heaven's time is endless and eternal: timeless, like the divine.

The heavens describe many stories of time through mythological epics, philosophical discourses, scientific dissertations and astrological symbols. Symbols are not fixed, but free to move between the past and future. Astrological symbols disregard linear time – through them we can return to a time past or consider future time while still being in the present. Being multi-dimensional, astrological symbols reveal both literal and soul time.

Time and Soul

Astrology images time through planetary transitions and cycles. Although planets are physical and have time-measured orbits and patterns, in astrological practice their movements are symbolic. This allows them to become archetypal symbols, existing outside the bounds of chronological time; therefore their character is not subject to ageing nor inhibited by clock time. Astrological time is trans-temporal as it can move freely between the archaic past and the expectant future through the imaginative medium of planetary cycles. The planetary cycle that is happening today has happened before and will again; hence when the present is linked with the past and the future, not causally or temporally, but imaginatively, then the soul is freed from its temporal patterning to glimpse its eternality. Viewed through the windows of the soul, time is like 'the moving image of eternity'.[5]

To an astronomer the planets are physical wonders, ageless icons in our miraculous solar system; to an astrologer the planets are also metaphors of life, archetypal symbols of reflection and revelation. As physical representations, planets mark out the passages of sequential time through their cycles around the Sun and with each other. As archetypal symbols, planets are not bound by physical laws or chronological time, but exist out of time and through time. Paradoxically, planetary symbols can reveal time unbound by the constraints of incarnation, while simultaneously referring to a calendar time period. When concerned with both the law and the wisdom of the planets, astrologers can skilfully move in and out of chronological time. Planetary symbols have two eyes: one looks to external events in real time while the other illuminates layers of the soul.

Astrological time links seemingly random events together through planetary symbols and cycles. Telling a story using astrological time is akin to a technique known as 'ring composition', which loops back and forward through time, utilized in oral traditions and epics.[6] Chronological time is suspended to gather together the narrative. Astrological time is connective, associating past events with current ones, even circling forward to anticipate future consequences. Ultimately, astrological time tells us about the mystery of the soul using present, past and future verbs.

Two Timing: Qualitative and Quantitative Time

Astrological timing is both quantitative and qualitative. Yet in both practice and theory, astrological timing is most commonly utilized quantitatively, fixing the planetary movement to an event in clock time, whether that is hours, days, weeks, months or years. In this way the astronomical image is literalized, disconnected from its poetic voice. Prediction becomes limited when planetary symbols and movements are explained and then projected onto future events or episodes. When time is fixed to actual events, astrological practitioners are coerced into anticipating future possibilities. When we are anticipating time, we are no longer participating in it. Pulled into linear time and objectivity, we lose access to the cycles and subjectivity of the subtle world that astrology reveals. When divination is severed from prediction the porous boundaries vital to subjective involvement are obscured by literality and objectivity.

From a quantitative point of view, astrological periods are measured by the time it takes for a planet to pass through a particular point in the heavens, whether that is a zodiac sign, a degree of the zodiac or an aspect to another planet. For instance, Pluto moves into Aquarius on 23 March 2023 for the first time since its discovery and will move back and forth across the zodiacal cusp of Capricorn and Aquarius three more times until on 19 November 2024 it enters Aquarius, where it stays for nearly two decades. Uranus ingresses into Gemini in 2025, and in 2026 Saturn and Neptune conjoin in the first degree of the zodiac at 0♈45. In 2025 Neptune wavers on the cusp between Pisces and Aries; finally it enters Aries in 2026 at the midpoint between Uranus and Pluto. Depending on an 'orb of influence',[7] we can time these planetary periods. Quantitative time compares these planetary positions with a natal chart to personalize the advance of time. But how we engage with this symbol of time is the key: do we interpret, divine or imagine time?

Qualitative timing is imaginative and symbolic, encouraging participation with the moment. It is not read in the context of a calendar, but is considered and reflective. Through imagination we make time for soul,[8] not by marking out time but by being in time. Astrology happens in the moment. The astrological alignment of both quantitative and qualitative time promotes soul-making by honouring the subjective symbols associated with 'real' time. We respect the signs of the cosmos by delineating planetary movements; then we value the symbol's meaning through imagination, participation and reflection.

When speaking to an astrology conference James Hillman suggested that by 'setting aside the literalistic attachment to time we might also be free of another dangerously compelling power in astrology: the temptation to predict'.[9] A refreshing thought. But 'setting aside the literalistic attachment to time', given astrology's deeply entrenched roots in the Ptolemaic model, is not a simple task in a world whose dominant mythology is scientism.[10]

Astrological tradition espouses the meaningfulness of time; yet its value is diminished when set amidst a literal and chronological rhetoric on time. Even 'quality time' often suggests an intentioned period of time, defined by human will for a measured outcome with little room for divine intervention. Similar to the wandering planets, astrological practice needs time and space for the soul to wander along its course until it reveals the significance of its symbols.[11] Astrological perception does not operate on a cause–effect spectrum, but considers the qualities intrinsic in the moment through the symbols of that moment.

Astrology and astrological practice are commonly denigrated by science, sceptics and systems, yet it is not astrology that is maligned, as most sceptics have not taken the time to actually become familiar with the tradition. What is degraded is its mystery and unknowing, its randomness and wanderings that inspire self-revelations. As astrologers we must struggle with our questions about time in a world smitten with explanations and evidence.

In astrological thinking each sign of the zodiac contains attributes and essences that characterize the mood of the time. For instance, when the Moon is in Scorpio, time has different features, qualities and properties to when it is in Gemini. As Pluto transits through Capricorn, the collective experience of time is characteristically different from when it is in Aquarius. While planetary archetypes contribute to the timing of the moment, it is the imaginative skill of the astrologer that tells the condition of time. Active imagination and reflection are fundamental to releasing the symbol from its chronological restraints and limited range of expression.

Participation is a subjective practice, a way of experiencing the non-linear and non-rational world through instinct and intuition, not concepts or theories. It is an anthropologic idea inspired by animistic cultures where nature was imbued with soul and unseen forces animated the universe. A characteristic of participation fuses the observer and the observed together, resulting in feelings of unity or oneness. Astrology is also animistic, as astrologers perceive the planets as subjective, respecting the unseen forces that give life to the universe. But when caught in the grooves of linear time, celestial timing can be explanations of truthful facts, rather than participation with the eternality of time. We become stuck in delineating what is happening rather than what is becoming.

The Passing of Time

Time does not exist in the same way as physical objects; nor do we have a sensory perception of time. Time is cerebrally constructed; for human beings time is mainly experienced through movement and change. We are acutely aware of time because of ageing and our ability for episodic recall, to remember past events, time and time again. A collection of incidents and a network of events echoes past time.

In the natural world, rhythms of time are instinctual. Living organisms have various inbuilt clocks such as molecular, neuronal, chemical and hormonal.[12] Animals do not perceive time in the same way as us; it is instinctual and momentary.[13] Without the complexity needed for time perception or episodic memory, animals live in the natural world.

If we were immortal would we feel time? Ageing or the passing of time does not seem to be an immortal concern. Chronos will always be reliably old; Hermes will always be mischievously young; Artemis, lithe and fit; and Aphrodite always sexually active. In a way each immortal deity is aligned with certain passages of time when their presence is more psychologically and emotionally evident. It is as if they are fixed in a phase in time, which is a way of thinking built into the tradition of astrology. Humans live in a temporal world, bound by the passing of time, unlike animals or gods who exist in a relatively time-free zone. At a crossroads or meaningful moment in our lives, another time is experienced. Time, as we habitually know it, is not always bound by corporeal parameters – it is the unbound time of which poets and mystics speak.

One of the ways time is deeply felt by humans is through ageing. Ageing confirms our mortality; yet, at times, we can also be astonished by momentary feelings of immortality. The ancient Greeks wisely differentiated between ageing and immortality through the myth of Tithonus, one of the sons of the Trojan king Laomedon, whom 'cruel immortality consumes'.[14]

Eos, the goddess of dawn, fell wildly in love with the youthful beauty of Tithonus. Eos, sister of the Sun god Helios and Moon goddess Selene, was mother of the stars and winds. Aphrodite cursed Eos for seducing her lover Ares. This meant Eos continually fell in love with the attractive, yet ephemeral, energy of youth: the seductive, translucent light that heralds the fullness of day, yet is short-lived. Like dawn, youthful beauty is fleeting. Eos fell in love with the Trojan prince Tithonus and carried him away to her home in the Far East where they dwelt on the horizon that divides night from day.

Not wanting her love to ever end, Eos petitioned Zeus to make her lover immortal. Zeus granted her appeal, but Eos failed to specify that Tithonus must remain eternally youthful. The goddess did not differentiate between ageing and immortality. As the years passed, immortal Tithonus grew older, greyer, stooped and demented. While the original myth ended with Eos locking Tithonus away from sight, a later addition suggested Eos turned him into a cicada so she could eternally hear his voice. The myth so eloquently contrasts human and immortal time, a helpful distinction for discriminating between mortal and divine time and between growing old and being spiritual.

Does time really slip away, as Eos tried to prevent, or does it just rearrange itself? From an ageing point of view we might find it difficult to do what we once did, but what we can no longer do still exists in another time. While I may no longer be able to do what I did as a nine-year old, an experience of this time exists. I can remember and re-collect that image of this adventurous young boy, who still wants me to take him on yet another escapade. Memory is a storehouse of time, not just of our own past experiences but of those of the ancestors and the ancients.

Time and Memory

The Greeks knew of this visceral memory, personifying her as one of the twelve Titans. Her name was Mnemosyne, mother to the nine Muses. She embodies feeling memory, not linear or cognitive, but instinctual, stored in the aches and pains of the body, recalled through images, symbols, reactions, impulses, impressions and gut feelings. She is neither linear nor rational. Mnemosyne does not learn by repeating dates and statistics, but re-members through dreams and feeling responses, re-collecting the soul's experience before cognitive impressions set in.

Mnemosyne's voice is poetic; her memoirs are stored in the fragments of a song, a myth, an epic story or fairy tale.[15] Hermes remembers the details and features of the moment while Mnemosyne recalls its quality and mood. In the Homeric Hymn to Hermes, the god's first honour is to Mnemosyne,[16] an apt archetypal pairing that reminds us of subjective and objective memory. Both Hermes and Mnemosyne are present at any moment in time. When we reach a turning point or are in a dynamic transition, the memory of times past arises. At crossroads we encounter all the other times of life that are resonant with this present. Therefore time 'is not only perceived, imagined and conceived, but remembered as well.'[17] We inhabit a remembered present.

Memory is the seamstress of time, embroidering fragments of ourselves, threading processes and experiences of our past together, whether distant or near, stitching up the splits. She stores the strands of feeling until they can be entwined with our identity. Mnemosyne invites us to be in time, to muse on who we are through time so we can be at ease with ourselves.

Time is also entwined with events. While we can time an event and record its circumstances, there are many subjective factors in any particular time: moods, feelings, fantasies, reactions, senses, expectations, hopes, desires and reminiscences. Time is not free from past sorrows or future wishes. The present is punctuated with recollected time and future aspirations; therefore it is rarely released from its past, nor free of its future. We not only inhabit a remembered present, but also an expectant future.

What is it about this particular time that is different from any other time? Each minute is unlike the next, as each moment of time shapes a different pattern in the cosmos. The passing of time is characterized by the ever-changing arrangements in the universe. This is the nature of astrology: it uses the momentary arrangements of the cosmos to give meaning to the times that we are passing through. Astrology is a powerful paradigm of time, as it charts each unique moment of time as a reflection of planetary arrangements. Each horoscope is configured according to the pattern of the cosmos as we know it at that moment at this place. While the time recorded by astrological measures may be a literal date, it is also fictional, as it tells a story about this moment. Outer events are bound by literal time; soul time is unbound by material constraints. Like the heavens themselves, the astrological clock reveals an expansive time.

Horoscopic Time
The horoscope is the documentation of this causal temporal beginning, based on the first breath of life, the symbolic moment that separates us from the symbiosis with the biological mother and mythological Great Mother. This is the defining moment for the individual horoscope; the blueprint becomes the archetypal map for the human journey of the soul. It is fixed, unchanging, yet is constantly responsive to and shaped by the punctures of time. The four angles of the horoscope give rise to a four-dimensional authenticity that contains our multi-dimensional experience of time. The birth moment marks this crossroads when the soul incarnates, no longer suspended between worlds but locked onto the mortal grid. As we take our first breath, an independent human life begins.

The moment of birth marks the entry of the soul into temporal time. There will be other significant and crucial times within the lifespan, but the first breath symbolizes the soulful animation of the mortal body which is subject to ageing and temporality. Astrological doctrine recognizes this as the defining moment of the natal horoscope. Each moment, every event or critical time after birth will have its own horoscope, but these will be secondary to the primary birth chart. These times will exert their unique influences, shape the emerging archetypal responses and even alter the life path, but astrological tradition grounds the authenticity of the soul's response in the moment of birth. As a result of this fixed time, astrologers are susceptible to becoming caught up in the constraints of literal timing.[18]

While astrological techniques allow us to consider the horoscope through time, essentially the horoscope does not change over time. It remains the same. An exercise I do with students is to have them make three photocopies of their natal horoscope. The first copy we label 'the past'; this is the chart that contains what has happened to them, reflects who they were, how they developed, where they have been and also is the chart that is consulted for reflection and meaning as to the why of these occurrences. The second chart is tagged 'the present' and points towards current circumstances, while the third chart is marked 'the future' and signifies what lies ahead.

The symbols in all three charts are the same: the angles, the planetary houses, signs and aspects. An astrologer can apply past, current or future transits and progressions to the chart to place it in a context of time, but ultimately the natal horoscope is timeless, and although the symbols move in and out and through time, they remain constant. As consciousness develops and our awareness deepens, the astrological symbols become ensouled; therefore our relationship to them becomes more coherent through time. While all three horoscopes are the same, awareness of the archetypes in the present encourages a more collaborative participation with the planetary arrangements in the future and a more reflective engagement with them in the past.

All time is contained in each horoscope and the movement of time that is reflected through planetary cycles, returns, progressions and transitions confront and encourage us to return to who we are through ensouling these symbols.

1

COSMOLOGICAL TIME
Justice, Peace, Order

Inherent in the astrological discourse is a natural treatise on time centred on observable and measurable planetary periods that are cosmetic in their order and beauty. The discipline of astrology is horological, a study of time, and each horoscope is a testament to its mystery. A horoscope ensouls time, inviting us to imagine and animate it with the spirit of the moment. 'Horoscope' is derived from the Greek *hora*, meaning 'hour' and *skopein*, meaning 'to look at'; therefore a horoscope is a view of time. Mythologically, *hora* refers to the Horai, the trinity of goddesses whose collective name refers to the seasons and the eternally ordered round of time. Individually, the Horai were known as Dike, Eirene and Eunomia, who embodied the values of justice, peace and order respectively. They hold the imaginative, feminine and cyclical threads of time.

Together, the Horai personified the hours, the dance of the seasons and the passing of time. As seasonal goddesses the Horai oversaw the turning of the heavenly wheel, which determines the natural movements of time. Being daughters of two orderly gods, Zeus and Themis,[19] the natural impulses towards organizing time were embedded in their parentage. Each horoscope and horary chart invokes these early goddesses, who were custodians of justice (Dike), peace (Eirene) and order (Eunomia), virtues that underscore time. Astrological seasons are enriched by these qualities and as astrologers we find justice, peace and order underscoring each transit, progression and return.

The Horai were also sisters to another trinity of goddesses known as the Moirai, or the Fates. As weavers of time each sister had a particular role: Clotho spun the thread, Lachesis measured its length and Atropos cut the cord. The length of the woven cord not only epitomized the lifespan but its severance from the spool marked the seminal moment of birth. Fittingly, time and fate are sisters in Greek mythology, enmeshed in our collective and personal cosmogonies, our personal cosmogony being the horoscope. Both the Horai and the Moirai were imagined as apportioning time through their participation with nature and the heavens. This measure of time was metaphorical, part of a greater and more mysterious process that involved our relationship with the gods.

The Mythic Language of Time

There are many ways of thinking about time. The ancient Greeks knew *chronos* as the unyielding passage of time. Like the eponymous Titan who devoured his children, time was seen to consume all things.[20] Images of the passing of time, such as the hourglass and crutches, became linked with Chronos. Being an early agricultural god, his symbol was also the sickle, associated with power and prosperity and the cutting down of time. Ironically, Chronos presided over a Golden Age, an era when man lived in peace and prosperity with the gods, and 'miserable age rested not on them'.[21] While this paradox of time is unsettling from a rational point of view, the soul is not constrained by the inconsistencies of human perception. In context of the soul, time is eternal.

Once upon a time Chronos was benevolent, but now his time is all-consuming. Ambivalence towards Chronos underpins the astrological archetype of Saturn. Chronos time enters our vocabulary through words that represent the passing and recording of time, and include *chronological* or the arrangement of recorded time; *chronicle*, a detailed account of events arranged sequentially; and *chronometer*, an instrument that measures time. But perhaps the word that reminds us most of the troubling relentlessness of time is *chronic*, a mnemonic for the inevitability of temporal decay. Chronos remains a powerful symbol of time embedded in our language, and his surrogate Saturn remains one of astrology's great chronocrators. As a god of time, astrological Saturn inherits the problematic dilemma of the incarnated soul in chronological time.

The Greeks knew another time, and that was *kairos*, which had a subjective, even supernatural quality. While *chronos* characterized linear and measurable time, *kairos* referred to a critical or appointed time - the 'right' moment. In early usage it was linked with opportunity or the moment when possibility penetrated the present. In ancient Greek terminology *kairos* referred to an opening, the critical moment to enter into and take advantage of that moment. *Kairos* is the mysterious process when a fissure between the worlds creates crucial and life-affirming opportunities. It is the rupturing and ripening of time.

In the Homeric Greek *kairos* was the 'penetrable opening' which may have originated with the archer who aimed at cracks in the armour to seize the right moment,[22] an early symbolic association between arrows and time.[23] The word was also associated with weaving, which is frequently connected to fate and time, conjuring up the sisterly alliance of the Horai and the Moirai. Eternal moments are woven into the web of fate and *kairos* time is when these eternal moments breach the surface of our everyday lives. In that instant the veil of time lifts and an opportune moment arises, akin to the idea that the time has come. *Kairos* could be likened to the birth moment, which opens us up to the vital opportunity of life, or other times when a fissure between the worlds materializes.

While *kairos* is the Greek image for 'opportunity', our English word is more associated with the Latin *opportunitas*, whose root is *portas*, from which we derive our word 'portal', meaning an opening or an entrance.[24] Opportunity constellates this sense of opening onto a new space. These two concepts of *chronos* and *kairos* embody the quantitative and qualitative nature of time, both its literal and fictional qualities. As astrologers we constantly work with both, investing the literal planetary cycles with meaning, using *chronos* timing to become aware of the *kairos* moments of life. It is not the mechanism of time that creates the opportunity, but the willingness to participate freely in the imagined possibilities that astrology aptly outlines.

Seeing through the realities to foresee the opportunities veiled in the moment is the interchange between *chronos* and *kairos*, the movement from predicament to possibility. As astrologers we are always moving between *chronos* and *kairos*, similar to our interchanges between fate and free will. Like free will, *kairos* invites us to seize the opportunities and be proactive. *Kairos* is more than a word: it is a symbol that characterizes timing and opportunities released by problems generated by the crisis. Chance is born out of the occasion of misfortune. *Kairos* implies that at times of tension and crisis, the 'right' time arises, but it is our choice and our determination that help us to seize the opportunity.

The ancient Roman god associated with thresholds, gateways and doorways was Janus, the patron of beginnings. As the spirit of the doorways his blessing was essential at the birth of each life, as well as the beginning of each day, month and year, as evoked each January. Janus had two faces, one that looked east to the rising Sun and the other west, to its setting. As a two-faced god of time he reminds us of the different attitudes towards time in eastern and western cultures, the objective and subjective nature of time, its measurable and mystical aspects, as well as the ancient Greek ideas of *chronos* and *kairos*. And as a god of time one face glimpses the past world; the other looks forward to anticipate the future.

By the later Hellenistic period the image of Aion had made his way into contemporary mystery cults. Immigrating from the East into Egypt he found his way into the writing of Plato and Aristotle, and developed into a Hellenistic deity connected with time. Our modern word 'aeon', which suggests an indefinitely long period of time, is his modern incarnation. As the god of eternity, Aion was depicted within an orb representing the zodiac or the eternal cycle of life. By Hellenistic times the ouroboric orb of the zodiac had enclosed infinity and become the perpetual symbol against which man measured time.

Astrological Time and Timing

As time is measured by the rotation and revolution of the Earth, it has its footing in the heavens. The starry heavens were the earliest timepiece, whether that was the rising or setting of the constellations, the lunar orbit or the synodic cycles of the planets.[25] Astrological time is cyclical, comprising the orbits of all the planets, not just Earth's. Each of the planetary cycles maps out its own calendared time. The cycle of planetary pairs from one conjunction to the next also charts passages of time; therefore, there are numerous astrological times in each moment of time.

These cycles are metaphorical meters for personal, social and collective timing. For instance, lunar time is recorded by the cycle of the Moon and is a metaphor for instinctual time and feeling memory such as the unconscious assimilation of every nuance, reaction, sense, desire, etc. It is a 27.3-day cycle. The Neptune–Pluto cycle lasts 492–94 years and is symbolic of the emerging motives and aspirations of the collective. This cycle is imagistic of the emergence of deep-rooted urges, intentions and ideals that may dominate and influence mankind's direction and ways of being. Since Neptune and Pluto symbolize energies beneath the foundation stones of all systems, the cycle represents the compelling human attitudes that are awakened during each cycle's epoch. These are only two of many planetary time cycles; inherent in each astrological cycle is a symmetry and order that inspires confidence in the intelligence and beauty of the cosmos.

In the 5th century CE, the Bishop of Alexandria, Synesius of Alexandria, summarized an ancient belief that history repeats itself 'because the stars return to their former positions'.[26] Images of return and renewal are embedded in astrological cycles, as each planet returns to the same zodiacal degree or to its conjunction with the Sun at some defined point in its cycle. Underlying each astrological cycle is the inevitability of return and the enduring image of the eternal return.

Early ways of thinking about time imagined it to be cyclical, like the natural phases of the Sun–Moon cycle. At the Dark phase of the cycle the Great Mother would bring the dead back into her womb to be reborn at the next Crescent. With the advent of rational thought, time became more linear, with the beginning and the end no longer entwined at the same point. In this way of thinking, rebirth and return are relinquished and detached from the cycle of life. In astrological philosophy the concept of the eternal return is preserved in planetary cycles, as their ending is the gateway to another beginning, with each new cycle being reborn from the previous one.

The road leading from the past and the road which stretches out into the future cross at the return. The forward-looking Promethean spirit is influenced and shaped by his backward-looking Epimethean counterpart. Returns are a time of transition, suspended by two ways of being. A return is an ending, yet like all endings it has seeds for the future, distilled from the past cycle. Like all beginnings it is subjective, unknown, anticipatory, hopeful and fearful. No light is visible in this pre-dawn phase. It is pre-historic; the future has not yet come, yet instincts and feelings from the past await rebirth.

Another perpetual image of the eternal return is the Sun as it returns from its night journey every morning to swallow the darkness; the dawn threshold marking where day, or the creation of new light, devours the dark. Astrologers also utilize the image of the Sun's annual return to make meaning through ingress and solar return charts. Not only the Sun, but the planets and other celestial bodies and points, such as the asteroids and planetary nodes, make returns to their original positions in the horoscope. Returns are natural to human experience. They are homecomings. As each planet in the horoscope returns, it returns home with a new cycle of experience.

While we may not be familiar with the philosophy or the concept of the eternal return, we are instinctually familiar with the experience of return. It is deep-seated and imprinted in the soul, having been impressed upon the psyche for millennia through the experience of daily, monthly and annual cycles, reflected by these astrological returns:

- The Diurnal Return or daily cycle traces the Sun as it rises, culminates, sets and descends to its lower meridian. This cycle marks the Sun's crossing of the horizon and meridian and defines four critical times during the day: sunrise, midday, sunset and midnight. This daily return marks out 24 hours of time, defining the rituals of our everyday lives.

- The Lunation Return or monthly cycle includes the aspects between the Sun and Moon that form the four quarters of the solar-lunar cycle. This return occurs every 29.5 days.

- The Seasonal Return or annual cycle charts the four seasons of the year, as the Sun crosses the Celestial Equator at the equinoxes and is at its greatest distance from the Celestial Equator at the solstices. This annual return of 365.25 days commemorates the seasons of our lives as well as the anniversaries and annual celebrations, rituals and festivals of personal, family and communal life.

These three cycles are prototypal as they mark out a beginning (the conjunction), two critical turning points (the squares), a middle (the opposition) and an ending (the subsequent conjunction) which returns the cycle to its new zodiacal inception point. Turning points of these cycles are defined by aspects or divisions of the circle, which are linked to the natural cycles and returns as in the following table. Embedded in the aspects, angles and signs of the zodiac are ancient images of the passing of time.

The Diurnal Return	The Diurnal Angles	The Lunation Return	The Return of the Seasons	The Return of the Aspect
Midnight	IC	New Moon	Winter solstice	Conjunction
Sunrise	Ascendant	First Quarter	Spring equinox	Waxing square
Noon	MC	Full Moon	Summer solstice	Opposition
Sunset	Descendant	Last Quarter	Autumn equinox	Waning Square
Midnight (next day)	IC	New Moon (next cycle)	Return of the winter solstice	Return to the conjunction

The end of each astrological cycle begins the next; every round embraces this knowledge of return. Astrological timing links these times together to reflect on deepening our understanding of the patterns of time. For instance, from a lunar perspective this moment is linked to the moment 27.3 days ago; from a Martian perspective this time is linked into the previous cycle and the ones before at intervals of approximately two years or, more precisely, 17–23.5 months; Chiron draws a plumb line into the previous cycle 50 years ago, while Uranus's present position evokes a moment 84 years ago. Astrology can draw the qualities of time together from many differing perspectives to reflect on and stimulate meaning for the present experience.

Astrological Moments in Time
Astrological tradition has cultivated procedures that help its practitioners read the moment of time so as to bring meaning to it. This act of investing time with meaning can be seen as one of soul-making. When we collaborate in time we are mindful of creating rituals for the appropriate moment, more conscious of the phases of time and more likely to be participating than anticipating.

From past astrological traditions comes a toolbox of techniques such as planetary transits, ingresses, annual profections, time lords, planetary periods, ascensions and directions, which give rise to more contemporary methods such as progressions and return charts. Like any profession, the debate amongst practitioners about the authenticity and dependability of certain systems persists; however, the success of any technique rests with the practitioner. An astrological student learns to be technically proficient, yet it is not the technique itself that reveals meaning but the practitioner's participation and ability to think symbolically, liberated from the literality of measured time.

Many ancient time techniques are sophisticated in their measurement of planetary periods and the rulers of these periods of the life cycle. I feel it is essential to not only understand the engineering of each technique, but also its context and purpose. For the student beginning to open the toolkit of time techniques, it is necessary to recognize which techniques are best used in specific situations and which ones are most compatible with their own philosophical approach. You may be overwhelmed by the complexity of astrological methods, confused by the multiplicity of procedures and disheartened by the contradictory formulas available; however, these are necessary initiations into the rituals of astrological practice. We sort through the endless array of tools to see which ones are best suited for us. Whilst we might marvel at the accuracy of a technique, we can never say that one technique is better than another. If we do, then astrology is brought to the level of intellectual debate and proof, rendering it factual, limiting our access to what we may not know. Astrological perception does not operate on a cause–effect spectrum, but pictures the qualities intrinsic in the moment through the symbols arising in that moment. Considered reflection on the symbols engenders understanding.

A technique that invites our participation with time is planetary transits, one of the most common contemporary methods used for timing. Simply, transits are the current planetary placements referenced to the zodiacal sphere. As snapshots of situations in time, phases of life and processes of change, each planetary transit characterizes moments in the shifting tides of humanity. The zodiacal sphere that contains twelve distinct regions or signs has linear demarcations or cusps, as well as other important reference points. The planets travel along this route. As they move against this backdrop, the possibilities of the present moment are symbolized.

Each planetary transit tells a tale of time and witnesses the synchrony of outer world events that mirror the inner world of soul.[27] Like a cosmic clock the transits tell time; they do not make it, or judge it.

Progressions are a time-based technique using one clock to measure a timeline in another dimension. In speaking on the nature of time, Manoj Thulasidas states that 'time is a secondary sense without any direct sensory percept or reason for its existence' and argues that its measurement is open to interpretation. As part of his thesis he likens the time elapsed from the birth of the universe 15 billion years ago to a time span of 45 years. By this reckoning the beginning of Christianity 2000 years ago would represent three minutes and nine seconds.[28] Time is relative and qualified.

In a way, Thulasidas's premise is analogous to astrological progressions because we link the symbols of the past to give meaning to another period in time. This method distances us from timing events in fixed or sequential periods. When using progressions, astrologers are more focused on a secondary expression in time, a more subjective and inner time frame. Progressions challenge us to move away from fixed concepts and deconstruct our inclination to understand time logically.

Astrology provides ways to open the doors of perception onto the complex and multi-layered dimensions of time. When reflecting on time frames highlighted by techniques such as transits, students often try to equate an event to this time period, as if the event represents the transit. But events are not the whole experience. Techniques point to significant time periods and, rather than trying to tell the time, it is often best to let the time reveal its meaning through the symbols and images. Although an event may manifest at a certain time, it is connected through time by the symbol. While life events such as the onset of an illness, the beginning of an important relationship, the loss of a loved one, moving house or a career change may be implied by the astrological clock, the experience and effect of these life events are not solely confined to this time. Astrological timing techniques are connected to symbols that may or may not have manifested as an outer event. To remain true to the astrological symbol through time we must return to the imagination because 'imagination is very much part of our being in time – in fact, intrinsic to it.'[29]

Imagining Symbols Through Time

Astrologers are often criticized for their self-assurance when analysing the past and their lack of confidence in deciphering future events. This does not imply that astrologers cannot envision the future, only that they cannot see the specific appearance of the symbol. Symbols in time past have already materialized and become wedged in the linear grooves of time, but the symbols of the future have not yet become available to consciousness.

Since archetypes are so diverse they can manifest in countless ways. Imagining the possibilities and reflecting on them in the context of their symbolism allows the soul to be more present in time. Astrologers become caught in the tracks of linear time when a symbol is projected forward in the same way that it has displayed itself in the past, or when symbols are presented as facts or clear-cut images of what is, was or will be. To see a symbol through time we must imagine it. Imagination extends us into the fullness of time and encourages meaningfulness beyond the present.

We can imagine what might happen next January. Like the planets, imagination wanders; but astrological timing contextualizes time, allowing the imagination to roam freely focused on symbols. Rather than delineate an astrological premise, we can use astrological techniques to frame time, allowing insight and intuition. In this way, transits and progressions become like active imagination, using astrological timing methods to imagine the future, not predict it.

Measuring time is ritualistic, not explanatory. It prepares us for participation with the unknowable where time exists. As we move forward to consider astrological time, we must honour the quantitative and qualitative aspects of time, allowing the astrological symbol to reveal the soul within the planetary precincts of time.

Life Transitions

One of astrology's many marvels is that it maps out the stages and phases of life using planetary cycles in an organic way. Anthropologists, sociologists and psychologists too have charted the life journey and so often their theories echo the astrological wisdom inherent in planetary cycles. At the age of 16, Dane Rudhyar, one of the 20th century's foremost astrologers, was inspired by the idea that the nature of time is cyclic and that the Law of Cycles controls all existence. This would influence the course of his life's work and design a framework for a deeper appreciation of astrological cycles.[30]

Rites of Passage: Separation, Initiation and Return
Initiatory times of life are constellated around the 'critical phases' of planetary cycles, whether the cycle is in relationship to itself (generic) or to individual placements in the chart (personal). When thinking about the development of these cycles, there is a strong temptation to see these as linear, unfolding sequentially over time. As much as possible it is important to imagine time from a multi-dimensional perspective to keep the integrity of the cycle intact. Age is an important factor in considering how we ascribe meaning to the events of our lives. Journeying through the life cycle will allow us to re-visit, re-imagine and re-connect with our story as well as move our narrative forward. I acknowledge these stages as initiatory times to participate in and ritualize life's transitions.

In the early 20th century, anthropologist Arnold Van Gennep wrote Les Rites de Passage,[31] bringing attention to the need for ritual, celebration and acknowledgement of the passing of time. While acknowledging the difficulty in systemizing ceremonial rites across cultures, he did identify a commonality of rites of passage which could be subdivided into 'rites of separation, transition rites and rites of incorporation'.[32] Influenced by Van Gennep's seminal ideas, Joseph Campbell reworked the stages as Separation, Initiation and Return. While these are imagistic of the heroic life cycle they can also be employed as metaphors for stages and phases of the life cycle as well as all astrological transitions.

Planetary Cycles
All planets have defined cycles; their cyclic returns symbolize homecoming and mark the maturation of a cycle of life. With reference to the life cycle, many planetary cycles demarcate phases of life. Saturn and the progressed Moon are valuable markers because they measure distinct cycles of 29.5 and 27.3 years respectively, marking out three stages of life: childhood and young adulthood; the adult phase; and finally a more mature elder phase of life. This trinity has deep roots in matrilineal tradition.

Three cycles map out the current lifespan for many individuals living in developed countries. Three cycles of the progressed Moon measure 82 years, the approximate life expectancy for individuals in countries such as Japan, Switzerland, Israel and Australia, according to statistical research. Three cycles of Saturn encompass 88 years. The lunar nodes also map out the lifespan, with 4–5 phases of 18.6 years each. Four nodal cycles span 74–75 years, which is the average life expectancy in other countries.

Planetary Cycle	The 1st Cycle		The 2nd Cycle		The 3rd Cycle		The 4th Cycle	
	Age at 1st ☊	Age at 1st Return	Age at 2nd ☊	Age at 2nd Return	Age at 3rd ☊	Age at 3rd Return	Age at 4th ☊	Age at 4th Return
Saturn	14–15	**29–30**	44–45	**58–59**	73–74	**88–89**		
Progressed Moon	13–14	**27–28**	41	**54–55**	68–69	**81–82**		
Lunar Nodes	9–9.5	**18–19**	27–28	**37–38**	46–47	**55–56**	65–66	**74–75**

The above table *approximates* the opposition and return ages which we might consider in terms of our own and the family's development. When contemplating the life cycle with its initiatory times and crossroads, the social planets, Jupiter and Saturn, are important in demarcating familial and social rites of passage. Chiron and the outer planets are significant in differentiating psychic and psychological phases of life, while the cycle of the lunar nodes might be described as vocational and spiritual passages. The progressed Moon's cycle identifies the emotional layers of transition.

Another cycle spanning the whole life is the Uranus cycle of 84 years. The squares and oppositions in this cycle are important turning points instinctually embedded in our own development as well as that of the family.

Planetary Cycle	Age at the Waxing Square	Age at the 1st Opposition	Age at the Waning Square	Age at the 1st Return
Uranus	20–21	38–42	62–3	84

2

PLANETARY CYCLES
The Ring of Time

The study of astrological cycles immerses us in the question of time; each cycle, no matter its length, has a beginning, a middle and an end, thereby renewing itself in the birth of another cycle. There is a past and a future in every present moment. Each astrological cycle has occurred before and will again; hence a body of feeling, knowledge and experience, as well as apprehension and expectation, is embedded into our understanding of each celestial cycle. Given that the cycle is repetitive and eternal, astrology applies correlative methods to link planetary cycles with the wheels of human affairs, be they external, internal, physical or soulful, looping backwards and forwards through time like the aforementioned ring composition of the ancient oral tradition.

Planetary Cycles

Our word 'cycle' comes directly from the Latin *cyclus*, derived from the Greek *kyklos* which means circle, ring or wheel. Cycles are the spirit of astrological time. The cyclic movement away from and back to a seminal moment in each planetary cycle evokes the mystery of the eternal return. With every return a new cycle emerges; its essence evokes the possibility of consciousness. Astrology invites us into the reverence of this recurring process, exquisitely mapped by the orbits of celestial bodies. Astrological cycles are numerous, including not only the planets but any other points which complete a zodiacal round, such as the lunar nodes. Astrological cycles are mostly categorized as *sidereal* or *synodic*.

Dane Rudhyar differentiated these as 'cycles of position' (sidereal) and 'cycles of relationship' (synodic). A 'cycle of relationship' involves aspects between two planets. Rudhyar said 'this is best exemplified in the lunation cycle from New Moon to New Moon',[33] suggesting the lunation cycle is an informative image for all planetary pair cycles. A 'cycle of position' measures the course that a planet takes to transit the horoscope and return to its starting position.

A sidereal cycle measures one complete planetary cycle. Sidereal is from the Latin *sider*, meaning 'star';[34] therefore the cycle refers to measuring the planet's return against the backdrop of a 'fixed' star. Generally it is used to express the average time it takes a planet to orbit the Sun. Specifically, the term tropical period conveys the average amount of time a planet takes to complete a full round through the zodiac. Each return, after one full orbit of the zodiac, is referred to as a tropical cycle. All planets' sidereal and tropical cycles are similar except for those of Mercury and Venus, which are internal to the Earth's orbit. Since they are between the Earth and the Sun, they are always viewed in proximity to the Sun. While they will complete an orbit of the Sun in a shorter period, their path through the zodiac from the Earth's perspective stays close to the Sun's. Therefore, their sidereal period and tropical period are not the same, as follows:

Planet	Sidereal Cycle *One complete cycle in reference to a fixed star*	Tropical Cycle *One zodiacal revolution*	Synodic Cycle *One complete cycle with the Sun*
Mercury	88 days	11–13 months	116 days
Venus	224–5 days	10–14 months	584 days

A synodic cycle refers to the relationship between two planets and to the time that elapses between successive conjunctions with a planet and the Sun, as viewed from Earth. Each planet's synodic cycle with the Sun occurs in phases and creates its own predictable retrograde sub-cycle. The term can also apply to other planetary pair cycles, such as the Jupiter–Saturn cycle. In Greek and Latin, *synodos* suggested a meeting or assembly. In astronomy this is applied to a conjunction of planets. In Greek, *syn* is the prefix for 'together' while *hodos* refers to a path, road, a journey or going a certain way. Used in an astrological context, 'synodal' refers to the two planets that have met and forged a path together. Astrologically, planets are referenced to their synodic cycle either with the Sun or with one another.

For instance, the Moon's sidereal orbital period is 27.3 days, whereas its synodic period, measured from one conjunction with the Sun (the New Moon) to the next, is 29.5 days. The synodic period of Jupiter and Saturn with the Sun is just over one year, because annually the Sun conjuncts each planet to start a new cycle. However, it takes Jupiter 11.8 years and Saturn 29.5 years to complete one orbit of the Sun. This difference is because the synodic cycle measures a planetary pair cycle, while the sidereal cycle examines one planet's cycle. The Mercury–Sun and the Venus–Sun cycles capture the imagination of astrologers, as their patterning in the heavens sketch the sacred figures of Pi and the Golden Mean respectively onto the heavenly canvas.

The pairing of the social and outer planets, Jupiter, Saturn, Uranus, Neptune and Pluto, form ten possible planetary pair cycles that are of great interest when studying the impact of astrological time on the collective. These synodic cycles often comprise a larger pattern which returns to a specific zodiacal position. The term *synodic recurrence* period is used to describe the average time it takes for planets to conjoin at a similar zodiacal degree as in the past. For instance, the Sun and Moon will return to a similar degree every 19 years while the Sun and Venus will conjoin at the same degree every 8 years. The social and outer planets also create repetitive degrees in their synodic cycles.

Astrologically there are numerous ways to reflect on the cycles of time as well as various techniques that assist in recording time. Astrological techniques such as transits use the actual positions of the planets to measure time, whereas other methods such as progressions and directions use symbolic placements to tell time. Ancient techniques brought into contemporary practice use planetary periods based on recurrent synodic cycles with corresponding time lords. Horoscopes can be drawn when a planet returns to its natal position in order to consider its next cycle, while other charts can be used to research a particular time period. Yet, with every technique, it is crucial to contextualize the planetary cycle, whether that be its orbit around the Sun, its synodic cycle with the Sun or its cycle with another planet. Each planetary cycle has a unique timetable through the zodiac, whether that is the fast-moving Moon orbiting the Earth in 27.3 days, or the slow-moving Uranus which takes a lifetime of 84 years to encircle the Sun. In 84 years, Uranus has made one complete cycle through the zodiac whereas the Moon in the same period has completed well over 1000 orbits.

Sidereal Cycles

When considering cycles astrologically, our reference point is the zodiac, tracing the cycle of a planet through its degrees and signs. Here is a summary of the time it takes for each planet to complete one zodiacal round. For the slower-moving planets, the quarter and halfway markers are significant.

Planet	Approx. cycle through the zodiac	Approx. time transiting 1/12th of the zodiac (one zodiac sign)	Approx. time transiting 1/4 of the zodiac (the square)	Approx. time transiting 1/2 of the zodiac (the opposition)
☽	27.3 days	2.25 days	1 week	1 fortnight
☉	365.25 days	29–31 days	3 months	6 months
☿	11–13 months	14–45 days	*This time period is dependent on whether the planet is moving direct or retrograde*	
♀	10–14 months	25–125 days		
♂	17–23.5 months	1.5–7 months		
♃	12 years	1 year	3 years	6 years
♄	29.5 years	2.5 years	7.5 years	15 years
⚷	50 years	2–7 years	*Time period is dependent on its sign in the birth chart*	
♅	84 years	7 years	21 years	42 years
♆	165 years	14 years	41 years	82 years
♇	248 years	13–30 years	*Time period is dependent on its sign in the birth chart*	

When considering planetary times and techniques, I find it helpful to differentiate the planets into three categories:

- *The Inner Planets*, including the Sun and Moon, Mercury, Venus and Mars. Although Mars is external to the orbit of Earth, it can be considered an 'inner' planet due to its speed. Since these planets transit our horoscope frequently, they are often used for timing processes in return charts, event charts, using their synodic cycles and by progression. Their transits can be very useful for scheduling and planning the timetables and calendars of daily life.

• *The Social Planets*, Jupiter and Saturn, are experienced through the socialization process, such as education, training, relating and working, as well as ageing and maturing. They demarcate important passages of the life cycle and are highly suggestive of environmental change and focus as they transit the houses of the horoscope.

• *The Outer Planets* are those outside the boundary of Saturn: Uranus, Neptune and Pluto, as well as Chiron. These slower-moving planets represent forces beyond our control and perception, even beyond our time and place; hence they are powerful agents of awakening and growth.

Cycles of the Inner Planets

Each of the five inner planets (Sun–Mars) has a unique cycle. Being shortest in duration, they represent instinctual and habitual timing, unlike the outer planets which represent the major epochs of our lives. As these cycles pass quickly and frequently, their experience in time becomes familiar and routine, embedded in the everyday events that are taken for granted, such as fleeting thoughts, momentary pleasures, emotional reactions and dream images.

Cycles of the inner planets are experienced as the diurnal and seasonal rhythms of life, describing personal qualities of time. For instance, the transiting Sun defines the four seasons and marks personal anniversaries, framing the daily rhythm of life. In the southern hemisphere, when the Sun passes through Cancer we are attuned to the quality of winter, the changing of the season, the beckoning hearth. In the northern hemisphere summer is announced; family holidays, the school break and the return home. The Sun's yearly transit of the sign evokes the qualities of identifying more with home and family (♋). Every year at the same time the Sun transits through the house/s of our horoscope which contain/s the sign Cancer, identifying the recurrent anniversaries, rhythms and schedules of our life.

The transits of the Moon encapsulate the ever-changing oceanic tides of feelings, moods and bodily rhythms that occur without our will, symbolizing instinctual and bodily memory. Because lunar transits occur so frequently they embody an innate or intuitive time, told through our reactions and responses, which are often involuntary.

When we are in Mercurial time, it is the time for communication and interaction. A Venusian occasion marks out a period of pleasure, while Martian time distinguishes a period of action. Because these are fast-moving cycles they are beneficial in understanding the patterns and cycles of our everyday life. They are also constructive in planning personal agendas and rituals. The lunar cycle maps our moods, our changing needs, the patterns of eating and dieting; therefore, it can help to plan appropriate times of rest and retreat. The lunar cycle monitors the sequence of our dreams and helps to decode the images inherent in them. Many avid gardeners use lunar timing to plant, weed, feed and harvest their gardens. All the inner planetary cycles can be employed to help us understand the tempo of our natural rhythms and disposition.

Planetary Cycle	Notes
☉ 12 months	The solar cycle can be traced through the signs of the zodiac each year, starting with the vernal point (0°♈ in the northern hemisphere). The Sun circles the horoscope annually, transiting a house every year during the same period, marking annual and personal seasons for each individual as it transits the quadrants of the horoscope.
☽ 27.3 days	The Moon circles the zodiac in 27.3 days, moving through each sign and house in 2–2.5 days, distinguishing emotional and feeling time. Recording the transits of the Moon in a dream journal or personal diary reveals interesting recurrences in our dreams, repetitive habits, emotional cycles and moods. The synodic cycle of 29.5 days differentiates the month into lunar phases which follow a course of development from New Moon to New Moon.

☿ 11–13 months	Mercury cycles close to the Sun, within 28°. Each year Mercury goes retrograde three times for approximately three weeks. Mercury retrogrades through the elements, and links to the degree where it went direct previously, creating a pattern in our horoscope that connects our thoughts and ideas together through time. Its synodic cycle with the Sun averages 116 days, shape-shifting from evening to morning star at its inferior conjunction with the Sun and from morning to evening star at its superior conjunction. Its synodic cycle reflects its phases of thinking, conceptualizing, judging and reflecting in the heavens.
♀ 10–14 months	Venus also cycles close to the Sun, within 48°. Venus's synodic cycle with the Sun is approximately 19 months. Once every cycle Venus is retrograde for approximately six weeks. Every eight years the synodic cycle repeats its zodiacal position within a few degrees, creating a pentagram in the heavens when traced on the backdrop of the zodiac. Its symmetrical pattern in the horoscope reminds us of beauty and balance in our lives. Venus is critical when she is retrograde because she stresses a particular house of the horoscope. Her cycle is a meditation on our innate values, love, relationships and self-worth.
♂ 17–23.5 months	Mars returns every 22 months, although due to its retrograde cycle it may return as early as 17 months. It is retrograde once every cycle for 2–3 months. During this time one area of the zodiac will be highlighted. The first return of Mars is known as the 'terrible twos', when the child's will and desire emerge. As the first planet exterior to the Earth's orbit, Mars embodies the urge to be independent and motivational. A Mars transit acts as a stimulant, motivator or trigger to an outer planet transit that is occurring simultaneously.

Nodal Cycles

The lunar nodes are not planets but points where the orbits of the Sun and Moon are at a crossroads. These points where their orbits intersect have a cycle of 18.6 years, averaging 18.6 months in a sign and opposing one another in their cycle every 9.3 years. The North Node (☊) is where the Moon crosses the ecliptic in a northward direction rising into the northern ecliptic hemisphere, while at the South Node (☋) the Moon crosses the ecliptic in a southerly direction. Solar and lunar eclipses occur near the nodal axis; therefore, the nodal cycle through our horoscope indicates where a series of eclipses will take place. The cycle of the nodal axis and the corresponding eclipses are very useful in astrological timing.

The Nodal Cycle	Notes
☊ ☋ 18.6 years	The nodal cycle retrogrades through the zodiac, distinct from the forward motion of the planets. This reverse movement assists in contemplating the nature of this cycle, as it represents soul time, not necessarily chronological time. Four significant returns at age 19, 37, 56 and 75 usher in new chapters in our spiritual quest for meaning and purposefulness. The nodal cycle through the houses of the horoscope herald the location of solar and lunar eclipses. Eclipses too are cyclic, repeating every 18 years and 10–11 days (Saros Cycle). The nodal cycle has the following harmonic: one cycle of the zodiac is 18.6 years; one transit of a sign is 18.6 months and one degree of the zodiac is regressed in about 18.6 days. The movement of the True Node plateaus for 2–3 months every 4 months.

Cycles of the Social Planets

The social planets measure out important chapters in the life cycle, because their returns and critical aspects in their cycle herald initiatory phases in every human being's life. For instance, the first return of Jupiter at age 12 signals the dawning of adolescence while Saturn's return at age 29 heralds adulthood. Working with these planetary cycles can pinpoint recurring passages in an individual's life; for instance, imagine transiting Saturn is opposing an individual's Sun. Because Saturn's cycle is 29–30 years we know that approximately 15 years ago (half of the cycle) transiting Saturn would have been conjunct the Sun. It is informative to link these time periods together, as themes and issues from the past may be infiltrating the present. Jupiter and Saturn mark societal rites of passage.

Planetary Cycle	Notes
♃ 12 months	Jupiter's cycle is just under 12 years, spending an average of 1 year in each sign of the zodiac. Every year it retrogrades 10° of the zodiac for 4 months. When direct it moves forward about 40°, thereby covering a total of about 30° of zodiacal territory in a year. Important ages in the Jupiter cycle are its oppositions near ages 6, 18, 30, 42, 53, 65 and 77 as well as its returns near ages 12, 24, 35, 47, 59, 71 and 83. Each return marks a new phase of hope, discovery and growth.
♄ 29.5 years	Saturn transits a sign in about 2–2½ years, covering about 10°–15° of the zodiac each year. When direct it can travel up to 20°; when retrograde it backtracks nearly 7°. Each year it spends nearly 4½ months retrograde. Saturn returns to its natal place for the first time at age 29–30; the second return is at 59 and the third is at 88. At each of these times, an initiation into a different task of the individuation process takes place. Other important times in the cycle are its waxing squares at approximately ages 7, 37 and 66; its oppositions at ages 15, 44–45 and 74; and its waning squares at approximately ages 22, 52 and 81.

Cycles of the Outer Planets

The cycles and transits of the outer planets differ from those of the social planets Jupiter and Saturn, as they take us beyond the realm of familial, social and cultural expectations into a deeper experience and understanding of the Self.

Transits of the slower-moving planets characterize major transitions and life-altering experiences; in essence, events that awaken the soul to the authentic self. These transits are part of larger cycles that symbolize rites of passage when social maturation calls us into a new phase of life. As Howard Sasportas described in his brilliant treatise *The Gods of Change*, Uranus, Neptune and Pluto 'break us down so that we can break through to a new way of being'.[35] Each planet has its own methods of deconstructing the outworn remnants of the past that are no longer useful to the future direction; hence each planetary transition is an initiatory step in the process of individuation. Each of these transitions allows us to make contact with deeper layers of the psyche, levels not drawn on in the everyday routines of life.

An outer planet's cycle also marks times of important life cycle initiations. For instance, Uranus's first square to itself at the age of 21 announces the coming of age and the launching of the individual on their self-determining road of life, while Neptune's first square at 41 announces the shifting seas of midlife.

Planetary Cycle	Notes
⚷ 50 years	Chiron completes its cycle in 50 years but, due to its elliptical orbit, the timing of the waxing and waning squares and oppositions is different for each Chiron sign. At 50 Chiron initiates us into the second half of life.

♅ 84 years	Uranus's cycle of 84 years corresponds with the current life expectancy for many. It transits a sign in approximately 7 years, being retrograde each year for about 5 months. It travels approximately 8° direct then retrogrades about 4°, traversing each degree of the zodiac at least three times. The important transitional points of the cycle are the waxing square at approximately age 21, the opposition between 38 and 42, and the waning square between 61 and 63.
♆ 165 years	Neptune has the most circular orbit of the outer planets and moves steadily through the zodiac, spending about 14 years in each sign. Neptune is retrograde each year for about 5¼ months, travelling about 5° forward then 2°–2.7° backwards. The waxing square occurs at 41, synchronous with the progressed Moon square. The opposition occurs near age 82 at the same age as the third progressed Moon return.
♇ 247–8 years	Like Chiron, Pluto has a very elliptical orbit; therefore its passage through the signs is irregular, spending about 30 years in the sign of ♉ but only 12 years in ♏. Each year it spends over 5 months retrograde. Each generation will receive its waxing Pluto square at differing times; the Pluto in ♍ and ♎ generations received this square in their late 30s while the subsequent generations will experience this aspect much later.

Synodic Cycles

The lunation cycle from New Moon to New Moon is the synodic cycle most employed in astrological practice. The synodic cycles of Mercury and Venus have recently become more utilized in terms of astrological timing and cyclic phases. The synodic cycle of Mars is close to its sidereal period of two years while the other planets conjoin the Sun every year. The synodic periods of Jupiter and Saturn are just over one year. The following table demonstrates the difference in the synodic and the return cycle of each planet having completed one zodiacal round.

Below: The Planetary Rounds
Tropical, Sidereal and Synodic Cycles

Planet	Astrological Cycle		
	Tropical Period *Average amount of time for one full round of the zodiac along the ecliptic*	**Sidereal Period** *Average amount of time for one full orbit of the Sun*	**Synodic Period** *Average amount of time elapsing from one conjunction with the Sun to the next*
☽	27.3 days	*One full orbit of the Earth* 27.3 days	29.5 days/ 1 month
☿	11–13 months	88 days	116 days/ 3.8 months
♀	10–14 months	225 days	584 days/ 19 months
♂	17–23.5 months (average 22.5 months)	22.5 months	780 days/ 25.6 months
♃	12 years	11.88 years	399 days/ 13 months
♄	29.5 years	29.5 years	378 days/ 12.4 months
⚷	50 years	50.4 years	373 days/ 12.3 months
♅	84 years	84 years	370 days/ 12 months
♆	165 years	165 years	368 days/ 12 months
♇	248 years	248 years	366 days/ 12 months

Mundane astrology utilizes the ten synodic cycles that take place between the social and outer planets. The longest of these cycles occurs between the two slowest-moving planets, Pluto and Neptune. This cycle runs for over 490 years and last occurred in 1891–92 at 7°–8° Gemini. During the last half of the 20th century and first half of the 21st century, a waxing sextile between these two planets formed when Neptune entered Libra and sextiled Pluto in Leo, which lasts until Neptune is in Aries sextiling Pluto in Aquarius. During this phase Pluto averages the same speed as Neptune. This period of the long sextile covers nearly 100 years from the early 1940s to the late 2030s.

The table below summarizes the ten planetary pairs and is inspired by Leyla Rael Rudhyar's three classifications of these cycles.[36]

Overviews: The Big Picture *Evolutionary epochs of transformation*	Saturn Synods: Clash of the Titans *Boundary making and breaking*	Jupiter Synods: Progressive Ideals *Discoveries and visions*
♅–♇ 113–142 years (varies due to Pluto's elliptical orbit)	♄–♇ 31–38 years	♃–♄ 20 years
♅–♆ 172 years	♄–♆ 36 years	♃–♅ 14 years
♆–♇ 492–494 years	♄–♅ 45 years	♃–♆ 13 years
		♃–♇ 12–13 years

The shortest of the planetary pairs is the Jupiter–Pluto cycle, which astrologers have related to the growth of international terrorism and economic cycles. Mundane astrologers work with the unfolding of the planetary pairs over the course of their cycles, focusing on the periods when the two planets form important angular relationships with each other. For instance, the period from 2012 to 2015 was of astrological interest as this included seven exact waxing squares in the Uranus–Pluto cycle. 2020 was highlighted due to the three major conjunctions of Saturn-Pluto, Jupiter-Pluto and Jupiter-Saturn. Often some aspects, such as the Neptune–Pluto sextile and the Chiron–Uranus opposition, are elongated when planets are moving at similar speeds.

Synodic Cycles of the Social and Outer Planets			
	Saturn	**Uranus**	**Neptune**	**Pluto**
Jupiter	20 years	14 years	13 years	12.5 years
Saturn		45 years	36 years	31–38 years
Uranus			172 years	113–142 years
Neptune				492–494 years

Advancing the Horoscope

Although the horoscope is a permanent moment, fixed at the crossroads between two worlds, it continually participates in the passing of time. Shaped by our first breath, our horoscope continues to respond to every heartbeat that follows. In a way it is renewed with each breath and each moment in time. The living horoscope testifies to the cycles of time, which constantly remind us of the inevitability of endings, yet embedded in all transitions is the hope of renewal that follows each closure of the cycle.

The horoscope itself does not change but it will unfold through time, as if it were a seed growing or a plant blossoming. While the natal chart's configuration is fixed, transits and the other forms of timing techniques account for how an individual's life, as reflected by the horoscope, is constantly in flux. Transits and progressions or directions can be used in tandem to ascertain not only events and potential manifestations in the external world, but also how inner psychological shifts and developments synchronize with these changes. As mentioned, planetary symbols of time look both outward to the external life and inward to the soul. Let's introduce the contemporary techniques of transits, progressions and returns in an attempt to deepen and ensoul our work with planetary time.

Transits

The dictionary defines 'transit' as passing over or through something or traversing it; a change or a transition. When applied to a celestial body it suggests passing over the meridian of a place or another celestial body. Astrologically, a transit is the actual movement of a planet, asteroid or other point, such as a planetary node, through the zodiac. A personal transit compares a particular planetary position at any given date with the natal planets and angles of an individual's horoscope, noting the movement of that planet through the signs and houses of the horoscope. Transits are a snapshot of a moment in time, a phase of life, characterizing the shifting tides of our lives. They symbolize the influences on our personal development and augur change and possibly transformation. Simply, a transit is the position of any given planet at a given time in reference to the natal horoscope.

The term 'transit' also refers to the passage of a planet in relationship to its natal placement. These transits record the process of ageing and correspond to the initiatory stages in the life cycle; therefore, they are common to the same generation. Aspects in these larger cycles occur for everyone at similar ages, and are known as generic cycles or cycles specific to a generation.

Transits are pictures of the sky at any moment in time; therefore, they are collective images, in that all humanity experiences these images on differing levels. However, each individual will have their own unique orientation and experience of the transit. When the moving picture of time impinges upon our horoscope, then we may feel this personally and respond to the times in our own unique way. Transits are often experienced in the outer world first since the encouragement towards consciousness often comes from an external source. When experienced as an external event, a transit can awaken an innate psychic structure that forces us into a more authentic way of being. Confusion arises when we are awakened to latent aspects of our self or when a dormant psychic complex begins to unravel. Life's rhythms symbolized by the transiting planet awaken the potential in the natal horoscope and confront us with a more authentic way of being. As we awaken to unknown aspects of ourselves, disengagement, confusion or trauma may be aroused. We may respond defensively, yet also be excited by the potentiality of change.

Transits, especially of the social and outer planets, are catalysts of change that challenge our habitual patterns. Outer planetary transits can be frightening to the personality as they confront us to become more authentic, let go of outworn attachments and encourage us to move forward. These transits augur consciousness, separation and change. An ancient adage suggested that when a god was pursuing you, it was imperative to make a sacrifice to the divinity, metaphorically the divine in us: an offering, a votive, a sacred object, a prayer or a symbolic gesture. An offering symbolizes participation, consciousness and the willingness to shine light on the situation. Transits invite preparation and participation in the process of transition.

Progressions and Directions

Progressions and directions use a symbolic framework to advance the horoscope, unlike transits, which refer to the actual planetary positions. Progressions and directions are closely related systems which move the planets and angles of the natal horoscope either forward or backward using a secondary rate of motion. The two most popular systems in contemporary use are secondary progressions and solar arc directions. Since each system yields quite different results, it is important to understand how these are derived and to develop a consistent way to work with each one.

Progressions are based on the actual orbital motion of the planets. With progressions, the planets move at their own rates of speed, akin to their natural orbits, thereby retaining their ratio of speed to one another. The most commonly used progressions are secondary progressions, which advance the horoscope 'a day for a year'. One day after birth symbolizes the first year of life; the second day after birth symbolizes the second year of life, and so on. For instance, the Sun moves approximately 1° a day, so it moves 1° a year by secondary progression, whereas the Moon averages 13° a day and therefore 13° a year by secondary progression; this means the Moon's speed is approximately 13 times faster than the Sun's. Planets also move in the appropriate direction from birth, either direct or retrograde, and may also change their direction after birth in the secondary progressed horoscope.

Directions advance all the planets at the same speed in the same direction: the Sun, Moon and the planets all move at the same speed in the same direction. The most popular form of direction is solar arc direction, which equates one year of life with the true movement of the Sun in one day. All the planets are advanced each year by the daily motion of the Sun in the horoscope. The Sun's daily motion can vary from anywhere between 57'12" per day when it travels through Cancer, to 61'10" per day as it moves through Capricorn. Therefore, all planets will be moving forward at approximately 1°

a year by solar arc. In this method the social and outer planets are directed at a much greater speed than in a secondary progressed horoscope. Like all techniques, both progressions and directions are valuable when used in context for identifiable outcomes.

To me, secondary progressions consider the development of the inner life and allow reflection on purpose and meaning throughout an individual's life. Secondary progressions are a natural outgrowth of the natal chart, like genetic material embedded in the horoscope. Over the course of a lifetime secondary progressions reflect the unfolding of the soul's intention in the world. Transits are descriptive of the relevance of planetary energies during a specific time frame, while secondary progressions are more indicative of inner development over a longer period; hence I like to think of them as the 'soul's diary'.

Unlike secondary progressions, solar arc directions are not intrinsic to the horoscope. I feel that advancing all the planets of the horoscope by approximately 1° a year tells time like a real clock. Each planet becomes a dynamic symbol of quantitative time which is more outer-worldly. However, as a symbol, each planet is still highly imaginative and soulful in the hands of a symbolist or an astrologer who works psychologically. Perhaps we might suggest that solar arc directions tell a story of the outer times while secondary progressions are inherent timing, embedded in the individual's DNA. Outer and inner events mirror one another; therefore, both techniques need to be respected in the context of the archetypal symbols and time frames they reveal.

Both systems are of value when the astrologer deepens their working knowledge and uses them in context of the question or the situation.

The following tables compare the different positions of secondary progressions and solar arc directions at the same moment in time. Two US presidents, Barack Obama and Donald Trump, are contrasted using secondary progressions and solar arc directions for the day each of them won their presidential election: 4 November 2008 (Barack Obama) and 9 November 2016 (Donald Trump). Note the variations that occur with the differing systems, as well as how these connect to the natal planetary positions. Of particular note is the movement of the social and outer planets: with secondary progressions there is minimal progression, while with solar arcs the movement is considerable. Also note the angular advance. In each case the progressed and directed MC is the same, based on the solar arc at the time. However, in the secondary progressed charts the Ascendant and Vertex are derived from the progressed MC, whereas in the solar arc directions the solar arc is added to the natal Ascendant and Vertex.

Here are Barack Obama's secondary progressed and solar arc planets for 4 November 2008. His birth details are 4 August 1961 at 7.24 p.m., born in Honolulu, Hawaii.[37]

	Natal	Sec. Prog.	Solar Arc		Natal	Sec. Prog.	Solar Arc
		at 4 November 2008				at 4 November 2008	
☉	12♌32	28♍14	28♍14	♅	25♌16	28♌08	10♎57
☽	03♊21	16♒18	19♋02	♆	08♏36	09♏32	24♐17
☿	02♌19	23♎14	18♍01	♇	06♍58	08♍33	22♎40
♀	01♋47	27♌21	17♌28	ASC	18♒03	20♈33	03♈44
♂	22♍34	23♎02	08♏16	MC	28♏53	14♑35	14♑35
♃	00♒51℞	27♑19℞	16♓32	Vx	12♍54	08♎09	28♎35
♄	25♑19℞	23♑16℞	11♓01	☊	27♌18	26♌56	12♎59
⚷	05♓19℞	03♓06℞	21♈00				

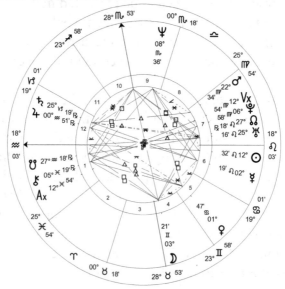

Here are Donald Trump's secondary progression and solar arc planets for 9 November 2016. His birth details are 14 June 1946 at 10.54 a.m., born in New York, NY.[38]

	Natal	Sec. Prog.	Solar Arc		Natal	Sec. Prog.	Solar Arc
		at 9 November 2016				at 9 November 2016	
☉	22♊55	00♍15	00♍15	♅	17♊53	21♊16	25♌12
☽	21♐12	22♋55	28♒31	♆	05♎50℞	06♎59	13♐09
☿	08♋51	12♌15	16♍10	♇	10♌02	11♌59	17♎21
♀	25♋44	15♎47	03♎03	ASC	29♌58	26♎50	07♏17
♂	26♌46	09♎10	04♏05	MC	24♉21	01♌41	01♌41
♃	17♎27	23♎56	24♐46	Vx	22♑54	01♊52	00♈13
♄	23♋48	02♌40	01♎08	☊	20♊48	18♊11	28♌07
⚷	14♎54	19♎21	22♐14				

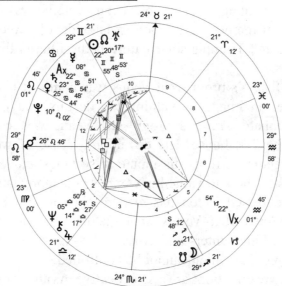

How might we consider the secondary progressions and solar arc directions for different personalities experiencing a similar event? First, I would differentiate the solar arc directions as pertaining to the event, the atmosphere of the times and how the event may have impacted their lives. I would reflect on the secondary progressions as the emotional and psychological impact of the situation, the natural maturation and development accompanying the event as well the soul quality of the time. I would not be trying to fit the event to any of the astrological symbols, but would use the symbols to amplify the outer and inner landscape of this period.

Looking at the major secondary progressions for Donald Trump when he was elected President, it is interesting to note that his progressed Sun at 0♍15 was conjunct his natal Ascendant at 29♌58. For the previous year and the one to follow, this highlighted his character coming to the foreground, a potent image of rebirth and new beginnings, the soul task of projecting his authentic self or aligning character with persona. Barack Obama's progressed Moon was 16♒18 on the day of his election, conjunct his natal Ascendant at 18♒03. For the next few months, as he approached his inauguration and stepped into his position at the White House, the progressed Moon journeyed across the horizon. A cycle had ended; another one was beginning. His challenge was to align his feeling and soulful side with his personality. In the previous cycle he was coming out of college; in this following cycle he was coming out as the voice of the people. A contrast is evident between Obama's lunar nature and Trump's solar nature being filtered through their personalities.

Barack Obama's progressed Venus was conjunct his 7th house North Node, an image of valuing his destiny that had become manifest. Donald Trump's progressed Venus was conjunct his Chiron in the 2nd house. His developing sense of worth, value and self-esteem confronts his innate misgivings and weaknesses. The soul task is how to value his wounds and appreciate his flaws. Trump's progressed Moon has also reached an angle – the 3rd angle of the Antivertex–Vertex, an angle that resonates with hidden agendas, fated encounters and crossroads – an emotive encounter with accepting that which cannot be controlled.

The solar arc directions are also evocative. As already mentioned, my perspective on these directions is in amplifying the nature of the times. If we use a 1° orb, then each direction will have a time frame of two years. Obama's solar arc Venus at 17♌28 is conjunct his Descendant at 18♌03, an image that speaks of the warmth and affection received from others, new contacts as well as a revaluing and engagement in his own partnerships. It is an echo of his progressed Venus conjunct his 7th house North Node. His solar arc Mars at 8♏16 conjoins his 9th house Neptune at 8♏36. This archetypal image speaks of many possibilities such as championing the underprivileged, asserting his own beliefs and moral values, yet also feeling and reacting to collective ideals and dreams, confronting the ambiguity, confusion and treachery beyond his known world. He is challenged to be a warrior for divine principles.

Trump's solar arc Moon at 28≈21 conjoins his Descendant at 29≈58, symbolizing both his relationship with the public and his private affiliations, which become public. His solar arc Chiron at 22♐14 is conjunct his Moon at 21♐12 and opposite his Sun at 22♊55, echoing the progressed Venus conjunct his natal Chiron. Perhaps a core wound to his identity and security festers – no doubt his maverick nature is exposed. Whether his reaction to his vulnerability drives him to behave as a wild and rowdy Centaur or as a wise teacher is in his own hands. Chiron is from the Greek meaning 'handy' and this solar arc is indicative of handiwork needed to heal the past. Solar arc Uranus at 25♌12 is approaching natal Mars at 26♌46 and the Ascendant at 29♌58, directions that will last until the later part of 2022. This synchronizes with his surprise win and his rocky rise as a media magnet and public figure, as well as his 'expect the unexpected' persona, which has a hold on him throughout his presidency.

While secondary progressions and solar arc directions are very different techniques, they can both be employed effectively when used in context and with a considered and focused approach. When either is used in tandem with transits, they are highly lucrative as they amplify the current state of affairs for either an inner perspective (secondary progressions) or as a magnification of the situation (solar arc directions).

Planetary Return Charts

A return corresponds with the ending of one cycle and the beginning of the next. Astrologically we use the concept of return when describing the complete cycle of a planet. The social planets are especially significant in marking the initiations of the life cycle. For instance, the Jupiter return every 12 years marks the beginning of a new phase of the life cycle. Each return of Jupiter is an initiation into a broader perspective of one's life. The Saturn returns mark three distinct phases of the life cycle and Saturn's return initiates the individual into a new sphere of reliability, responsibility and maturity. The first return at 29 signals the maturation, self-responsibility and authority of an individual as they claim their place in the world, while the next return at 58–59 demarcates a shift away from the outer to the internal world. Chiron returns at 50 to initiate a return to the authentic and spiritual aspects of the self that have been imprisoned by the necessity to conform. Planetary returns demarcate lifetime thresholds and reveal vital transitional periods in the life cycle.

Astrologically, a technique called a return chart can also be constructed when a planet returns to its natal position. These charts encapsulate the energies that are prominent during the pivotal return time. Return charts delineate major themes for an individual during the next cycle of the planet.

Throughout the course of the book we will be examining and applying these techniques to astrological practice. I am aware that there are many valuable texts on this subject available and these are summarized in the bibliography. Since we will be concentrating on modern timing methods I have also included recommended texts for traditional methods. My intention is to help bring imagination and ways of thinking to contemporary astrological timing techniques to help you build your confidence in your forecasting work.

PART II

TRANSITS

The Soul in Transition

Yesterday is gone.
Tomorrow has not yet come.
We have only today.
Let us begin.

Mother Teresa

3

TRANSITS AND TRANSITIONS
Moving Through Time

Having a strong Mercurial temperament, it came as a big surprise that not everyone embraced the prospect of change the way I did. Ever since I can remember I have loved the road, packing a suitcase, boarding a train and heading off. I have always been more comfortable *in between* places than I have *in* places. I like leaving and arriving, but staying is never easy. Then again Mercury, my planetary patron, is the god of the road and transition. Whenever this deity appeared in these in-between times, clothed as either trickster or guide, my journeys turned out to be unpredictable and exciting. Not knowing what was around the corner or next on the agenda was exhilarating.

But when I began leading tours and retreats, it became clear that not everyone shared the same outlook or approach to transition as I did. I began to be aware of each individual's unique approach to transition. Being mindful of different personal styles helped me to be more accepting of myself and others in changing times, as well as revealing what might be needed to maximize a safe and successful passage.

Transition is generally recognized as a period of change from one state to another, a passage of time, an alteration or changeover – all recurring states throughout our lifetime. Quintessentially, life is a state of transition between birth and death. Life's intermediary adjustments can seem to last an aeon or a moment and are often referred to as liminal states.[39]

Liminality is the time in-between what has passed and what is to come. Liminal states are times of feeling suspended between what was once familiar, yet is now the past, and what will be, yet is not known. While confusing and disorientating, the space opens up a world of new possibilities. Therefore liminal periods are often depicted as initiations or rites of passage and are appropriate times for ritual observances that assist in activating these transitions successfully.

Planetary movements symbolize transitional times, identifying initiatory passages of development. The planetary god seeking attention is personified by its transits to the natal horoscope. Each planet's progress embodies qualities particular to transition and the atmosphere of the times. Planetary movements do not make time, but are astute for reading time. While the birth chart remains unchanged, endless planetary transits animate the horoscope through time. Our astrological transit-system identifies the transport that you board to make the transition.

The punctuations of time, as witnessed by the planets' present positions and their interconnection to your natal horoscope are the symbols of transition. The word 'transit' can be used either as a verb, implying an action and a process, or as a noun identifying a place, a person or a thing. As an action, transit implies passing from one state to another. As an astrological verb, it points towards transformative patterns that invite consciousness and participation. As an astrological noun, the word accompanies a planetary adjective such as a 'Saturn transit', which is objective and descriptive of the nature of the process, which is often void of the feeling life underpinning the ongoing experience. As astrologers we use transits to narrate time; however, we also listen for the underlying felt experience that arises from remembered disturbances during past cycles.

Temperament and Transition

Before we look at transits, it is important to appreciate your personal style of transition. Reflecting on elemental temperament, it is apparent that Fire's zealous approach to transition differs from Water's emotive or Earth's cautious style. I have observed that our unique brand of transition is primarily symbolized by our Ascendant. The horizon of our horoscope is connected with emergence and disappearance, symbolized by the Sun's rise at the eastern horizon and its setting at the western portal. Birth and death, the two most powerful moments of transformation, are resonant images along this axis of transition.

Metaphorically, the Ascendant marks a birth point, symbolizing the soul's entry into incarnation as well as the personality's lifelong attitude and reaction to new situations and stages of life. Our Ascendant is a potent image of how we approach transition;

therefore, transits to the Ascendant–Descendant axis synchronize with significant life changes.

To reflect on your style of transition, contemplate your Ascendant sign's modality. It is immediately apparent that the cardinal style of transition will be very different from the fixed or mutable style. Cardinal signs may be more inclined to initiate the change and confront any impasses that arise; however, they may find it difficult to sustain the momentum as the transition advances. The element will differentiate whether the response may be more conceptual (Fire), hands-on (Earth), logical (Air) or emotional (Water). Fixed signs may approach the transition more warily, needing more time to plan and gather the skills and techniques which make the passage more coherent. However, they may also procrastinate, stall and get stuck in the process. A mutable rising may be in the change before they realize it, responding to situations as they arise and reacting on the spur of the moment; however, this expenditure of energy may deplete the stamina needed to maintain the transition. The astrological combination of the modality and quality of each sign outlines twelve unique styles of transition.

Any planet on the horizon of the horoscope is summoned in times of transition; therefore, this planetary archetype can be used as a supportive orientating force during passages of change. The ruler of the Ascendant also plays a major role, as it is like the chauffeur at the wheel of your vehicle during transitional times. This planetary archetype helps us to imagine how our transitional process may be handled and which path is best to follow. As a guide in transition, the condition of and aspects to the Ascendant ruler reveal the ease or effort that accompanies the change.

The Moon is also significant in considering your style of transition. How we defend, respond and react to change is all part of our lunar constitution. At its core the Moon is our symbol of home, a deeply felt sense of belonging that needs emotional constancy and psychological stability. In a way, transition and change are a return home, a homecoming to an aspect of the Self. Pointers to how we might protect and nurture ourselves through the process of change are represented by the natal Moon. The sign reflects the qualities needed during transition while its aspects are a key to which patterns and memories will be stirred through the upheaval.

The trinity of the Ascendant, its ruler, and the Moon illustrate our personal style of transition. It is important to recognize that there is no one way or right way to transition through life, but our temperament revealed by the natal chart helps us to appreciate how we might manage change. There is only our way, and tuning into our natural response to transition assists us to move through the passages of our life authentically.

Transitions are recurring features in our lives, symbolized by the transits of the planets along their zodiacal path in the heavens. Each transition, like each horoscope, is unique; therefore each transit, while having similar archetypal themes, is experienced in a personal way. There is no standard manual for the way transits manifest. The transiting planets' archetypal natures will be our guide to understanding the patterns of time, both personally and collectively.

Considering Transits

When working with transits, finding a system for organizing the data is a priority. What follows is an approach that I have developed from working with transits over time. This approach is not definitive, simply ways to consider differentiating the complexities and priorities of transits. Clarity of understanding does not come through a formulaic approach to transits, but through the persistent honouring of the symbols that are involved in the astrological images.

Planetary transits are multi-dimensional because they occur on all levels of human experience. A transit may reveal itself through an inner experience, an emotional or psychological crisis, a spiritual shift or an external event. The planetary transit evokes images of the soul in transition, but these can be experienced in various ways in several dimensions.[40] Symbols are multi-layered as they can reveal different levels of meaning simultaneously – they can represent the literal world as well as emotional and psychological conditions.[41] Being systemic by nature, transits are not isolated to just one part of the system. When a major transit impacts one area of the horoscope, its affect ripples through the whole system. This is also apparent in the family system where a transit to one member's horoscope affects the other family members as well, due to planetary links in the family organism.[42] Personal transitions affect the systems of our lives.

The most apparent manifestation of a transit is an event or incident in the outer world – a crisis, a change of status or an episode that is consistent with the planetary archetypes involved. This is the *literal level* of the symbol – a tangible and material level of manifestation. The law of correspondences reminds us of the connection between the inner and outer; therefore, the worldly event, no matter how dramatic or how small, is reflective of the inner world. If an individual is unconscious of their inner need for reorientation and change, an incident in their outer world is often the impetus that provokes reflection and action.

An inner situation becomes more conscious when an outer event or situation is recognized as our own projection. We often recognize the transit in the outer world first through a circumstance or incident that confronts our identity and direction. It is useful to reflect on the astrological symbolism of the transit, together with the impact of the event, as being symptomatic of an underlying need for change and redirection. What is happening, coupled with the symbolism of the transit, allows the astrologer and client to reflect meaningfully on the process of time.

Transits also evoke the feeling life, memories, emotional reactions and moods – the *emotional* level. Major transits could synchronize with a wide range of feelings that induce memories, physiological responses, symptoms or reactions, fantasies or images, mood swings or uncharacteristic behaviour. The feelings evoked by the transit are the medium through which the soul invites psychological reconnection and reparation. In this way the transit manifests as an invitation to reflect on the emotional changes that are occurring.

When psychological changes are afoot, repressed feelings and painful memories may rise to the surface for recognition and healing. Working with the symbols of the transits connects past times when similar feelings may have been present. Outer planetary transits are soul-awakening when authentic feelings surface. For instance, during a Pluto transit, feelings of loss, grief, despair, rage or betrayal may have to be confronted. A Neptune transit may flood the individual with feelings of confusion, fatigue or hopelessness, while a transit of Uranus may awaken feelings of anxiety, panic, disconnection and/or terror. Transits reveal the psychic territory in need of attention. Astrological counsellors are witnesses to the retrieval and healing of painful feelings.

On a deeper level, transits engender meaning and the recovery of purpose – the *soul level* of the transit. At the core of the transit is a calling to be valued and authenticated. While the outcome may lead to a greater self-acceptance and knowledge, what is demanded is often uncertain and unclear. At the soul level of the transit we are challenged to find purpose and meaning in the current context of our lives. We are invited to accept the necessity of the transition, even if we are not yet able to understand it.

It would be normal for all these levels to be enmeshed during the process of any transit. Experiencing a critical event leads to the realization that change is necessary, heralding the beginning of the transit. Emotional reactions follow, unearthing archaic and repressed feelings. Finally, the understanding and integration of the transition strengthens identity and consciousness. While major transits awaken potentiality and possibilities, like all opportunities, it is incumbent on the individual to respond with confidence in the process, consciously cooperating with the potential of the transit and facing what needs to be confronted.

In Chapter 1, I referenced Joseph Campbell's reworking of Van Gennep's *Rites of Passage* into the transitional cycle of separation, initiation, and return.[43] Applying this sequence of initiation to transits is helpful in recognizing stages of the transitional process. The first stage is *separation* from what has been familiar, known and habitual, which occurs as the transit is applying. This may also be accompanied by an outer event or a significant development. As the transit retrogrades back and forth, the individual experiences the trials and ordeals of separating from the past towards an uncertain future. This phase of *initiation* could be characterized by the emotional catharsis and psychological insights that accompany transition. As the transiting planet separates, the *return* evokes new images for the initiate returning to life, not as it once was, but as it is meant to be.

Types of Transits

Transits can be categorized in many ways. However, I find it worthwhile to differentiate between the transit being unique to an individual, a *personal transit*, and the transit being part of a generational cycle, a *generic transit*.

The *personal transit* suggests that a planet is transiting a key feature of the horoscope. Generally, a personal transit takes into account the movement of an outer planet (♇, ♅, ♆, ♇) or social one (♃, ♄) that forms a major aspect to an inner planet (☽, ☉, ☿, ♀, ♂) or one of the four angles. I first note any outer planets in transit to natal angles or inner planets. Then I consider the transits of the social planets in the same way.

Nodal transits, along with eclipses, are also noteworthy, as the transiting lunar nodes focus on certain house polarities and aspects to natal planets. In the footsteps of the transiting nodes are eclipses, which impact the similar houses and planets.

Personal transits also include the transit of planets through the houses of the horoscope. The social planets are highly significant, as their timetable through one house of the horoscope is approximately one year (♃) or two and a half years (♄). Jupiter transits the horoscope in 12 years or about 7 times in an average lifetime. Saturn takes 29–30 years to cycle the horoscope, completing almost 3 series in an average lifespan. Jupiter and Saturn focus their attention on the area of the horoscope they are transiting. The outer planets spend considerable time in each house; therefore, their influence is felt more acutely in the early stages of transition into the new house. If you remain consistent with your house system, the transiting planet's ingress into a house is an evocative image of environmental change. Since the outer planets spend a large amount of time in one quadrant and each house, these areas of the chart become strongly influenced by this transiting energy.

Generic transits are the social and outer planets transiting in aspect to their natal placements. We will differentiate the generational passages more in Chapters 6 and 7 and their returns in Chapter 15. These transits can be identified in two ways:

• Aspects that occur within the planet's unique cycle; for
  instance, transiting Saturn opposite natal Saturn, at ages 14–
  15 or 44–45, or the Jupiter return nearly every 12 years, etc.
  These aspects define the passages of the life cycle and stress
  the importance of certain times of life that we have come to
  know as: *adolescence* (Jupiter return, Saturn opposition),
  Midlife (Uranus opposition, Neptune waxing square) and *The
  Fifties* (Chiron return), and so on.

Transiting planets make critical aspects to their natal placements, such as transiting Neptune square natal Neptune at age 41. Critical times are defined by the waxing square, the opposition, the waning square and the return to the conjunction to begin the next cycle. All outer and social planets form these aspects at similar ages in the life cycle. Pluto and Chiron are the exceptions, due to their elliptical orbits. However, each generation will experience their cycle at more or less the same ages. These transits differentiate the ethos, intention and concern of different generations.

• The dance of the outer planets between themselves occurs near the same age for everyone of that generation; for instance, for the Neptune in Capricorn generation, Pluto is conjunct Neptune in their mid-twenties. For the Pluto in Virgo and subsequent generations, transiting Neptune opposes Pluto in the decade of the fifties.

These two levels of transits differentiate personal changes from intrinsic rites of passage in the life cycle. One of the most profound transits is when both the personal and the generic cycles occur simultaneously. For example, consider the aspect of Pluto conjunct the Moon in a natal chart. When Pluto squares the Moon by transit, the generic cycle of Pluto squaring Pluto will also be in effect. Therefore, the Pluto–Moon aspect in the natal chart is recapitulated by transits in both a personal and generic sense. Hence when an outer planet is natally in a key aspect to an inner planet, at some point in the outer planet's cycle it will reconfigure the planetary combination by transit.

Transits are continually occurring, because change and movement are inevitable. Transits validate everything being in flux. Each generation experiences the atmosphere of the times differently because, astrologically, the constellation of planetary energies for each generation differs. Since so many cycles occur simultaneously, it is important to prioritize them. Which transits are the most important and which ones should be given precedence?

Prioritizing Transits

To help classify which transits will be the most potent, let's differentiate major themes from minor ones. Note that this system is only a guide in considering the multiplicity of transits that can be concurrent at any given time. To begin, let's establish which transiting planets have higher priority.

i. The Transiting Planet

The slower the transiting planet, the greater its impact, since its influence persists over a longer period. Outer planets evoke complexes that are often in conflict with the personality. By transit, outer planets awaken a depth of feeling that illuminates what may previously have been unidentified or unfelt and is often of great concern or uncertainty. I would prioritize the planets as follows:

Pluto	248 years
Neptune	165 years
Uranus	84 years
Chiron	50 years
Saturn	29–30 years
Jupiter	12 years

ii. The Planet Being Transited

Aspects made to the inner planets and angles are of great personal importance. Consider the speed of the planet being transited as the main prerequisite. Transits to the Moon and Sun are of first importance, but angles are also very sensitive; therefore, transiting planets conjoining angles are also high priority. Transits to the inner planets signify changes that are taking place on a personal and intimate level; therefore, transits from the slower-moving planets to the faster-moving planets are crucial, as they suggest profound shifts in personal understanding and self-realization.

When combining these priorities, the outer planets' transits to the angles and inner planets have highest precedence.

The Four Angles	The Ascendant, MC, Descendant and IC complete a cycle in 24 hours
The Moon	27.3 days

The Sun	12 months
Mercury	11–13 months
Venus	10–14 months
Mars	17–23.5 months

Aspects made between transiting outer planets and natal outer planets are generic transits indicating changes within the context of the life cycle. While important, they affect a generation. The changes and modifications needed are due to age and the stage in the process of life. Although these transits may be experienced as deeply personal, they are inherent to our developmental process. These are rites of passage and age-appropriate life cycle shifts. Transiting aspects made between the outer planets to the social planets are also generational, yet they are often felt as deeply personal because the individual's opinions, values, social systems, education, status, traditions and security may be challenged, confronting the individual to be more authentic with their own beliefs and ideals, becoming more autonomous and less influenced by the social and familial systems.

iii. The Aspect Formed

The conjunction marks both the beginning of the new cycle and the end of the previous one, while the opposition occurs at the cycle's midpoint. Although there is only one conjunction and one opposition, all other aspects occur twice in the cycle: one in the waxing and the other in the waning phase of the cycle.

Evaluate the stress-type aspects in contrast to the supportive ones. These different aspects have a particular feeling tone. For instance, the 8th harmonic aspects are multiples of 45°: squares, semi-squares and sesquisquares. These are considered to be more stressful or demanding than some of the 12th harmonic aspects (multiples of 30°) such as the sextile and the trine. However, the 12th harmonic aspects of the semi-sextile (30°) and quincunx (150°) could be considered stressful, as they combine incompatible elements. Personally, I find the five Ptolemaic aspects of the conjunction, opposition, trine, square and sextile, along with the quincunx most helpful when considering timing, perhaps because of the way they unfold over the course of a cycle. The following table summarizes the priority I give to the aspects, but again this is only a guide, a way of reflecting. I assign more significance to the square and the quincunx than the trine and sextile due to the tension and conflict involved when combining incompatible elements.

Priority	Aspect	Harmonic	In the Context of a Cycle
1	Conjunction	1	The beginning of the new cycle
2	Opposition	2	The midpoint or culmination of the cycle
3	Square	4	The crisis points in the cycle
4	Quincunx	12	The adjustment phase of the cycle
5	Trine	3	The coming together of the cycle; synthesis
6	Sextile	6	Forward-striving in the cycle; opportunity

It is essential to differentiate the impact of several transits that occur at the same time. From the listing above, we are suggesting that transiting Pluto conjunct a natal angle or the Moon would be very high priority. Transiting Neptune opposing the Sun is also very important, whereas transiting Jupiter trining Mars would not be the main transit if there were other major ones.

I am proposing that faster-moving transits occur within the context of the 'greater' or slower-moving transits; consequently, the themes of the faster-moving transits serve those of the greater ones. This is a working theory and in practice this may change with each individual. As mentioned previously, a very important priority would be when a personal and a generic transit occur simultaneously. This will happen when an aspect between an inner and an outer planet is re-formed by transit at one of the four critical times in the outer planet's generic cycle.

Timing
When considering the timing of a transiting planet, we must be mindful that each planet has its own timetable according to the length of its cycle. The inner planets move quickly, so their influence is seen as passing quickly. They are highly effective when reflecting on a particular event such as an accident, celebration, emotional

reaction, unusual experience or even a dream. The faster-moving planets are often triggers for these types of event.

The social planets – Jupiter and Saturn – may also transit an area of the horoscope fairly quickly; however, due to their retrograde sub-cycle they can also pass over an area of the horoscope three times, elongating the duration of their transit. Outer planets always pass over an area of the zodiac three times and sometimes five, depending on their retrograde pattern. Therefore, these transits last longer, with the planet moving back and forth to highlight a particular area of the horoscope. Timing of astrological cycles can be very empowering for individuals when they realize that there is an order and rhythm to transitions. The retrograde periods of the planetary cycle emphasize and deepen the experience of the transition.

Traditionally, the first thing to consider is an orb of influence for the planetary transit under consideration. Orbs of influence help to focus astrological timing; however, personal timing of transits is highly subjective and this cannot be measured by the imposition of orbs. Although orbs help to frame the period of an astrological transit, gauging the timing of psychological, emotional and spiritual change is never as easy. Therefore, it is always important to keep in mind the difference between astrological timing and soul timing.

While orbs for the slower-moving planets are often set at 1° or 2°, individuals who are responsive and sensitive to change may feel the transit much earlier than others, maybe at an orb of 5°. The symbolism of the planetary transit may appear in dreams or through experiences in the outer world. These experiences may not impact the individual directly, but they become subtly aware of changes and shifts around them. At the beginning of the transit the consequences may feel impersonal, yet, as the transition is underway, the transit becomes individualized. For instance, imagine transiting Uranus opposing the Sun in the 6th house – an individual may hear of occupational changes in his father's or brother's workplace, or suddenly a male in their environment becomes sick, leaves the workplace or takes on a new role of boss, a leader or a father. The symbols are around them, but not directly affecting them. As the transit develops then the changes become more personal: the individual realizes their work identity is shifting.

Imagining the Transit
To begin to picture how the transit may be experienced, we need to take many factors into account. Begin by considering the nature, the archetypal characteristics, the cycle and the symbolism of the transiting planet itself.

i. The Nature of the Transiting Planet
The following points are designed to reflect on the transiting planet:

- Is the transiting planet personal, social or transpersonal?

- What is the archetypal nature of the transiting planet and what role does it play in psychological development? What might it be asking or inviting us to do?

- Which aspects does the transiting planet make? Prioritize the planetary transit by its speed, the planet it aspects and the aspect made.

- How is the transiting planet situated in the natal horoscope? Consider its astrological aspects, sign and house, as well as the role the planet plays in the life. Do you think the planetary energy is astrologically well supported and developed? Is the natal design and orientation to this archetype heightened in the current situation?

- In what house is the transit occurring? Which environmental factors may be influencing the current situation?

- Is the individual consciously aware of the transiting planetary archetype and its potential impact? Do you consider this energy to be operating functionally for this person?

- Does the individual have adequate support and resources to deal with the changes?

ii. The Nature of the Planet Being Transited

Now, let's consider the archetypal nature and astrological condition of the planet being transited.

- What role does this planet play in the natal horoscope? Is this planet well supported? What is the archetypal essence of this planetary energy? Take into account the sign, house, aspects and full nature of the planet receiving the transit to reflect on what is emerging for the individual.

- Which aspects does this planet make in the horoscope? Will these aspects play a role in supporting or hindering the current situation?

- Which house does this planet rule and how can this area become more developed?

Put the transit in perspective. For instance, if this is a Jupiter or Saturn transit it may have happened before. When did this last happen? If it is a slower-moving transit, when was the last time this transiting planet made a major aspect in its cycle? Reflect on the current cycle and any former times in the cycle that are linked to the present.

iii. The Planetary Cycle

- Has this transit happened before? If so, when?

- When was the last time that this planet made its last major aspect by transit to this natal planet?

- Reflect on the nature of the current cycle and place the transit in this context.

- What are the recurrent themes, issues, dilemmas and patterns that might manifest in this astrological combination?

Keep in mind the nature of planets, their natal aspects and the houses they rule. The houses that these planets rule are affected by the transit, therefore it is important to take into account the affairs of these houses. There are many possibilities in the way that the images of the houses may be experienced during the transit.

iv. The Houses
- The natal house of the transiting planet may describe where underlying issues are being uncovered and brought to the surface in the current environment.

- The house where the transit is occurring is most likely to be where the majority of change takes place. What is evident and needs changing? What is the effect of the underpinning attitudes that this transiting planet brings to this area?

- The house that the planet rules locates where allies and strengths can help to support the change.

- The planet being aspected describes the innate aspect of one's self being awoken, and the house/s it rules shows where there may be consequences due to the changes.

Reflecting on the Technique of Transits
Before beginning to work with transits, contemplate the larger questions concerning time. It is helpful to question our beliefs, define our parameters and be mindful of the complexities involved when working with the timing of transitions. For instance, do significant events always need to synchronize with major transits? Consider whether you believe that an accompanying experience or situation will always be revealed during a transit. It is important to remain open and non-judgemental when studying and understanding the process of how transits work.

Accuracy of Birth Times
If a birth time is not accurate then transits to angles are compromised. Astrological timing, especially transits to the angles and the Moon, is also unreliable. If the chart is calculated for noon at the birthplace, the Moon will be accurate within 6°–7.5° and this discrepancy can

be taken into account when ascertaining transits to the Moon. Even with an unknown time, transits to all the other planets can still be considered.

Precession-corrected Transits

Some astrologers put forward a case for amending transits due to the precession of the equinoxes, which retrospectively alters a planet's position by approximately 1° every 72 years. Should the planetary positions of natal planets be altered to take this into account? Since we are using a tropical framework, I suggest this is not necessary. While it is important to be mindful of this 'discrepancy', I imagine this is more a moot point for those who are inclined to regard astrology as a technical process rather than a symbolic language.

Techniques that Work for Others Do Not Necessarily Work for Us

Some astrologers are very enthusiastic and convincing about certain techniques. However, they may be subjectively giving excessive significance to a minor transit, based on personal rather than unbiased experience. Since astrology is so subjective, particular techniques may not speak to you. It is important to discern which astrological techniques are most comfortable for you.

Do We Bias Our Interpretations Through Our Personal Reactions to Planetary Archetypes?

Recognize the difference between the will of the gods (the planetary archetypes) and the will of the client which could influence your personal interpretation of the situation. Not all individuals may be conscious of their feelings, as they may be defended or split off from the transition they are undergoing. Their denials, wishes and projections may be convincing enough to influence the reading of their current situation. Unconsciously colluding with the client weakens our ability to be impartial to the horoscope's signs and symbols. Our unspoken wishes for the client and our own philosophy can distort how we present and understand the transits.

Psychological and Ethical Considerations

Richard Tarnas, author of *Cosmos and Psyche*, said: 'Astrology is archetypally predictive, not concretely predictive.'[44] This is a heartening quote to remember when working with transits, as astrology is astute at articulating the psychic atmosphere and symbolic realm. How this translates into real time is the mystery, as the symbolic and the literal are two different paradigms. I have found that working psychologically, metaphorically and meaningfully with the symbols leads to an understanding of how they manifest in our world. It is not through cause and effect, but soulful exploration, that the transits reveal themselves to me.

When working with clients I differentiate between astrological timing and psyche's timing. While we can predict the time of an astrological transit precisely, using defined orbs, the human psyche does not always respond in a similar fashion. Underpinning all events are subjective factors such as moods, memories, senses and responses. One of the mysteries of astrology is how soul images literalize in real time.

The Question of Prediction

If we accept that the astrological model is a predictive mechanism, then we are prone to reading a chart from a literal and event-orientated point of view. However, if we view transits from an archetypal perspective, many different nuances of meaning can arise from the chart and certainly more possibilities can be explored.

When reflecting on prediction, Dane Rudhyar reiterated that astrological forecasting was the art of knowing the possibilities of time inherent in the symbol.

> ... if we look at this matter of prediction with intellectual honesty, we have to realize that when the astrologer predicts future events he is rarely able to pinpoint ahead of time (1) exactly what the events will be, (2) under precisely what circumstances they will take place, and (3) how they will affect the consciousness and the psycho-physiological health of the person.[45]

The past can be reflected upon, while the present is often uncertain and the future remains even more so. Astrologers are often consulted to make the future evident or knowable; but is this plausible? For over two thousand years the oracle at Delphi was consulted and one of the main questions asked of the oracle is similar to the question asked by astrological clients: 'How have I offended the god and what reparations can I make in my relationship to this deity?' A common question still asked of modern oracles is 'What is going on?' and 'Why is this happening to me?'

The site of the oracle was a sacred space where one's intention was to enter into an exchange with the divine through the intermediary of the oracle. In doing so the connection between the mortal and the deity, and the sense of one's place in relationship to the divine, was experienced. Oracular sites served the petitioner's psychological life by creating a sacred space or *temenos* where attention could be focused on their questions in a respectful and ritualistic way. Similarly, the *temenos* created between astrologer and client encourages an oracular space where revelation might take place. In this way, astrological divination is more an oracular art, where insights and knowledge of the unconscious can be revealed. While astrological practitioners read the images and transits of the chart, the actual revelations and oracular messages arise spontaneously through participation with the symbols. Astrological forecasts are possible when we remain attuned and open to the astrological symbols of the horoscope.

In my experience the 'prediction' is not read or consciously known, but reveals itself during the exchange between myself and the person whose chart is being examined. Many astrologers claim predictive ability, but in most cases their techniques are not able to be authenticated. The urge to have a mechanistic astrology that predicts is a defence against the uncertainty of the future. Astrological transits supply a richness of signs, symbols and metaphors that can help us reflect and consider future options. Working with transits in an enquiring exchange can spontaneously reveal what is important to know.

What do we believe astrology is capable of revealing? Is it astrology, the astrologer or the client who reveals, or a combination of all three? The fewer expectations we have about the way transits manifest, the more we may be able to hear what is going on with the individual whose chart we are reading. The consideration of ethics when using forecasting techniques honours the astrological tradition and the part we play in promoting its professional image.

When Bad Transits Happen to Good People – or 'It Didn't Begin With Me'

Planets do not moralize or judge; therefore, in examining and interpreting transits it is imperative to remember that we cannot judge, nor criticize, others for their life experiences. While the responsibility may be in the hands of the individual, liability is not easily attributed to one person, one experience or one time. So often the complex did not begin with the person who is suffering or in pain. Whether a past life offence, an ancestral transgression or a personal misdemeanour is at the core of the story, it is not the astrologer's place to judge, nor to form an opinion about what is happening in the person's life. More importantly, it is vital to listen and offer the insights that astrological symbols can provide. In the cosmic design no one is free from the pain of living, no matter how well intentioned or virtuous the individual is or has been.

The Greek myth of Oedipus reminds us of the complex design of fate. Oedipus brilliantly answers the impossible riddle of the sphinx to save the town of Thebes from the menacing monster. Yet he is unconscious of the riddle of his own fate and how this impacts the choices he has made and will make.

Transits, especially of the slower-moving planets, awaken deep-seated psychological puzzles. They shift the natural order that is familiar to us, involving us in mystery and questions which cannot be answered by the intellect or appeased by beliefs. Transits invite us to participate in the process of our own discovery.

4

GOING THROUGH THE PHASES
Styles of Time

'Phase' originates from the ancient Greek word *phasis*, suggesting 'bringing to light', an 'appearance' or 'showing'. In the ancient world, a planet showing itself after being absent from the heavens was a time of reverence, a time of annunciation; a time that ancient astrologers considered auspicious. 'Phase' also suggested a recurrent planetary cycle with reference to its illumination and visibility, most apparent with the phases of the Moon.[46]

The word is now used in many ways; when referring to time, it suggests distinct periods in an ongoing process of change. Psychologically, these perceptible periods are defined as life cycle transitions. Astrologically, we also refer to phases of time, most commonly in reference to the lunar phases. The Moon is illuminated by its reflection of light from the Sun, its phases formed by their changing relationship throughout their 29½ day cycle.

Planets in their relationship to the Sun have different phases that mark transitions in their cycle as they become visible and disappear from sight. A phase also describes distinct stages of change in a planet's aspects, speed, brightness and planetary distance as it orbits the Sun. The planets moving slower than the Earth (from Mars to Pluto) disappear into the Sun beams when approaching their conjunction with the Sun and brighten at their opposition, when they are retrograde and closest to the Earth, but do not go through visible phases of illumination. Since Mars is close enough to the Earth there is some partial phasing. But Mercury and Venus, when viewed from our vantage point, do form a sequence of illuminated phases. This astronomical phenomenon becomes a vivid metaphor of time when seen through astrological eyes.

Mercury and Venus are both closer to the Sun than the Earth is. Being interior to the Earth, they are said to have an 'inferior' orbit. This is why they are often referred to as inferior planets, while the planets exterior to Earth's orbit (Mars to Pluto) are known as superior planets. Although the visual impact of Venus's phases is more impressive and observable than Mercury's, nonetheless they both follow a course of distinguishable phases through their cycles.

Astrologically, the term 'phases' catalogues planets in their synodic cycles with the Sun, with each other, or one zodiacal revolution through the signs or houses. Significant too are the phases of human maturing and development that are synchronous with planetary cycles, such as infancy, adolescence, midlife and later life. These phases are symbolized by aspects that occur within the planet's cycle or with another planet, such as the first Jupiter return at adolescence, the Uranus opposition at midlife or Pluto conjoining Neptune during our twenties. These are life cycle phases, which can be mapped by the zodiacal track of the planets in aspect to their natal position.

Aspects as Phases of Time

Like the chapters of a good book that slowly unveil the plot and develop its characters, every planet has recognizable phases as it progresses from the beginning to the end of its cycle. We have considered how cycles can be defined by aspects, starting at the conjunction (☌) through to the opposition (☍), then back to the following conjunction. We also take note of the two critical turning points or squares (□) that occur halfway between the ☌ and the ☍. These four aspects define the critical phases of astrological cycles and characterize significant developmental phases in the course of the planetary cycle.

Aspects initiate a new phase of a cycle that has its own style and purpose. An aspect between two planets represents a moment of time in their relationship illuminating the phase, style and purpose of their connection. Let's imagine the 12th harmonic (30° multiples of aspects) as phases of a cycle. First note the order of the aspects between the conjunction and opposition and how they are mirrored in the second half of the cycle from the opposition back to the conjunction. The following table is a way of thinking about the development of a cycle and how aspects play a role in its unfolding. An aspect indicates a significant moment in the cycle, as if it were a milestone in the cycle's progress. Each aspect brings to light and reveals a new phase of development.

Below: Twelve Aspects and the Quality of Time
– the 12th Harmonic

Aspects in the First Half of the Cycle	The Waxing Phase and Styles of Time		Aspects in the Last Half of the Cycle	The Waning Phase and Styles of Time
Conjunction 0°	Starting out; at the beginning; an initiation	☌		
		☍	Opposition 180°	Realizing the goal; taking advantage of what it offers
Semi-Sextile 30°	Sorting out the last cycle; adjusting; reorganizing	⚺		
		⚻	Quincunx 150°	Realigning and readjusting the presentation and process
Sextile 60°	Developing the new cycle; bringing together available resources to create opportunities	✳		
		△	Trine 240°	Enjoying the fruits of the labour and the creativity involved; sharing in the produce of the cycle
Square 90°	Taking action; accepting the challenges, following the signs and making innovative changes	□	Square 270°	A critical confrontation with what may still be possible but did not reach fruition in the current cycle
Trine 120°	Ensuring success by stabilizing the project and advancing towards the goal	△		
		✳	Sextile 300°	Accepting the possibility of change and re-visioning new possibilities for a later time
Quincunx 150°	Fine-tuning and last-minute adjustments to ensure that all that can be done has been done	⚻		
		⚺	Semi-Sextile 330°	The wisdom of withdrawal to await and welcome a new cycle; a time of active waiting and clearing away
		☌	Conjunction 360° (0°)	The seeds from the past cycle are fertilized to begin anew

Aspect Phases of the Lunation Cycle

In the 20th century Dane Rudhyar's inspirational work highlighted a cyclical approach to timing in astrological practice. He identified that 'every existential process has a beginning and an end, and passes in-between these two events through a series of recognizable and measurable phases or critical points of transformation.'[47] An ideal astronomical example of this, visible in our heavens, is the cycle of the Sun and Moon, which moves through 'recognizable and measurable phases' every month. It was this luminous cycle that inspired Rudhyar's modern articulation of the eight phases of the lunation cycle.

This mandala (pictured right) depicts the eight phases of the lunation cycle, commencing at the New Moon which is shown at the bottom of the ouroboros where the head and tail of the snake are joined. The face of the Moon is invisible lost in the light of the Sun. The cycle moves clockwise through its phases. The depiction of these eight phases is from a northern hemisphere viewpoint. Southern hemisphere phases would appear in a counter clockwise direction as depicted in this diagram.

Lunation Phases

The ever-changing relationship between the Sun and the Moon has always measured time and agricultural seasons. The shifting phases of light on the countenance of the Moon were of great importance to the ancients who associated the three faces of the Crescent, Full and Dark of the Moon with their goddesses. The threefold round of the Moon was often personified by three goddesses or three aspects of the goddess, who not only embodied three times of life – youth, adult and elder – but also three phases of the passing of time. Over time, the trinity ceded to the quaternary and four distinct phases of the Moon were delineated. We are familiar with these quarter phases depicted on monthly calendars and commonly referenced by science. Like the quarter-times of a football match, these four phases of the Moon symbolize the beginning, First Quarter, halfway and Last Quarter time in every cycle.

Below: Eight Phases and Qualities of Time

Aspects in the First Half of the Cycle	The Waxing Phase and Styles of Time		Aspects in the Last Half of the Cycle	The Waning Phase and Styles of Time
New Moon 0°	Starting out; the beginning of a new cycle; an initiation	♂		
		♋	**Full Moon** 180°	Realizing the goal; taking advantage of what it offers
The Crescent Phase 45°	A critical encounter with the past; remnants and uncompleted issues surface to be relinquished or integrated	∠		
		♐	**The Disseminating Phase** 225°	The challenge to disseminate the creative products and harvest the cycle; tension between productivity and publicity arises
The First Quarter 90°	Taking action; accepting the challenges, following the signs and making changes	□	**The Last Quarter** 270°	A critical confrontation with what may still be possible but has not yet reached fruition in the current cycle
The Gibbous Phase 135°	An awareness of crucial elements needed to ensure the success of the project are revealed; decisive and supportive action is needed	♐		
		∠	**The Balsamic Phase** 315°	A crucial crossroads in the cycle has arrived; time to gather together the successes of the past and create the seeds for future growth
		♂	**New Moon** 360° (0°)	The seeds from the past cycle are fertilized to begin anew

In contemporary astrological practice we refer to the lunation cycle as having eight segments. This division divides the lunation cycle into eight phases of 45° each.[48] Each phase can be measured and quantified, but it also symbolizes a unique quality and essence of time. As we track the cycle through its eight phases we encounter a living image of the passing of time – a seed falling on the ground, germinating, developing its root system, branching out, flowering, producing, thinning, receding, then dying to release the seed potential for the new cycle. The measure of each phase is one-eighth of the cycle. The character and soul of each phase is born out of one's ability to participate with the qualities of this time. In this way the lunation cycle is an ideal prototype for any cycle.

The **New Moon** begins at the conjunction of the Sun and Moon when the Moon is obscured by the light of the Sun. It is an intensely subjective time when there is receptivity to feelings and impressions, as new images and ideas are taking hold. When the Moon conjuncts the Sun, she loses herself in his light, allowing impregnation of a new focus. As the cycle develops the solar light reflected by the Moon increases. Towards the end of this phase the Moon appears as a sliver of light in the western sky at dusk. The Moon is waxing. The growing light symbolizes the maturing of consciousness and up until the Full Moon the cycle is more instinctual, reactive and responsive.

The incubation of the new cycle occurs in the Dark of the Moon when fertile ideas are germinated. As the Moon moves away from the Sun, she begins to reflect its light; the seed now begins to find its roots in the new cycle. It is a time of projection into the new and movement away from the past.

At the **Crescent Phase** the seed action or idea planted at the New Moon pushes forward and shoots up. There can be a struggle to move in the new direction, as challenges from the past need attention before the new cycle can fully develop. Instinctively, the action is to expand that which was birthed at the New Moon, but a firm commitment to the new cycle is needed in order to exorcise the past. At this phase of development, the amount of energy, desire and commitment that will be directed towards the success of the new cycle is established.

The Moon is now increasing in light; therefore, the past begins to challenge the new cycle. Previous actions or ideas may arise for revision. It is a time of struggle, as what is still incomplete from the past cycle seeks objectification; therefore, actions implemented at this time may feel ambivalent or confused. This developmental process calls for growth and expansion with a strong need for mobilization of resources and effort.

The **First Quarter** is a time when action is taken. A severance from the past cycle and a turning towards the future takes hold. Dane Rudhyar described this phase as 'crises in action', where the impetus to act is strong and the desire for change increases. Energy now is directed towards bringing the seed planted at the New Moon into being. This is the time when inner urges surface to be released into activity. Anything that is left over from the Crescent phase is now cleared away. The Moon is increasing in light; therefore, action may still be rooted in unconscious patterning, which is a strong and motivational force for change.

The First Quarter Moon begins as the waxing Moon squares the Sun about one week after the New Moon. The Moon is now 90° west of the Sun and rises across the Ascendant at about noon, crossing the MC near sunset. As the Sun sets, the Moon culminates. At the time when the solar light is being withdrawn, the Moon is at her highest point. Instinctual action comes to the forefront. The Moon sets near midnight, leaving the night sky lit by the stars.

The **Gibbous Phase** begins the transition from instinctual to conscious action. Objectivity is important in considering the growth of the new cycle. The past cycle's structure has been altered and it is now important that the clear focus of the new cycle is visible. A formulation of plans and conscious ideas, as well as analysis, prepares the way for realizations at the Full Moon phase. Techniques and tools are necessary to facilitate the functioning of the cycle. The Moon is swelling with light and consciousness; perseverance is necessary as the cycle increases.

Since more light is able to be reflected, the purpose of the cycle is more conscious; therefore, focus and determination are needed to meet the goals. Decisions that have been made need to be accepted and adapted to the new cycle. At this stage the developmental process is well underway and the time to work and develop it is at hand.

The **Full Moon** is the culmination of the cycle and potentially the realization of the seed purpose. What was begun at the New Moon can now be illuminated, because the midpoint in the cycle reflects understanding and consciousness. As the Sun sets, the Full Moon rises over the horizon to rule the night sky.

The Sun and Moon oppose each another, allowing the Moon to reflect maximum sunlight. Metaphorically, the unconscious is illuminated as much as possible; the seed can begin to bud. At this point the cycle's purpose can be realized and the opposing forces can now be seen clearly. Perception and self-expression begin to replace instinct and feeling as the motivational factors of the cycle.

A conscious cooperation with the instinctual forces that structured the first half of the cycle is being tempered. Objectivity, clarity and self-awareness are needed to understand the purpose of the cycle, as the capacity for reflection and unconscious potential becomes more apparent.

During the **Disseminating Phase** what became illuminated at the Full Moon is distributed in the world. The purpose of the cycle is realized and the momentum generated disseminates the knowledge that has been gained. The cup is full, the flower is in full bloom and the urge to share is heightened. But with dissemination and sharing comes emptying. At the Crescent phase it was necessary to struggle out of the old cycle into the new; at the Disseminating phase the push is to consciously demonstrate the fruits of the new cycle.

The lunar temperament is now purposeful, but the challenge is to sustain the dedication and momentum of what has been realized. By sustaining the vision, the lunar self is able to disseminate the information from a deep source, which is influential and inspiring. Without this dedication information is disseminated in a confusing and superficial way. The realization of the Full Moon phase can now be integrated and shared.

At the **Last Quarter** the Moon makes a waning square to the Sun, calling for re-polarization of the cycle. It is a time of revision, as goals that were not reached in the current cycle are assessed and examined. Dane Rudhyar portrayed this phase as 'crisis in consciousness' when awareness of the process is intensified. Different resolutions are possible: at the First Quarter the urge was to action, at the Last Quarter the tension is more conscious, so the impulse is to reflect and contemplate.

The cycle is nearing completion. It is not the time to act, but rather to reflect and look back on what was not completed. That which cannot become manifest must now be realigned. Goals are revised in an effort to consciously move forward in the present cycle. This phase marks the reorientation of values and the wisdom to know what is no longer useful and to be able to let that go. In the harvest of the cycle is also the awareness of obsolescence and the need for revision and amendments. At the Last Quarter we become aware that the cycle is coming to an end and that realignments must be made.

At the **Balsamic Phase** the reflective light of the Moon is decreasing and once again becomes lost in the brilliance of the Sun. It is a time of release, relief and endings. As the past is relinquished, new seeds for a future cycle can be sown. The Dark of the Moon brings a period of fecundity and incubation, retreat and solitude. Future goals are distilled at this crossroads between the past and the future. The time has passed for the ideas that did not take root, but they may once again be transformed into new ideas, which become re-established in the upcoming cycle. It is a time of metamorphosis as the old gives way to the new.

This is the final letting go of the old cycle. Symbolically, the Moon once again enters the kingdom of the Sun, bringing her needs and seeds for the future. Transition and transformation are thematic of this phase. Something dies but its essence is reseeded at the New Moon. A commitment to the future is made.

Labours of the Lights

The changing phases of light visible in our heavens each month have always served as the living symbol of the quintessential round. Rudhyar's work on the lunation process reintroduced this classic astrological round as the prototype for the phases of every cycle from beginning to end. Its eight phases suggest the inevitability of growth, struggle, change, enquiry, maturity, distribution, decay and death. As an archetypal cycle its essence underpins all cycles. Knowing its sequence helps us to instinctually identify the conventional stages within other cycles.

Psychologist Erik Erikson also formulated eight stages of the life cycle. With each stage comes a task, a challenge and maturation. Although his psychological theory was geared towards the life cycle, we could also apply this metaphorically to all cycles. To reflect on the qualitative nature of astrological cycles, I have placed Erikson's model alongside Rudhyar's lunation cycle. While we cannot impose one system of thought directly on another, other ideas can inform and amplify astrological wisdom. I present this as a way to honour the embedded intelligence at each stage of any cycle.

The Lunation Cycle	Keyword for this Phase	Erikson's Life Cycle Virtue	Erikson's Life Cycle Task	Erikson's Life Cycle Challenge
New Moon	Birth	Hope	Trust	Basic Trust vs Mistrust
Crescent	Struggle	Will	Autonomy	Autonomy vs Shame and Doubt
First Quarter	Action	Purpose	Initiative	Initiative vs Guilt
Gibbous	Preparation	Competence	Industry	Industry vs Inferiority
Full Moon	Culmination	Fidelity	Identity	Identity vs Role Confusion
Disseminating	Convey	Love	Intimacy	Intimacy vs Isolation
Last Quarter	Edit	Care	Generativity	Generativity vs Stagnation
Balsamic	Withdraw	Wisdom	Ego Identity	Ego Integrity vs Despair

The Lunation Cycle as Metaphoric of All Cycles

This recurring movement of the Sun and Moon from their conjunction at the New Moon through their waxing phases to their opposition at the Full Moon, back through the waning phases to return to their next conjunction, not only regularly marks out a passage of time but is an illustration of every cycle. Using this image we can divide every cycle into two main phases: waxing and waning. We can measure the waxing phase from the beginning of its cycle to the midpoint; the waning half runs from its midpoint to the beginning of the next cycle. This can be used as a map for all cycles as long as we define the starting point as the conjunction.

The lunation process is a cyclic model of time that embraces definable phases, analogous to every cycle of life, no matter its context, duration or intention. As a symbol for the phases of any cycle the lunation cycle of phases is evocative and revelatory. The round of time so well illustrated by this cycle is an enduring aspect of all astrological time, which offers astrologers a profound glimpse into the *moving image of eternity*.

Mercury and Venus Phases

Mercury and Venus orbit between the Earth and the Sun, and from our vantage point each one progresses through a series of phases, growing and decreasing in light and speed. While the planets will reflect solar light as the Moon does, there is a difference: the Moon reflects maximum light during its full phase, whereas Mercury and Venus do so at their crescent phase, before and after their inferior conjunction with the Sun.[49] This is due to the proximity of the planets to the Earth, so they appear much bigger than when they are fully lit on the other side of the Sun, at their 'full' phase.

Astronomically, there are four important configurations during the synodic cycles of Mercury and Venus:

- The inferior conjunction when their synodic cycle begins.

- The greatest elongation west (GEW) when the planet is west of the Sun at its greatest angle with the Sun (Mercury's greatest elongation is 28° while Venus's is 48°). It is the morning star.

- The superior conjunction when the planet is on the opposite side of the Sun from the Earth.

- The greatest elongation east (GEE) when the planet is east of the Sun at it greatest possible span from the Sun. It is the evening star.

To ancient astrologers these times during the cycle were important, but other times were significant as well. These included the first appearance of the planet in the morning sky after the inferior conjunction, as well as the first appearance of the planet in the evening sky after the superior conjunction. Similarly, the morning and evening setting and the planets turning retrograde and direct were key turning points. During its complete cycle the planet changed speed, shape, distance and direction, disappeared then reappeared: all phases that symbolized time.

Since Mercury and Venus are interior to the Earth's orbit, they are contained between the Earth and the Sun, limiting their aspects to the Sun. Rather than having a conjunction and an opposition like superior planets, their cycles include two conjunctions. One conjunction occurs when they are closest to the Earth and retrograde. This is known as their inferior conjunction. The other occurs when Mercury or Venus is direct on the other side of the Sun to the Earth. This is known as the superior conjunction.

Mercury and Venus begin their synodic cycle at their inferior conjunction while they are still retrograde and absent from the heavens. At this time each planet shape-shifts from evening to morning star. By its morning heliacal rise, it has separated enough from the Sun to become visible, announcing the rebirth of its cycle. Shortly after, the planet turns direct and reaches its greatest elongation from the Sun. The gap between the planet and the Sun begins to close as the planet moves towards its superior conjunction. Before this, the planet disappears from the morning sky, but reappears as an evening star after the superior conjunction. The planet then decreases its speed until it reaches its greatest elongation once again on the way to its station retrograde. Shortly after, the planet disappears, ending its cycle at the next inferior conjunction.

In the following chapter the Mercury and Venus phases will be amplified. For instance, Mercury's planetary phases are supportive timetables when considering study, writing, travel, movement, research, communication, etc. Venusian phases can be helpful when considering her domains of budgeting, relating, relationship planning, purchasing valuables, investing, etc.

5

WANDERERS OF HEAVEN
Rhythms and Rhymes of the Personal Planets

Astrological time is differentiated through each planetary cycle which has its own purpose and pattern. Plato, in *Timaeus*, observed that it is not just the course of the Moon and Sun through the heavens that mark out time in months and years, but the other planets do so as well:

> … the month, complete when the moon has been around her orbit and caught up with the sun again; the year, complete when the sun has been round his orbit. Only a very few men have thought about the periods of the other planets; they have no name for them and do not calculate their numerical relationships. They are indeed virtually ignorant of the fact that their wandering movements are time, so bewildering are they in number and so amazing in intricacy.[50]

The 'wandering movements' of the other planets is astrological timing, which practitioners discover is 'amazing in intricacy'. In Plato's age, two and a half millennia ago, five other wanderers or planets were known, each differentiating qualities of time: Mercurial, Venusian, Martian, Jovial and Saturnine time. Through these traditional timepieces, periods and phases of life can be imagined, as each planetary cycle has its own quality of time.[51] While it is tempting to see time as chronological rather than cyclic, planetary cycles demonstrate the multiplicity and complexity of time. Working astrologically reminds us that time is symbolic, rather than metric. Although we read time by our watches, phones or clocks, astrological cycles have their own characteristic timing which reveals their nature and purpose.

In this chapter we will muse on the three personal planets and their purposeful patterns in the *moving image of eternity*. The transits of Mercury, Venus and Mars move relatively fast; therefore, their cycles in reference to our natal chart are regularly repeated throughout life. Due to their recurrent transitions, the affect of the inner planets becomes familiar and habitual. Our thoughts, values and desires are expressed naturally and routinely. Focused around these planetary transitions are the rituals, observances and celebrations of our everyday life. Here is a summary of the sidereal, synodic and tropical or zodiacal cycles of the three personal planets.

Planet	Traits in Time	Approximate Sidereal Period in Months/Days	Approximate Synodic Period in Months/Days	Approximate Time to Transit Horoscope
Mercury	Time to Imagine	88 days	116 days	11–13 months
Venus	Time to Appreciate	225 days	584 days	10–14 months
Mars	Time to Act	22 months	25–26 months	17.5–23 months

Like other cycles, their influence is important in a variety of ways, particularly as they transit through the houses, form aspects to natal planets and when they are in their retrograde sub-cycle. While they may not play a lead role in major transitions, they are significant in the everyday rituals, exchanges and events of life. These are the gods of everyday activity.

Transits of the inner planets also act as triggers to the larger cycles that are already operating. This is especially so when an inner planet transits an outer planet in the similar time frame reciprocally: for instance, the time frame of Uranus transiting in aspect to natal Mars can be about 15 months, using a 1° orb. However, within this time frame transiting Mars will aspect natal Uranus. The planetary transition is mutual, reinforcing the archetypal interchange at this time.

Retrograde Sub-cycle
Mercury, Venus and Mars all have unique retrograde periods which occur when each planet is closest to the Earth. The phenomenon of retrograde planets occurs because we observe the heavens from our perspective on Earth, which is also orbiting the Sun. Imagine two trains on parallel tracks. When one overtakes the other, a visual distortion occurs as the train being witnessed appears to be moving backward.

Each retrograde period occurs once in the planet's synodic cycle with the Sun; therefore, the retrograde process is a sub-cycle occurring within the larger context of the cycle. It occurs at a predictable and critical time in the cycle and represents an important chapter within the context of the whole cycle. Since the synodic cycle of the planets from Jupiter to Pluto lasts nearly a year, these planets will be retrograde once a year. Mars's synodic cycle suggests it will be retrograde once in its 2-year cycle; Venus is retrograde once in its 19-month cycle, while Mercury is retrograde nearly every 4 months. It is important to honour this phase within the context of the planet's full cycle.

At the midpoint of their retrograde periods, Mercury and Venus are at their inferior conjunction with the Sun beginning their new cycle. Therefore, there are two segments to their retrograde periods – one before the inferior conjunction, which ends the previous cycle, and the one after that ushers in the new cycle. At the inferior conjunction the planet begins to rise before the Sun, leading the way as the 'morning star'. At the superior conjunction the planet again changes, from rising before the Sun to following the Sun, becoming visible in the western skies as the 'evening star'.

Mars, Jupiter, Saturn and the outer planets turn retrograde as they approach their opposition to the Sun. At the midpoint of the retrograde sub-cycle, these planets are directly opposite the Sun and shine brightly in the night sky. Each retrograde period is an intrinsic part of the planet's cycle and tells time in its own unique way. Retrograde time is more reflective and internal, a phase of reconsideration and review. The following table summarizes the retrograde sub-cycles of all the planets.

Planet	Frequency	Length of Retrograde Period	Critical Degree Where Planet Turns Retrograde
Mercury	3 times per year	19–24 days (3 weeks)	Mercury stations anywhere between 13° and 22° from the Sun, about 10–12 days before its inferior conjunction
Venus	Once every 19 months	40–43 days (6 weeks)	Venus will station when it is approximately one sign ahead of the Sun (approximately 28°–30°). This occurs about 3 weeks before its inferior conjunction

Mars	Once every 2 years	58–82 days	The critical degree of separation from the Sun at which Mars turns retrograde is variable
Jupiter	Once a year	4 months	The critical degree of separation from the Sun when Jupiter turns retrograde is approximately 117°; therefore, Jupiter will be retrograde in a natal chart when trine (dependent on orb), quincunx or opposite the Sun
Saturn	Once a year	4.5 months	The critical degree of separation when Saturn turns retrograde is approximately 108°; therefore, Saturn will be retrograde in a natal chart when trine, quincunx or opposite the Sun
Uranus	Once a year	5 months	The critical degree of separation from the Sun when Uranus turns retrograde is approximately 104°; therefore, Uranus will be retrograde in a natal chart when trine, quincunx or opposite the Sun
Neptune	Once a year	5.25 months	The critical degree of separation when Neptune turns retrograde is approximately 101°; therefore, Neptune will be retrograde in a natal chart when trine, quincunx or opposite the Sun
Pluto	Once a year	At present about 5.25 months	The critical degree of separation from the Sun when Pluto turns retrograde varies. In 2020 it is approximately 101.3°; therefore, Pluto will be retrograde in a natal chart when trine, quincunx or opposite the Sun

☿ Mercury

Catching a glimpse of Mercury is not easy. The planet is only visible near the horizon in the transitional twilight before sunrise or after sunset, the in-between zone where Mercury is most at home. In myth, Mercury was also difficult to corner. Dual, dexterous and disappearing, Mercury is the god of the road and the marketplace, a guide and a traveller. Unlike the other gods he did not have sanctuaries or fixed places of worship; instead he was spotted on the road, in-between, in transition and in motion.

Being close to the Sun, the skies are never completely darkened when Mercury becomes discernible. Perched between day and night, Mercury can be fleetingly glimpsed after the Sun sets or before it rises. Even though Mercury will make three morning and three evening appearances each year, he remains elusive. In his morning face, mythic Mercury leads souls up from the underworld; as the psychopomp, he guides them down again. He awakens us, bringing the spirits up from the night realm so they linger in our imagination until they disappear into the dawning light. At nightfall, as shepherd of dreams, he guides us down into the world of sleep and dreams. Characteristically, Mercury lingers on the threshold of sleeping and waking. On the borderland of sleep, sensory phenomena such as voices and visions are often experienced while Mercury guides us into or up from the cavern of sleep each day. By transit Mercury symbolizes meaningful moments, in-between time, synchrony, times when there is a change of thinking or modification of plans or routines. He is at his best when in motion; therefore, under Mercury's guidance we often have our best conversations in the car or on the road, our best thoughts upon waking or when travelling, and our best ideas during a reflective moment.

Mercury is multifarious, mischievous and magical, residing between intellect and imagination. He is a master traveller and the zodiacal route he travels in the heavens maps out Mercurial time with regularity and order, signifying that the god is not as haphazard as we sometimes assume. Mercury has an affinity with the numbers three and six: it is retrograde three times a year, each for a period of about three weeks, and has a six-year pattern of retrograding through the elements.

Mercury's cycle illustrates the sacredness of geometry. Annually there are 3.14 synodic cycles; therefore, the mathematical constant of Pi is outlined on the heavens as Mercury orbits the Sun. This numerical paradigm states that the ratio of a circle's circumference to its diameter is approximately 3.14, re-minding us of the Mercurial link between infinity (circle) and linearity (diameter). Mercury is the god of the hieroglyph, a 'sacred carving', and his heavenly hieroglyph is Pi.[52] Mathematical Mercury is irrational in the truest sense, in that it is unlimited in possibilities, reminding us of the infinite possibilities of thoughts, ideas and movement. Mercury is at the helm of the horizon; no wonder the ancients said he en-joys the 1st house, always ready to transition from a night to a day personality.

Mercury is betwixt and between, inhabiting liminal and subliminal spaces, endlessly linking the narratives of our lives together. Being multi-focal, the god sees through lenses of intellect, intuition, interpretation and imagination. Tom Moore so succinctly describes Mercurial intelligence as the power 'to keep the soul in motion' and 'the carousel of interpretation moving'.[53]

When we are on thresholds, in transitions, between times, crossing borders or at crossroads, Mercury might appear out of the shadows to leads us into or out of essential experiences. He is the guide to the guru, the unexpected detour, the thought that reconnects us to the dream we had the night before; he is leader and follower, eyeing the landscape in front of and behind us.

The Mercury Cycle

Being egg-shaped, Mercury's orbit is eccentric, which is characteristic of this god. Its orbital speed varies considerably, ranging from a standstill near its stations to over 2.25° a day at its superior conjunction. Like the Moon, Mercury's synodic cycle goes through phases, a heavenly and helpful time frame when imagining and developing certain projects.

The Sun–Mercury cycle averages 116 days; however, each individual cycle may last 105–130 days. We might think of these as being like academic terms of a year or modules of a course. The cycle's two conjunctions are turning points. At the inferior conjunction Mercury leaves its post as the evening star to now rise first, leading the Sun into a new cycle.[54] At the superior conjunction Mercury is on the other side of the Sun, changing position to now follow the Sun. Through the technique of planetary sect our astrological ancestors respected Mercury's dual temperament by aligning him with the day sect, when he rose before the Sun, and the night camp when he set after the Sun.

This cycle accounts for Mercury's disappearance and reappearance, as well as its retrograde period three times a year. Shape-shifting between the twilight gods of dawn and dusk is consistent with the Mercurial disposition: adaptability in changeover times, proficiency in moving between hemispheres, acclimatizing to new arrangements, guiding in transitional zones and linking different states of consciousness.

At the inferior conjunction, a renewed facet of Mercurial development is set in motion. This 'new Mercury' begins a forward striving phase while it is still retrograde and closest to the Earth.

At the halfway period, Mercury is direct, fast-moving and farthest from the Earth, now at its most objective and informed point of this cycle. It enters its occidental phase, a more pensive and introspective period. About a week before each conjunction Mercury disappears from our skies, preparing to change focus, visibly rising about a fortnight later, having changed allegiance between the day and the night.

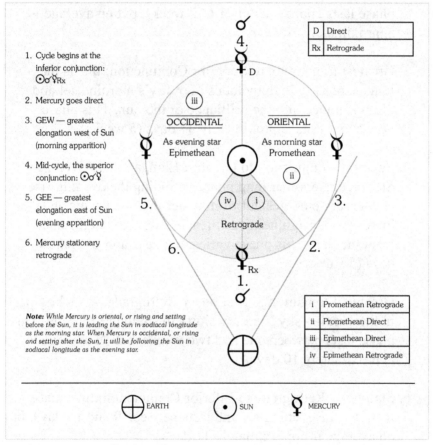

1. Cycle begins at the inferior conjunction: ☉☌☿Rx

2. Mercury goes direct

3. GEW — greatest elongation west of Sun (morning apparition)

4. Mid-cycle, the superior conjunction: ☉☌☿

5. GEE — greatest elongation east of Sun (evening apparition)

6. Mercury stationary retrograde

D	Direct
Rx	Retrograde

OCCIDENTAL — As evening star Epimethean

ORIENTAL — As morning star Promethean

Retrograde

i	Promethean Retrograde
ii	Promethean Direct
iii	Epimethean Direct
iv	Epimethean Retrograde

Note: *While Mercury is oriental, or rising and setting before the Sun, it is leading the Sun in zodiacal longitude as the morning star. When Mercury is occidental, or rising and setting after the Sun, it will be following the Sun in zodiacal longitude as the evening star.*

⊕ EARTH   ☉ SUN   ☿ MERCURY

Thanks to The Mountain Astrologer (www.mountainastrologer.com) for permission to reprint this table.

While we might use 8 phases, as in the lunation or Venus cycles, to characterize the chapters of the Mercurial cycle, I prefer to use 6 stages, a number resonant with Mercury. The length of each phase varies in each cycle, but the average days are listed below, forming the synodic period average of 116 days.

1. Inferior Conjunction to Stationary Direct: this phase includes the morning rise and lasts between 9 and 14 days but on average is approximately 11 days.

2. Stationary Direct to Greatest Elongation as Morning Star: this phase includes Mercury's increasing brightness and greatest brilliance in the morning sky, as morning Mercury reaches its greatest zodiacal distance from the Sun. This phase lasts approximately 1 to 2 weeks, but on average is approximately 10 days.

3. Greatest Elongation to Superior Conjunction: this is the longest phase which includes Mercury's morning set and disappearance into the brilliance of the Sun. This phase varies, but lasts approximately 37 days (5 weeks).

4. Superior Conjunction to Greatest Elongation as Evening Star: again, another long phase including the evening rise as Mercury emerges out from under the Sun beams and increases in brightness, as it reaches its greatest distance from the Sun. This phase varies, but lasts approximately 37 days (5 weeks).

5. Greatest Elongation to Stationary Retrograde: at its brightest in the evening sky Mercury slows to station retrograde. This phase lasts between one and two weeks, but on average is approximately 10 days.

6. Stationary Retrograde to Inferior Conjunction: this phase includes the evening set and lasts between 9 and 14 days, but on average is approximately 11 days.

Mercury Retrograde

The inferior conjunction is the midpoint of Mercury's retrograde period. Mercury turns retrograde 10–11 days before its inferior conjunction, ingesting the information, impressions, ideas, impact and senses from the past 3–4 months of its cycle. After the inferior conjunction, Mercury retrograde enables the essence of what has been digested to seed the new cycle. For these next 10–11 days the retrograde period is reformatting and reframing what has been distilled, nourishing the newborn cycle.

Therefore, the three-week cycle of Mercury retrograde can be seen in two parts: the ending of one cycle and the renewal of the next cycle. Mercury retrograde times are periods of review, clearing the backlog of work, filing completed reports, deleting old programmes, attending to the messages you have been avoiding. Now is the time to get caught up with the paper trail that has piled up, finish the assignment you have been postponing, complete the tasks you have been delaying, so that the new cycle can begin with a purer essence of the past cycle.

Mercury's patterning reveals the cycles of thinking and rethinking and establishes times to order and plan, times to communicate, write, learn and study. Mercury's retrograde design is a wonder, but too often this phase of its cycle is sensationalized and exaggerated, which is a Mercurial quality anyway! The traditional view of this period is that it invariably strains communication lines with wrong phone numbers, lost emails, cancelled appointments, misread contracts and a host of other frustrating communication delays. This is so often true but, when viewed in the context of a cycle, this period contains its own intelligence. Inherent in every planetary cycle is the retrograde phase containing the wisdom to slow down, take your time and reflect on what has happened during the past few months.

Mercury retrograde periods can be times of reflection, contemplation and re-thinking; ideas can be conceived and new patterns of thinking may emerge. I often think of this part of the cycle as slow motion, allowing us to retrace our steps to become mindful and more conscious of how we move through time. Seen from this perspective, Mercury retrograde is an essential part of its cycle, ending one cycle with the Sun and beginning another. While Mercury retrograde 'events' may seemingly appear indiscriminate, they invite us to be considered and reflective. A computer crash during Mercury retrograde could be embraced as a contemplative call to deliberate on the distractions that we mindlessly engage in. While it appears as a seemingly random act, it could result in mindfulness and consciousness if one listens, reflects and recognizes that the trickster at work might be our own unconscious response to being too chaotic, too busy and unfocused. The ancient Greeks recognized that moment in life when a critical discovery or event happens; they called this *anagnorisis* or recognition, the change from ignorance to knowledge, most apparent when there was a reversal of fortune. In Mercurial parlance this moment of reversal or retrograde potentially brings new understanding.

One of the features of the Mercury retrograde cycle is that it will turn retrograde at approximately the same zodiacal degree at which it turned direct eleven months previously. Mercury backtracks in its cycle to pick up the loose threads in the pattern of time. Notice that Mercury turns retrograde at 8♑29 on 13 December 2023; this is the zodiacal degree at which it turned direct three periods ago on 18 January 2023 at 8♑08, threading these two periods together. Mercury retrograde alerts us to the times when our thought processes recover previous ground, linking us back to a previous cycle. As Mercury weaves its way through the zodiac, it picks up the threads from the previous year which may have been overlooked, weaving them again into the Mercurial tapestry, as follows.

Year	Date Stationary Retrograde	Zodiacal Degree	Date Stationary Direct	Zodiacal Degree	Retrograde Element	No. of Days Retro
2020	17 Feb	12♓53	10 Mar	28♒12	Water	21
	18 June	14♋45	12 Jul	05♋29	Water	24
	14 Oct	11♏40	3 Nov	25♎53	Water	20
2021	30 Jan	26♒29	21 Feb	11♒01	Air	22
	29 May	24♊43	22 Jun	16♊07	Air	24
	27 Sep	25♎28	18 Oct	10♎07	Air	21
2022	14 Jan	10♒20	4 Feb	24♑22	Air	21
	10 May	04♊51	3 Jun	26♉05	Air	24
	10 Sep	08♎55	2 Oct	24♍11	Air	22
	29 Dec	24♑21	2023: 18 Jan	08♑08	Earth	20
2023	21 Apr	15♉37	15 May	05♉50	Earth	24
	23 Aug	21♍51	15 Sep	08♍00	Earth	23
	13 Dec	08♑29	2024: 2 Jan	22♐10	Earth	20
2024	1 Apr	27♈13	25 Apr	15♈58	Fire	24

Periods of Mercury retrograde are important times to clear the backlog of work, review, file what needs to be filed, delete old programs from the computer, service the printing machines, complete your assignments or return the phone calls that you have been avoiding. This is especially significant in the period before the inferior conjunction, at the end of this last synodic cycle. If we continue to try to instigate new projects during the period when Mercury is retrograde, we could put stress on the communication system, resulting in the photocopier packing up or documents disappearing. Being an in-between cycle, it is time for revision and completion, a time for rethinking and reflecting, so a new cycle can comfortably begin at the inferior conjunction.

When Mercury is retrograde in a natal horoscope, the ability to instinctually perceive meaning is self-evident, yet finding the words or means to express this is challenged. The clarity of comprehension can be lost in translation! Mercury retrograde individuals often intuit what another is going to say or what that person's reaction will be to what they have said, and this results in their restating or rethinking the situation. Mercury retrograde implies the possibility of retaining knowledge and a keen sensitivity of one's own thought processes. The retrograde Mercury individual has the natural aptitude to perceive symbols, think in images and be reflective. There is also a greater tendency to be individualistic in their thoughts and their communication style. People with Mercury retrograde often feel they are constantly rehearsing for something, going over and over it in their minds.

I encourage students to make a list of remedies for when Mercury is retrograde. Over time students have suggested:

- Rethink an important decision
- Release the negative thoughts
- Re-evaluate your goals
- Reflect on your communication skills and patterns
- Reconfirm your appointments and your travel plans
- Resolve the misunderstanding with a sibling, a friend, a workmate or a colleague
- Focus on what needs to be serviced or repaired – your car, computer, mobile phone, etc

- Edit your manuscript, study in depth for your course, rehearse an important appointment
- Research the material you need for your assignment, your job, your creative project
- Renew your commitment to finishing incomplete projects
- Restart the gym programme or the diet you gave up on a few months ago
- Take a break from your normal schedule to revisit some of your favourite places
- Resurrect the projects and plans you have let go but which are still on your mind

Mercurial Phases

The Sun–Mercury cycle is a useful metaphor when thinking something through. When considering a time frame for writing an article, completing a major assignment, launching a campaign, beginning a study programme, delivering an important presentation or planning the next school semester, the Mercurial cycle is a creative clock to consult. Each phase in Mercury's synodic cycle is an integral aspect of a sequence that symbolizes the way we process information, develop concepts, return to and renew ideas. In contemporary life, with so many decisions to be made, the Mercurial cycle offers us a unique timetable.

Mercury has distinct crossroads in its synodic cycle. Let's review these again: it begins at its inferior conjunction, then turns direct, reaches its greatest elongation from the Sun as the morning star, disappears into the Sun beams, then conjoins the Sun once again on the far side of the Earth. After its superior conjunction, it reappears out of the glare of the Sun to reach its greatest elongation as the evening star, turns retrograde and then re-news its cycle at the next inferior conjunction. This averages 116 days, approximately one third of the year. Each one of these phases could be seen as a development stage of an idea, a project, an article, a plan.

After the inferior conjunction, a new phase begins, born from seeds of the previous cycle. New ideas, brainwaves, innovative projects, ways of thinking and patterns of communication all come to light. These can be developed throughout the course of the new cycle. At the superior conjunction the initiatives, assignments and designs set in motion near the inferior conjunction mature and come to fruition. Mercury as the evening star is more introspective and reflective. The matured ideas can now deepen and be disseminated and shared. As the cycle moves towards the inferior conjunction that which was brought to light may be completed, refined or analysed for future cycles.

During the cycle Mercury reappears and disappears in the morning and evening sky. About a week before each conjunction Mercury withdraws, being 'under the Sun beams'. But during this time Mercury prepares to change focus, visibly rising about a fortnight later having changed allegiances between the day and the night sect.

As we move through the Mercurial cycle, each phase is an integral aspect of the sequence. It is reflective of the way the mind cultivates its concepts and matures its ideas, like phases of thinking something through – this is how Mercury outlines its plots. Let's imagine how these time periods could be beneficial in planning agendas, scheduling programmes or planning itineraries.

Phases of the Mercury Cycle	Mercurial Time
Inferior Conjunction to Stationary Direct	Mercury guides the spirits of the last cycle out of the underworld so their essence may serve in the reformation of a new cycle. A new phase begins, born from the seeds of previous cycles. Mercury becomes the morning star, now more forward-thinking and progressive in planning and scheming. New ideas, projects, ways of thinking and patterns of communication come to light to be developed throughout the course of the new cycle.
Stationary Direct to Greatest Elongation as Morning Star	Instinctive and remembered intentions, initiatives and ideas are at a crossroads, with new ways of thinking and developments taking place. Former projects, research, ideas or studies may return to be redeveloped. Directions and decisions are considered. What was left unattended or incomplete from the last cycle is reviewed and integrated or discarded.
Greatest Elongation to Superior Conjunction	At Mercury's greatest distance from the Sun, a critical change occurs. Ideas and insight forge a way forward with new plans. Application and attention to working on and managing the project is heightened. New ideas and insight inspire a way forward with new strategies. Discrimination, focus and craft bring the emergent and creative ideas into the public domain.

Superior Conjunction to Greatest Elongation as Evening Star	At the superior conjunction, initiatives, assignments and designs approach their fruition. Mercury becomes the evening star, more introspective and reflective. This is the time to reflect and harvest insights and initiatives that have been applied towards the goal; time to disseminate the design, share the products of the creative process, and articulate the process.
Greatest Elongation to Stationary Retrograde	Thinking becomes more introspective and philosophical. Time to edit, review, and articulate the process that has been experienced. It is the phase when adjusting the process, fine-tuning the project and correcting the mistakes will help to complete the assignment and offer insights and revelations into the process.
Stationary Retrograde to Inferior Conjunction	As the cycle moves towards the inferior conjunction, what was brought to light can be completed, refined and analysed for future cycles. It is the time to gather in ideas and, in the depth and privacy of the self, journal and contemplate what has taken place for personal development and future reference. It is time to complete the project for this round.

We can personalize the cycle by considering our natal Mercury – its phase, sign, house and aspects – and reflect on how we best adapt to Mercurial transitions. Transiting Mercury's zodiacal sign and aspects at any moment flavour the phase it is passing through. Being aware of this rhythm helps me to remember a broader perspective – that Mercury is going through a phase and this moment is part of a larger process, a fuller cycle.

On the following page is a table of these dates, given in UT, to help you to track the cycle. This table is generated from the Astrodienst Website www.astro.com – *Planetary Phenomena of Mercury from 1600–2101* – see https://www.astro.com/swisseph/ae/mercury1600.pdf

Below: The Sun–Mercury Cycle
(October 2020 to March 2026)

Inferior Conj.	Station Direct	Greatest Elongation as Morning Star	Superior Conj.	Greatest Elongation as Evening Star	Station Retro.	Inferior Conj.
2020: 25 Oct	3 Nov	10 Nov	20 Dec	**2021:** 24 Jan	30 Jan	8 Feb
2021: 8 Feb	21 Feb	6 Mar	19 Apr	17 May	29 May	11 Jun
11 Jun	22 Jun	4 Jul	1 Aug	14 Sep	27 Sep	9 Oct
9 Oct	18 Oct	25 Oct	29 Nov	**2022:** 7 Jan	14 Jan	23 Jan
2022: 23 Jan	4 Feb	16 Feb	2 Apr	29 Apr	10 May	21 May
21 May	3 Jun	16 Jun	16 Jul	27 Aug	10 Sep	23 Sep
23 Sep	2 Oct	8 Oct	8 Nov	21 Dec	29 Dec	**2023:** 7 Jan
2023: 7 Jan	18 Jan	30 Jan	17 Mar	11 Apr	21 Apr	1 May
1 May	15 May	29 May	1 Jul	10 Aug	23 Aug	6 Sep
6 Sep	15 Sep	22 Sep	20 Oct	4 Dec	13 Dec	22 Dec
2023: 22 Dec	**2024:** 2 Jan	12 Jan	28 Feb	24 Mar	1 Apr	11 Apr
11 Apr	25 Apr	9 May	14 Jun	22 Jul	5 Aug	19 Aug
19 Aug	28 Aug	5 Sep	30 Sep	16 Nov	26 Nov	6 Dec
2024: 6 Dec	15 Dec	25 Dec	**2025:** 9 Feb	8 Mar	15 Mar	24 Mar
24 Mar	7 Apr	21 Apr	30 May	4 Jul	18 Jul	31 Jul
31 Jul	11 Aug	19 Aug	13 Sep	29 Oct	9 Nov	20 Nov
2025: 20 Nov	29 Nov	7 Dec	**2026:** 21 Jan	19 Feb	26 Feb	7 Mar

♀ Venus

Unlike Mercury, Venus is easier to glimpse in the eastern and western skies – she is the bright star, never more than 48° from the Sun, transiting all 12 houses of the horoscope in 10–14 months.

Like many poets, dreamers and lovers, Emily Brontë was captured by Venus's beauty when she portrayed the planet as the *silent silvery star*.[55] Palaeolithic Venus figurines, the Hellenistic statue of Venus de Milo and Botticelli's *Birth of Venus* all attest to her earthy magnetism. She has always been honoured for her heavenly brightness and physical attractiveness, enshrined in the morning and evening skies. Intrinsic to this silent silvery star is the beauty of her brightness, her symmetry, her cycle and her myth.

The Five-pointed Star

Venus will travel direct for just over 17 months before it turns retrograde once again for about 6 weeks, completing its full synodic cycle in approximately 19 months. The 6 weeks, or 40 days and 40 nights, of its retrograde period are part of our folklore, religious stories and observances. This symbol of time is often depicted as the time of wanderings, retreats and soul-searching. During these retrograde periods Venus will transit a zodiacal zone three times, affecting a specific area of your horoscope. As the synodic cycle of Venus and the Sun lasts 584 days and each solar year is 365 days, the following harmonic shows there are exactly 5 Sun–Venus cycles in 8 years:

$$584 \times 5 = 2920$$
$$365 \times 8 = 2920$$

In reality, the solar cycle is 365.25 years. Therefore, when the Sun–Venus inferior conjunction repeats after eight years, it will be within a 2° orb. If we join together the five zodiacal positions of the inferior conjunction, a five-pointed star or pentagram is created. This pentagram pattern also occurs with the superior conjunctions as well as the positions when Venus turns retrograde and direct. At the inferior conjunction with the Sun, Venus is between the Earth and the Sun, closest to the Earth, travelling slowly and retrograde. She is now at the midpoint of the retrograde cycle and begins her new cycle, rising before the Sun.

Date of Sun–Venus Inferior Conjunction	Degree of Zodiac	Date of Sun–Venus Inferior Conjunction	Degree of Zodiac
3 Jun 2020	13♊35	1 Jun 2028	11♊26
9 Jan 2022	18♑43	6 Jan 2030	16♑15
13 Aug 2023	20♌28	11 Aug 2031	18♌17
23 Mar 2025	02♈39	20 Mar 2033	00♈21
24 Oct 2026	00♏45	21 Oct 2034	28♎22

The Sun–Venus Cycle

At the inferior conjunction Venus is invisible as she is 'under the Sun's beams'. However, the following week she reappears as Venus Phosphorus or Lucifer, the morning star or the 'light bringer'. She turns direct three weeks after the inferior conjunction, then reaches her maximum distance from the Sun about seven weeks after that. About one month before the superior conjunction, when Venus is on the other side of the Sun, she disappears from the night sky for nearly two months.

At the midpoint of the cycle Venus conjoins the Sun again, but this time she is farthest from the Earth, fast in motion and direct. A month later she is visible again, but now in the western sky after sunset; she is now known as Hesperus. Seven months after the superior conjunction, Venus reaches her maximum distance from the Sun and approaches Earth. A month later she is at her brightest, then, three weeks after this, Venus turns retrograde. Two weeks later, she disappears from the western sky, preparing for her inferior conjunction to begin the cycle anew.

The table on the next page traces the eight phases of Venus inspired by the lunation cycle.

Phases of the Venus Cycle	Corresponding Lunation Phases	Average Length: 19 months	Venus Time
Inferior Conjunction to Stationary Direct	New Moon	Approx. 3 weeks	Venus begins her ascent from the underworld, renewing, revaluing and fertilizing the new cycle
Stationary Direct to Greatest Elongation	Crescent	Approx. 7 weeks	New ways of being and appreciating our resources and relationships are at a crossroads with past attitudes and values
Greatest Elongation as Morning Star to Morning Set	First Quarter	Approx. 31 weeks; 27 weeks from the greatest elongation to morning set; 4 more weeks until the superior conjunction	Possibilities of new or renewed contacts emerge, social situations may arise or relationship values may change, offering a more balanced way of relating. Simultaneously we are building our resource base, as well as our self-esteem and personal worth
Morning Set to Superior Conjunction	Gibbous		
Superior Conjunction to Evening Rise	Full Moon	Approx. 31 weeks in total; 4 weeks from superior conjunction to evening rise and another 27 weeks to the greatest elongation	Time to celebrate and acknowledge the valuable relationships that contribute to our life. It is the time of sharing our worth and value with others as well as expressing and distributing the resourcefulness and artistry of who we truly are, through our creativity, imagination and self-expression
Evening Rise to Greatest Elongation as Evening Star	Disseminating		
Greatest Elongation to Stationary Retrograde	Last Quarter	Approx. 7 weeks	It is time to be reflective, engaging in an examination of what our deeper self truly values and appreciates
Stationary Retrograde to Inferior Conjunction	Balsamic	Approx. 3 weeks	A time of withdrawal and retreat to reflect on and integrate the past so that a creative and valued cycle can remerge at the conjunction with the Sun

Venus Retrograde

Nearly every 19 months, for approximately 41–43 days, Venus turns retrograde. In a period of 8 years, Venus will retrograde 5 times. After 8 years she returns to the approximate degree (less 2°) on the approximate date (less 2 days) that she occupied in the previous cycle. It takes 96–104 years for Venus to stationary retrograde through each sign at 8-year intervals.

The retrograde period signals a time of reorientation and a sense of renewal in relating to the world as a loving and spirited individual. Venus retrograde implies the time in the cycle when we may withdraw to reflect on our relationships and consider our commitments. Every retrograde period reconnects to a similar time eight years ago; therefore, Venus themes such as self-worth, resources and relationship may link back to a period eight, or a multiple of eight, years ago. Anything that was incomplete or left unresolved in an important relationship may surface again for consideration.

Venus Station Retrograde	Degree of Zodiac	Venus Station Direct	Degree of Zodiac	Days Retrograde	No. of Degrees Retrograde
13 May 2020	21♊50	25 Jun 2020	05♊20	43	16°30'
19 Dec 2021	26♑59	29 Jan 2022	11♑04	41	15°55'
23 Jul 2023	28♌36	4 Sep 2023	12♌12	43	16°24'
2 Mar 2025	10♈50	13 Apr 2025	24♓37	42	16°13'
3 Oct 2026	08♏29	14 Nov 2026	22♎51	42	15°38'

At the midpoint of the retrograde period, Venus begins its new cycle at its inferior conjunction with the Sun; therefore, the first three weeks of the retrograde period end the previous nineteen-month cycle. These weeks focus on letting go of what is no longer of value or resourceful. During the three weeks following the inferior conjunction, Venus integrates and appreciates the best of the past, preparing for the emergent new cycle. This is an insightful and visionary period for contemplating resources, re-visioning relationships and reflecting on personal self-worth and values.

Venus retrograde occurs less frequently in horoscopes than any other planet. Natally, it might suggest that an individual's values, their preferences, likes and dislikes are unlike those of others in their social environment. What appears as inhibition, shyness or lack of affection may be their acute perception of the difficulty in relating and their vulnerability when interacting. Relationships may be non-traditional and unconventional. Often this individual develops their artistic and aesthetic side, with their relationship to creativity and/or spirituality being the priority. Venus retrograde suggests refining and redefining relating. It often manifests as distancing oneself from the fashions, trends and values of consumerism and popular trends. Venus retrograde has highly developed values and individualistic likes and dislikes.

When Venus is retrograde it suggests that an important period is available to reflect on relationship patterns and possibilities. It is also a great time to plan retreats and time out. Over time, students have suggested these remedies when Venus is retrograde:

- Schedule a retreat
- Make an appointment for a massage or beauty treatment
- Review your wardrobe, clear out what is no longer your style and shop for what is
- Buy yourself a gift; however, if you are an impulsive buyer try to constrain your spending
- Redecorate the bedroom
- Visit an art gallery or a lifestyle exhibition
- Review your investment portfolio
- Prepare a financial and savings budget for the next 19 months
- Reflect on your relationship patterns: how are you not being valued? Where do you not feel equal? Do you feel you deserve more?
- Reflect on what needs to be reintroduced into your relationships with others
- Set aside time to review and renew your relationships
- Plan a holiday for only you and your partner
- Finish the novel, complete the painting, focus on your creativity

The Transit of Venus

When Venus is near her own nodal axis, the Sun, Earth and Venus are in alignment. Being close to the Earth she is retrograde, having disappeared from her throne in the western sky but not yet reappeared in the east. At this time both Venus and the Earth are on the same side of the Sun. As she moves in front of the Sun, at her inferior conjunction, Venus appears as a delicate spot, almost like a beauty spot, across the countenance of the Sun. No longer visible in the heavens, being in her underworld phase of the cycle, Venus reveals her exquisiteness in a rare passage across the face of the blazing Sun for a few hours, leaving behind the trace of a small precious necklace strung across the solar disc.

This is the known as the transit of Venus. Astronomically it is like an eclipse, due to the alignment of the planetary orbits. Because Venus's countenance is so much smaller than the Sun's, the Sun is still visible. Some refer to this as an occultation, but nothing is hidden here. Transits of Venus are exquisite in design, repeating every 243 years. Generally, they will occur as pairs of transits 8 years apart, separated by gaps of 121.5 and 105.5 years. For instance, the first recorded sighting of the transit on 4 December 1639 was the second in its pairing. The next transit was 121.5 years later on 6 June 1761, followed by its twin on 3 June 1769.[56] Therefore, the next transit took place 105.5 years later on 9 December 1874, followed by its partner on 6 December 1882. Our last transit of Venus occurred first on 8 June 2004, then 8 years later on 6 June 2012. Noticeably, the transits take place either in June or December in the tropical zodiac signs of Gemini or Sagittarius when Venus reaches her nodal axis.

Transit of Venus Pairing at her Sagittarius South Node
243 years apart:
7 December 1631 and 4 December 1639
9 December 1874 and 6 December 1882

Transit of Venus Pairing at her Gemini North Node
243 years apart:
6 June 1761 and 3 June 1769
8 June 2004 and 6 June 2012

Mundane astrologers link transits in the heavens with terrestrial events. With the transit of Venus in the signs of Gemini and Sagittarius, many historical events that encapsulate the values of communication (Gemini) and discovery (Sagittarius) have been correlated with these times. The transit brightens Venus's focus on the development of human values, resources, connection and distribution of wealth. During the recent transits Venus was passing through the constellation of Taurus (the tropical sign of Gemini) in the horns of the Bull, constellating the meaning of this part of the heavens: our standards, our resources, our natural world and the wise management of our global economy.

Venus is often thought of as the sister to Earth. As she makes her close approach to the Earth during this transit she rises from the unseen world to become visible against the brilliant backdrop of the Sun, our system's heart centre. From our civilized vantage point this is an impressive reminder of cosmic synchrony; yet from a soulful viewpoint we are reminded of the alignment of our values with our hearts, being global participants in respecting the resources of our home, the Earth. The transit of Venus reflects the beauty, grace and symmetry of heaven's time.

One of the most fascinating aspects of the cycle of Venus is her disappearance from the sky as she loses herself under the Sun's beams.[57] This occurs twice in her synodic cycle and is a feature of her duality. After a period of intense brightness as the evening star and her resurrection as the morning star, Venus disappears for about a fortnight. Many cultures thought of this period as the time when the goddess walked amongst the people or descended into the underworld.

Our oldest known myth that characterizes the goddess's descent into the underworld concerns the Sumerian Inanna, Venus's predecessor. Inanna abandons the heavens for the underworld in order to witness the funeral of her sister's husband. At each gate she is stripped of part of her identity, then killed by her sister and hung in the underworld to rot. Eventually she is resurrected and rises into heaven, renewed and reborn. Imaginatively, the account offers us a pre-rational narrative for the disappearance of Venus from our skies, but also characterizes the descent that frequently follows a period of great brightness. Resurrected Venus reminds us of return, especially the return of the feminine. Inanna's symbol is the pentagram, a pattern traced in the heavens by Venus, and one that inspired Leonardo Da Vinci to link the human body with the workings of the cosmos through the Vitruvian Man.

♂ Mars

Mars transits the horoscope between every 17 and 23.5 months. However, its cycle is commonly referred to as 22 months or 2 years. It is often equated with the 'terrible twos', the stage of development when a child's will and urge to explore is emerging. Mars's 22-month cycle suggests that it will spend an average of about 2 months in each sign of the zodiac. However, when Mars is retrograde it can spend over 6 months in a sign, focusing on a particular area of the horoscope. For instance, in 2022–23 Mars is retrograde in Gemini, entering the sign on 20 August 2022 and exiting on 25 March 2023, remaining for a total of 7 months in Gemini. Mars is retrograde for between 58 and 82 days every 2 years. Let's look at the character of Mars retrograde to get a sense of the qualities it may bring to its timing when it is retrograde in its cycle.

Retrograde Mars
Mars retrograde varies, but on average it will backtrack between 10° and 20° of the zodiac before it turns direct. While it does not have a consistent pattern like Mercury and Venus, the retrograde does follow a consecutive course through the signs of the zodiac, often skipping one or two signs at a time.

Mars Station Retrograde	Degree of Zodiac	Mars Station Direct	Degree of Zodiac	Days Retrograde	No. of Degrees Retrograde
9 Sep 2020	28♈08	14 Nov 2020	15♈13	66	12°55'
30 Oct 2022	25♊36	12 Jan 2023	08♊07	74	17°29'
6 Dec 2024	06♌10	24 Feb 2025	17♋00	80	19°10'
10 Jan 2027	10♍25	1 Apr 2027	20♌55	81	19°30'

Mars retrograde in a natal horoscope suggests that the impulse to act may be contained or redirected. The person may appear to be less competitive than others; however, the urge to compete is still strong, and they often compete with themselves by setting high goals and standards. Being retrograde, Mars may be better equipped to conserve energy and focus on the task at hand. Like the 'second wind' of a long-distance runner, Mars retrograde is more inclined to complete the task, no matter how difficult or impossible. The will and drive are strong: a sheer determination and a spirit that urges to succeed against impossible odds. On the other hand, there is the possibility of obsession, blind ambition and the urge to win, no matter the cost or expense. Mars retrograde works best singularly, in an area that is not conventional, relying on its own survival instincts. Often Mars retrograde has the tenacity to succeed against impossible odds, evidenced by the number of sports champions who have this placement. They can succeed in spite of what appears to be physical limitations. Unconventional forms of relationship are often more suitable.

When transiting Mars is retrograde it is time to find ways to channel and refocus the Martian energies. Mars retrograde periods are times when the urge to move forward is best slowed down, so a period of re-creation and reorganization of plans and goals can take place. The retrograde and direct stations of Mars are like psychic pressure points, both collectively and personally in terms of conflict, determination, targets and objectives. Contentious issues put on hold may erupt; therefore, anger and frustration need to be expressed in a manner that leads to resolution. When Mars is retrograde, energy is being rechannelled and results are not always tangible. Taking stock of goals and ambitions during this period helps to implement supportive actions when Mars turns direct. The retrograde and direct stations of Mars are noteworthy as these times suggest that built-up stress may now be released and redirected.

Mars retrograde is a time to recover and recuperate, an important period for reordering priorities and plans. By taking time to regroup it will be easier to move forward when the time is right. Over time, students have suggested these remedies when Mars is retrograde:

- Tackle the difficult parts of any projects that you are involved in
- Rechannel the aggressive instincts into activities which help you feel centred, perhaps yoga, Tai Chi, walking, swimming or bicycling
- Re-embrace a martial art or join a dance class
- Be aware of not overexerting yourself; be careful of pulled ligaments, torn muscles and strained backs
- Be careful of being overly busy or taking on too much; say no when you want to say no!

- Redefine some important goals
- Redirect your energy into self-examination, feeling centred and clear about what you want
- Assert your intention to be in touch with what you want
- Be alert for anger in the environment, such as temper tantrums, road rage and rude customers!
- Increase your fitness level by recommitting yourself to a physical exercise programme
- Be aware of sacrificing 'being' for 'doing'
- Don't confuse busy-ness with happiness; risk being happy

The Cycle of Mars

As mentioned previously, the sidereal cycle of Mars averages about 22 months, so it transits the horoscope nearly every 2 years. This time period assists in planning strategies to move forward, launch a programme of action, regrouping and attack or advance. I am using military metaphors to imagine strategies for Mars's development as its temperament is akin to assertion and taking charge. Mars acts like a trigger and responds to challenges, campaigns and crusades. Note how your natal Mars might be an invitation to action: in Fire signs, Mars may be inclined to be more impulsive, while in Air it may become tactical; in Water it may be motivated emotionally while in Earth it may find its incentive through necessity. When in stress aspects to slower-moving planets like Jupiter or Uranus, Mars's volatility may be heightened, yet its urge to act may be tempered when in aspect to Saturn, Neptune or Pluto. When aspecting the inner planets, it may trigger the temperament of the other planet; for instance, when in aspect to the Moon it may spark an emotional reaction, while with the Sun it may activate issues concerning identity and pride. Mercury–Mars aspects might activate a fiery exchange or heated conversation while its relationship with Venus might elicit strong feelings of desire and longing.

Understanding Mars's natal disposition assists us in imagining how it reacts in transition and how we can confront change most effectively. One exercise I find useful is to track transiting Mars through its cycle of the horoscope, noting when it is conjunct each planet. If there is a powerful aspect pattern then I particularly pay attention to the times when a T-square or a Grand Cross is activated. At times I have encouraged students and clients to actually mark these dates on their calendar so they can be mindful of slowing down. Mars can speed things up, ignite the urge to finish a project before its time, aggravate the current situation or stir up a simmering conflict. Being prepared to be proactive rather than reactive or passive improves the transition.

Mars acts like a trigger so I am aware of other transits that may be occurring at the same time. As the outer planets' transitions may continue for an entire Mars cycle, I am aware that Mars may reinforce difficult aspects to the transiting or natal planet. My experience has been that Mars's transits are active at times of important undertakings and initiations.

Clients often have made their first appointment with me under a strong Mars transit, especially a Mars return. Something new wants to emerge.

6

GUIDES IN THE WORLD
The Transits of Jupiter and Saturn

The transits of Jupiter and Saturn chronicle significant developmental phases of the life cycle. Jupiter's sidereal cycle is nearly 12 years; Saturn's cycle is 29.5 years, two and half times that of Jupiter. This ratio is especially evident near the Saturn returns: at the first return at age 29.5, Jupiter is approaching its third opposition. At the second Saturn return at age 59, Jupiter nears its fifth return. Being classified as social planets, rulers of the day world, Jupiter and Saturn define the communal and public landscapes of life. Jupiter's passage through the horoscope symbolizes educational, cultural, ethical, teleological and religious initiations, while Saturn's movement represents the development of personal and social responsibility, boundaries, observance of rules, accountability, personal authority, consequences and maturity. Each archetype inducts the individual into becoming a moral and responsible member and citizen in their familial, communal, cultural and national systems.

Jupiter and Saturn are significant when they transit through the houses of the horoscope, making major aspects to other planetary energies and forming critical aspects within their own cycle.

Planet	Qualitative Time	Quantitative Time			
	Traits in Time	Sidereal Cycle	Synodic Cycle	Tropical Time – One Cycle of the Horoscope	Time to Transit One Sign/ House
Jupiter	Time to envision and re-vision	11.88 years	13 months	12 years	1 year
Saturn	Time to structure and reorganize	29.5 years	12.4 months	29.5 years	2.5 years

Transits of social or transpersonal planets in aspect to their natal placements (generational or generic transits) mark rites of passage, initiations and critical points in the life cycle. Each quarter of the cycle defines turning points that highlight the main phases of every planetary cycle. For instance, transiting Saturn will be in a waxing square to its natal position between the ages 7 and 8; in opposition at ages 14–15; at its waning square around age 22, returning to its natal position between the ages of 28 and 30. The following table reviews a way of thinking about how these generic cycles might unfold for the slower-moving planets.

Aspect	Qualitative Time
Conjunction Beginning of the new cycle	Subjectivity; when a new cycle begins, an old one ends. Therefore there may be confusion during this transitional time, as the new direction has not yet taken shape
Waxing Square The first quarter, a critical turning point	Alteration; change is afoot. Action is instinctive and spontaneous, as the individual feels compelled to make things happen. The unfolding of the cycle lies ahead, guided by will and passion
Opposition Realization at the cycle's midpoint	Clarity; recognition of the process, awareness, more objectivity and purpose are present. One can look back to the past to make the best use of the future
Waning Square At the three-quarter mark the cycle winds down	Reflection; a reorientation is taking place, turning inwards, reviewing and letting go of the aspects of the cycle that no longer are viable or necessary
Return At the next conjunction a new cycle begins	Imagination; an initiation into a new cycle is underway based on the accumulated resources, experiences and understanding of the past. How this will unfold is not clear, yet the promise and potential are there

This cycle could also be viewed from the perspective of the lunation cycle, marking eight transitional times in the cycle, as detailed in Chapter 4. This could be extended to include other aspects in the unfolding of a cycle; however, these four main directional points remain the most important transitional periods. Contrasting aspects with the daily, monthly and yearly cycles gives a seasonal rhythm to the unfoldment of the cycle of aspects. For instance, the First Quarter is like sunrise or spring, whereas the Last Quarter is like sunset or autumn. The conjunction is akin to the New Moon or winter solstice, while the opposition is analogous to the Full Moon or summer solstice. The following table correlates critical times with natural images.

Cycle of Aspects	Natural Images	Key Images
Conjunction	Midnight, New Moon, winter solstice	Beginning, awakening, stirring, crossroads, initiating
Waxing Square	Sunrise, First Quarter, spring equinox	Action, encounter, projection, critical, change in direction
Opposition	Noon, Full Moon, summer solstice	Objectivity, awareness, polarity, understanding, consciousness
Waning Square	Sunset, Last Quarter, autumnal equinox	Acceptance, receiving, contemplation, review
Return (Conjunction)	Midnight, New Moon, winter solstice	Integration, renewal, recycle, seeding, starting over

♃ Jupiter

Since Jupiter's synodic cycle with the Sun is thirteen months, it will turn retrograde once during this period, remaining retrograde for approximately four months. Its retrograde stations occur in succeeding signs year after year. Jupiter's sidereal cycle is nearly twelve years; therefore, it spends approximately one year in every sign of the zodiac. It moves approximately 30° in one year, travelling approximately 40° of zodiacal longitude forward for the nine months when it is direct, and 10° backward in the four months when it is retrograde.

The Jupiter Return

Every twelve years of life are commemorated with the return of Jupiter to its natal position; in essence, a homecoming after having a full round of experiencing the archetype in many different ways. Each return marks a graduation into a higher form of understanding our culture, our beliefs and our quest for knowledge and experience. These periods may accompany a re-visioning of our educational and vocational goals, as well as questioning our philosophy, ethics and morals. It is a time of return to the core of what we believe or at least what we think we believe; nonetheless, it is a time of conceptualizing and conceiving of a world that we would like to be a part of. Therefore, it can often be a period of educational travel, pilgrimage or vision quest. Whether we are conscious of it or not, the world around us has changed. Having outgrown ways of being in the world it is time to discover newer and more authentic ways of life.

I am aware how often clients seek a consultation around this period of their lives, especially near the third return between 35 and 36. I have found it very helpful to guide these clients on an imaginative exploration of the next 12 years in terms of the path they would like to follow and the dreams they would like to embody, exploring what is possible and what is not. I encourage a short-range forecast for the first year, a longer one for the next 2 years and then a full-range forecast for the entire 12 years!

The Astrological Life Cycle from the Perspective of Jupiter
Each Jupiter cycle of nearly 12 years marks a phase of life. In nearly 84 years or one Uranus cycle there are 7 Jupiter cycles. Alchemists considered 7 stages in their alchemical opus; metaphorically, we might consider the 7 Jupiter cycles as being transformative passages in our life's work.

Jupiter Cycle	Life Passage	Age Span	Age at Opposition	Age at Return
1st	Childhood	Birth to age 12	6	12
2nd	Adolescence	12–24	17–18	23–24
3rd	Young adulthood	24–36	29–30	35–36
4th	Midlife	36–48	41–42	47–48
5th	Middle age	48–60	53–54	59–60
6th	Seniority	60–72	65–66	71–72
7th	Eldership	72–84	77–78	83–84

In context of the family it is significant how we and other living members of each generation in the family may be experiencing and re-experiencing similar planetary cycles. Note which cycles are repeating themselves, because other family members or members of your generation may be experiencing a similar stage.[58] Look back and reflect on these life phases. I have included some reflective questions for each phase; however, it is helpful to contemplate your own personal experiences and development throughout these passages and how these inform and shape the pattern of your life.

As you go through the Jupiter times of your life, reflect on the following:

- Which cycle of Jupiter are you presently experiencing?

- Reflect on the way each new Jupiter cycle began. How did you respond to the world at this time – your dreams, your principles, your possibilities? What were your beliefs and ideals during this period? What new avenues did you explore? How did you begin to expand your horizons and move beyond what was familial?

- Now consider the oppositional points of this cycle. What were the major developmental phases and experiences of your life as Jupiter opposed itself? Are there any similar images, feelings, urges or insights that occur around these times?

- Reflect on the fullness of the cycle and contemplate these 12-year phases of your life. What is thematic about these periods and how would you describe these in an imaginative way? What is a consistent theme that underpins each cycle?

With each Jupiter cycle, I have included other planetary cycles that are concurrent to illustrate the patterns and initiations that are embedded in every human being's life cycle. While the political, cultural and societal landscape may change, these archetypal initiatory periods do not.

The 1st Jupiter Cycle: Childhood, Ages 0–12

- Review the astrological cycles of childhood. Consider your own experiences and those of your children and parents. Reflect on the shifts in the family during this first cycle.

- What is your first memory? Reflect on this memory imaginatively, using metaphors, symbols and images. Do you feel this memory is soulful? Does your chart reflect this in any way, such as a lunar aspect or an aspect pattern?

- Consider the mystical and other-worldly experiences of your childhood. What were the religious/spiritual overtones you experienced? What were your magical experiences and what dreams or nightmares do you still remember from childhood?

- Note the powerful impact of the four inner planets returning in the first year of life.

Childhood Sub Stage	Age-related Developmental Period	Astrological Developmental Cycle	Initiation of the Planetary Return
Newborn	Ages 0–4 weeks	From birth to the first lunar return at 27.3 days	Moon
Infant	Ages 4 weeks– approx. 1 year	From the first lunar return at 27.3 days to first solar return which will also include the first Mercury and Venus returns	Mercury Venus Sun
Toddler	Ages 1–2	From the first solar return to the first Mars return	Mars
Pre-school	Ages 2–6	From the first Mars return to the Jupiter opposition	Mars, Jupiter
Primary school	Ages 6–12	From the Jupiter opposition to the Jupiter return, including the first Saturn square	Jupiter, Saturn

The 2nd Jupiter Cycle: Adolescence, Ages 12–24

Many psychological researchers confirm that adolescence can extend into the twenties, synchronous with the timing of the second Jupiter cycle. During this period the brain is still developing and growing. A cluster of other planetary cycles is evident near age 21, with 'the coming of age' repeating again in midlife. Reflect on your adolescent passage. What stage of life were your parents and grandparents experiencing when you were at these stages? How did your parents and other members of your family navigate adolescence?

Cycle	Adolescence	Midlife Phase	Later Life
Jupiter Return	12	35–36	59–60
Progressed Moon Opposition	14	41	68
Saturn Opposition	15	44	73
Nodal Return	19	37	55–74
Uranus Cycle	□ at 21	☍ at 38–42	□ at 61–3
Neptune Cycle	∠ at 21	□ at 41	♇ at 62–3

- Contemplate the way you handled the physical and psychological changes that occurred during your adolescence. Did any major transitions or changes of school or home take place?

- Reflect on how your beliefs and attitudes to life developed through this period. Did these have an impact on your directional and vocational choices?

- Were there any major illnesses, crises or traumas at this time that profoundly influenced the course of your life?

The 3rd Jupiter Cycle: Young Adulthood, Ages 24–36
Adulthood continues beyond this phase; however, I have used Young Adulthood to describe this powerful time of emergence into the responsibilities and experiences of becoming an adult. The midpoint of this period is the Saturn return, which is a living symbol and metaphor for this period of the life cycle, an initiation into autonomy and self-regulation, conscientiousness, dependability, responsibility and accountability.

- What major milestones took place during your twenties? Did these prepare you for your Saturn return at the end of your twenties?

- What significant changes took place for you at your Saturn return?

The 4th Jupiter Cycle: Midlife, Ages 36–48

Midlife embraces the fourth Jupiter cycle when all the outer planets are configured in difficult aspects in their generic cycle. Uranus is at its opposition; Neptune is at its waxing square. Each generation experiences the transition differently; with the Pluto in Virgo and Libra generations, the waxing Pluto square was experienced during this stage of the life cycle, whereas this was not the case for their grandparents. These generations will have their Uranus opposition earlier than others; therefore, the sequence of the Uranus opposition and Pluto square is altered.

Each planetary cycle becomes entwined with others throughout the life cycle. This is very apparent at midlife when planetary cycles converge. The table below illustrates the other planetary cycles that are highlighted during midlife and how the same cycles repeat throughout the life cycle. Astrological symbols can be moved backward and forward through time to assist in linking life events into a coherent pattern.

Planetary Cycle/Age	Previous Ages of Note	Forward Ages
3rd Jupiter Return 35–36	Previous returns at 12 and 24; the last opposition was between 29 and 30. Reflect back	Note the next returns between 47 and 48, 59 and 60, and reflect on how you might imagine yourself at those ages
2nd Saturn □ 36–37	The first waxing square at age 7; opposition at 14–15; waning square at 22 and the return at 29–30. Consider your ambitions and driving forces at these times	The Saturn opposition at age 44–45 and the next return at 58–59. How might your decisions and choices now influence the outcome at 59?
2nd Nodal Return 37–38	The first nodal return at 19; contemplate your soul's yearning at this period of life	The next nodal return at 55–56. How do you imagine you will participate with the soul's desire in this next phase of life?
Uranus Opposition ☊ 38–43	The waxing square occurs at 21 and launches us into the adventure of life. What risks and journeys did we undertake in our early 20s?	The waning square occurs in our early 60s to prepare us for the exploration of life beyond work and family responsibilities

2nd Progressed Moon ☍ 41	Previous opposition at 13–14 as well as the return at age 27–28. Look back on your sense of security and ability to nurture your needs	Age 54–55 ushers in the third cycle. The work done at midlife to ensure the safety and emotional well-being of you and your dependants allows an organic renewal
Waxing Neptune □ 41	The first semi-square at age 20–21. Consider your dreams and ideals at this time of life. Which dreams are still real and possible? Which ones are not?	The Neptune opposition at 82. The Neptune square marks the halfway point in the human life cycle, offering a review of your creative and spiritual self
4th Jupiter ☍ 41–42	The 2nd opposition at 18 is in focus – where were you heading and do you need to pick up any threads, such as lost educational opportunities or travel?	The next return at 47–48 will complete this phase. What necessary changes are needed to ensure that the vision and goals for you and your family are being supported?
2nd Saturn ☍ 44–45	A direct plumb line to the adolescent opposition at 14–15 awakens the fragility and the strengths in the self to succeed	The return at 59–60 reaps the rewards from the work done now – how can we be as honest as possible with our authentic needs and goals?

The 5th Jupiter Cycle: Middle Age 48–60
The fifth Jupiter cycle encompasses the decade of the fifties, which starts at the Chiron return and ends with the returns of Jupiter and Saturn. Besides these three returns, the progressed Moon and the nodes also return mid-decade.

- Reflect on the passage of your parents through their fifties. What occurred in their lives at the Chiron return and towards the end of this decade?

- How does this passage of time prepare the way for later life and old age?

The 6th Jupiter Cycle: Seniority, Ages 60–72
Note that this cycle begins with the concurrent returns of Jupiter and Saturn which harmonically coincide before the age of 60 (i.e. 29.5 years x 2 = 59; 11.88 years x 5 = 59). The Jupiter–Saturn synodic cycle is 20 years and at age 60 both planets return to their

natal place. Twenty years are known as a 'score', a way to keep a tally on life. At 60 we are three-score years and the achievements and experiences of life are transforming into wisdom, which is the great task of this Jupiter cycle.

- Reflect on the transition from your identification with regular work and status in the world to a new phase

- What can be offered and disseminated during this phase of the life cycle?

The 7th Jupiter Cycle: Eldership, Ages 72–84

Retrospection and contemplation of one's life is the key during this phase. This is the Balsamic phase of life when the accomplishments and disappointments of life are internalized to forge a sense of integrity at having lived and fulfilled an authentic life. These are often romanticized as the golden years and often they can be if care has been taken to prepare for this phase.

- What is my vision and hope for this phase of my life?

Jupiter's Transit by House

On average, transiting Jupiter will spend approximately one year in each house of the horoscope, depending on its size. Jupiter concerns the development of our social conscience, our faith, beliefs, morals and ethics, our educational experiences, our questions and journeys, as well as the urge to move beyond what is familial; therefore, each year brings these issues and the urge to understand different environments in our lives. Jupiter's cycle begins as it crosses the Ascendant into the 1st house to focus its questions on self-development. As it crosses the Descendant six years later it expands our familiarity and experience of relationships, focusing on understanding other sides of our self. It culminates at the MC, linking us back to the time nine years ago when the cycle began and now is apparent in the values and principles encountered in the world. Each cycle of Jupiter is like the Wheel of Fortune focusing on each house of the horoscope as the years turn.

Consider the following to help you understand the personal cycle of Jupiter through your horoscope. Focus on its current transit.

- When did Jupiter cross the cusp into its current house position? Did you notice feeling freer or more optimistic about this area of your life? Reflect back on this period.

- When will Jupiter leave this house by transit? Have you changed your attitudes and beliefs towards this area of your life?

- How many times has Jupiter transited this house? For instance, if you are between 12 and 24, then this is the second time that Jupiter has transited here. If so, what are you aware of? If you are between 24 and 36 then this is the third time that Jupiter has transited this house, and so on. Reflect on what happened 12 years ago (or 24 or 36) when it transited this house – what are your recollections from the previous times? Does a theme emerge?

- How could you expand the horizon of the house that Jupiter is transiting? What beliefs and principles need changing or attending to in this area? How can you feel liberated in this area of your life? Where do you need to be more conscious and open-minded?

- Reflect on whether your attitudes in this area encourage you to develop and grow.

- Are you aware that you are questioning this area of your life? Do you understand the environment of this house any better?

- What are you capable of achieving in this area of your life? How could you be more adventuresome and positive in this district of your life?

Jupiter's Transits to Natal Planets

As mentioned in Chapter 3, Jupiter can transit a degree of the horoscope once or three times, depending on its retrograde cycle. Orbs used for the transit of Jupiter vary the time period of the transition. For instance, using a 1° orb, Jupiter may pass over a zodiacal degree within the month. However, if Jupiter turns retrograde then direct again over this degree, this time frame may be extended to nearly eight months. Using a larger orb widens the time period; therefore, it is important to be consistent with the orbs chosen. While it is important to have a sense of the quantitative timing it is important to recognize that this is not a fact nor fixed, but merely a guide, a possible timeline. Jupiter is often equated with fortune, but recognize that the Wheel of Fortune also turns downwards.

Imagine what is possible as transiting Jupiter forms aspects with natal planets and how the natal energy is revealing itself in the context of this astrological transition.

- How might I be more conscious and confident of this planetary archetype in my life?

- What obstacle does this part of me present? How could I encourage this part of myself to be more open and positive and become more conscious of mastering this energy?

- What limits do I place on this part of myself that I can now change by being conscious? What part of me feels restless and longs for adventure?

- What teachers or courses could help me become more aware and functional in relation to this archetypal energy?

- What goals could I set for myself with regard to this planetary energy?

Retrograde Sub-cycle

Jupiter retrograde does not suggest that opportunities are any less but rearranges these opportunities in an unconventional way. Natally, Jupiter retrograde suggests that opportunities come in non-standard packages, in a different form to others. One of my favourite examples is an author whose paperback was published first and then, following its success, the hardcover was issued. Here the usual procedure (at least in his day!) had been reversed. Jupiter retrograde can be defiant concerning orthodox religion and philosophy. They prefer self-made law and their own individualistic brand of philosophy. At extremes there can be social withdrawal, but positively used it manifests as service to higher social principles.

With Jupiter retrograde, the individual most probably has moved away from the belief system or religious orthodoxy of their family of origin. There is a greater tendency to search for their own beliefs, so Jupiter retrograde individuals generally find their beliefs outside the familial norm, often adopting a belief system originating from outside their own culture. These individuals quest in their own way and are constantly questioning and searching for a set of beliefs closer to their heart. They question deeply in order to find a sustaining faith.

Jupiter retrograde proposes the re-examination of our beliefs, as symbolized by the sign it is retrograding through. For instance, with Jupiter retrograde in Scorpio this may be the time to re-vision and reflect on our innate beliefs concerning death, personal integrity, truth, healing, therapy, etc. Jupiter retrograding in Taurus signals the time to consider our resources, traditions and what is of real value. With Jupiter retrograding through the personal signs (Aries - Cancer), our personal beliefs and morals are deeply challenged and reshaped. In inter-personal signs (Leo – Scorpio), Jupiter inspires us to question our relationship values and principles, while in the trans-personal signs (Sagittarius – Pisces), Jupiter helps to shape our political and communal beliefs and values. A more introspective and philosophical time emerges during these four months each year when Jupiter is retrograde.

♄ Saturn

Since Saturn's synodic cycle with the Sun is just less than 12.5 months, it will station retrograde once in this period, remaining retrograde for 4.5 months. Each successive year Saturn retrogrades about two weeks later than the previous year and 11 to 12 degrees later in the zodiac. Saturn's sidereal cycle is approximately 29.5 years; therefore, it spends approximately 2.5 years in every sign of the zodiac. In one year it travels approximately 12°, travelling forward about 19° of zodiacal longitude for 8 months, and 6°–7° backward in the 4.5 months when it is retrograde.

Saturn symbolizes the development of our autonomy, personal and social responsibilities, our ability to discern, to mature, to parent and to set appropriate boundaries and rules for ourselves and others. Saturn is a planet of consequence; therefore, there is an effect when we break the law, whether that is parental, societal or personal, and a reward when we work hard. As the archetype of 'reality' it confronts us with the material, manifest and literal world in order that we can become more masterful.

The First Saturn Return

The first Saturn return at the end of the twenties is preceded by the progressed Moon return at age 27. This period from 27–30 emotionally prepares us for the initiation of Saturn's return between 29 and 30. This time returns us to the natal essence of Saturn, yet now we have experienced its archetypal resonance through every sign of the zodiac, through every house of the horoscope and in aspect to every planet in multivalent ways. It returns to its birth position, but we are no longer newborn. Its return marks a time of maturity, a re-engagement with the soul of the planet and our relationship to its archetypal nature. Being 30, we are now separate and self-governing; therefore it is a time of deep reflection and questioning. It is a time of consequences and responsibilities.

The period before the Saturn return could be likened to the period before incarnation. At the Saturn return there is a re-incarnation into a matured and experienced adult who seeks the actualization of his or her potential in the world. A critical passage in our vocational search begins as we test out what is possible. Near the Saturn return an inner clock tells us it is time to plan the future, to set goals and understand what changes are afoot. It is a time of restructuring and realigning life's purpose; in a way, a recommitment to life.

However, this period can also be an anxious time, feeling weighed down by responsibilities and pressures to perform or achieve what may not be of our choosing. The Saturn return is like a crossroads between what I must do to be true to my passion and what I feel I should do to be accepted by others. For this reason, it is often a time of existential aloneness. In a felt sense it is being at the crossroads between apprentice and master, child and adult, dependence and self-determination. During the next thirty years we will experience every face of Saturn as it cycles through our horoscope once again. As the adult we will feel the youth underpinning our experience during the second cycle of Saturn.

The Saturn Cycle

The spinal column is an apt Saturnian metaphor, as it provides the base support for our entire body, like the archetype of Saturn, which symbolizes the structures and reinforcement of our lives. It is the skeleton of the system and the scaffolding for every project we undertake. Therefore, the cycle of Saturn is intimately involved with providing and sustaining supportive systems throughout our life, whether they are personal, familial or vocational. Saturn is the process of maturation, responsible action and the development of autonomy in our lives.

Each Saturn cycle of nearly thirty years completes a major chapter of life. In an average lifespan there are nearly three complete Saturn cycles, reminiscent of the three life stages of youth, adult and elder or the three familial stages of child, parent and grandparent. Each Saturn cycle embodies our physical capabilities and the process of ageing. Like the bones of our body which become more vulnerable as we age, Saturn becomes both wiser and more receptive through time. During each Saturn passage we experience the changing dynamic of familial, social and professional roles.

With Saturn, the opposition and squares to its natal position mark significant initiatory passages, natural processes and vocational transitions. Here is a table outlining these transitional ages.

Saturn Cycle	Life Passage	Age Span	Age at Waxing Square	Age at Opposition	Age at Waning Square	Age at Return
1st	Youth	Birth to age 29–30	7–8	14–15	21–22	29–30
2nd	Adult	29–30 to 58–59	37–38	43–45	50–52	58–60
3rd	Elder	58–59 to 88–89	67–68	73–75	80–82	88–90

Consider the cycle you are now in so you can reflect on Saturn's timeline in your life.

- How old are you? Which cycle of Saturn are you presently experiencing? Reflect back to the previous cycle at the same time by reflecting on what occurred 29–30 years ago.

Consider the way that you began this cycle of Saturn as it returned to its natal position

- Now consider the oppositions and squares of each cycle. What were the major developmental phases and experiences of your life when:
  - Saturn was in its opening or waxing square at 7–8, 36–37 and 65–66
  - Saturn opposed Saturn at 14–15 and at 44–45
  - Saturn was in its closing or waning square at 21–22 and 51–52

Saturn's Transit by House

On average, Saturn spends approximately two to three years in each house, according to its size. During this period it will retrograde two or three times; therefore, each house will be thoroughly excavated by Saturn. As Saturn transits each house, it brings the issues of these environments to the fore in our life so we can be more authoritative and in control of these concerns. Its transit cycle begins as it crosses the Ascendant into the 1st house, focusing its questions on personal responsibility and the shaping of personality in a considered, authentic and responsible way. As it crosses the Descendant 15 years later the focus shifts to being mature and dependable in the formation of relationships. We question the commitment to our relationships. As it culminates at the MC, 22 years or three-quarters of its cycle later, Saturn facilitates the possibility of being in the world in a way that feels authentic and true to our soul's purpose.

Consider the following questions to help you understand the personal cycle of Saturn through your horoscope. Reflect on Saturn's current transit in your horoscope.

- When did Saturn cross the cusp into this house? What structural shifts and directional changes did you notice in this area of your life?

- When will Saturn leave this house by transit? What outdated aspects and issues from this environment have been brought to completion?

- If you are between birth and 29½, then this is the first time that Saturn has transited this house. If so, what are you aware of? If you are between 29½ and 59 this is the second time that Saturn has transited this house. What happened when it transited this house during the first cycle? If you are 59+ then this will be the third pass of Saturn – what are your recollections from the previous times that Saturn transited this house? Does a theme emerge?

- How could you be more organized and competent in the house that Saturn is transiting? Which structures need replacing or attending to? Which plans, goals, budgets or audits need to occur in this area of your life? Where do you need to be more disciplined or aware?

- Reflect on whether your structural organization of this area is too rigid or too loose. Which boundaries may need to be put into place and which ones need to be altered?

- Which measures can be taken so you feel more mature, more in control and authoritative over the concerns of this house?

- Are you aware that this area of your life is demanding more of your time and focus? Are you becoming more conscious of your commitments and responsibilities in this particular arena?

- Is your attitude towards this area of your life beginning to change? Are you aware of the consequences of your past actions in this area? Are resident authority figures more dominant than before?

- What are you capable of achieving in this part of your life? How could you be more realistic and constructive in this sphere?

Saturn's Transits to Natal Planets

Like Jupiter, Saturn can transit a degree of the horoscope once or three times, depending on its retrograde cycle. Orbs will vary the time period of the transition, but if using a 1° orb Saturn may pass over a zodiacal degree within four to six weeks, depending on its speed. However, if Saturn turns retrograde then direct again over this degree, this time frame may be extended to ten months. As mentioned before, using a greater orb widens the time period; therefore, it is important to be consistent with the orbs that are chosen. Let's imagine what is possible as Saturn transits another planet and how the archetypal energy might reveal itself in the context of the astrological transit.

- How might you be more aware and in control of this energy in your life?

- What obstacle does this part of you present? How could you parent this part more effectively or become more masterful with this archetype?

- Which fears do you recognize regarding this energy? How do you still hold back in regards to this area of your personality? Where do you still feel inefficient and unskilled? If so, what do you need to do to skill up in this area?

- Which teachers or elders could help you become more aware and functional in this region?

- Where does the work need to be done? What foundation work needs redoing? What needs reconstructing?

- Which goals could be set in regards to this planetary energy?

Retrograde Saturn
Saturn is retrograde for four and a half months each year. Natal Saturn retrograde implies that the authority principle manifests differently. This might be experienced as 'instant guilt' when a policeman, customs official or any authority figure hooks a feeling of guilt, even when no laws have been contravened. Since there is a highly developed sense of rules and regulations, obligations and duty, it can be difficult for a Saturn retrograde individual to shake off the need to do what is expected of them.

External images of authority, control and power carry a potent projection. The image of father figures is psychically weakened. Saturn retrograde implies that this archetype, the symbol of the foster or father figure, is in the opposite sector to the Sun, the symbol of the hero and the Self. Internally, the solar hero and ancient king oppose one another, psychologically suggesting a felt sense of lack of support from authority figures. The individual, as hero, is constantly aware of the rigidity and severity of rules and consequences. Early in life, seriousness and responsibility may have been heightened; on the other side of the coin, the development of autonomy and self-reliance was emphasized.

During the period that Saturn is retrograde each year is the time to be more committed and serious about your personal goals. It is a time of looking back over mistakes, oversights and missed opportunities to renew and recommit to these projects, or to let them go. It is the time to be more self-determining and conscientious about what is most important and authentic.

The Jupiter–Saturn Synodic Cycle
Weavers of time, Jupiter and Saturn forge an impressive 20-year cycle together, which exists within a much larger cycle. Each Jupiter Saturn conjunction every 20 years progresses consecutively through the elements of the zodiac, completing a full zodiacal cycle. There are between 9 and 12 conjunctions in one element over the 180–240 years before the conjunctions progress into the next element. The circle of the zodiac hosts the complete cycle of the elements in these years. In this cycle's role as a millennium marker, Christian, Islamic and Jewish scholars recognized it as a timing mechanism for the lifespan of nations, dynasties and religions.

This cycle inspired the two classical planets to be christened the Great Chronocrators. They formed the longest planetary pair cycle in antiquity, endowing the cycle with great significance in marking out epochs and the passing of time. The length of time of the cycle is also known as a 'score', a notch on the moving image of eternity. Its symmetry is unique, as its conjunctions occur near the beginning of even-numbered decades while its oppositions occur at the onset of odd-numbered ones, orchestrating the decades of our lives.

As both are social planets, the cycle symbolizes societal trends, community concerns, public principles and beliefs, political and governmental developments as well as cultural events and markers. To understand how the cycle could manifest in natural phenomena, social change, political events or cultural developments, consider the two planetary energies and how they might unite.

JUPITER Concepts and Principles	SATURN Structures and Systems
Morals and Ethics	*Law and Order*
• Shared beliefs, cultural customs, ethics, morals, human values, ideals and broad-mindedness • The religious instinct and racial tolerance of the people, clergy, religious sects, cults; the beliefs and faith of the people • Foreign policies • Justice, the courts, judicial inquiries, human rights • Education, colleges, university, changes in educational systems • Publishing and dissemination of ideas • Marketing and media • Prosperity and increase	• The governing body, law enforcement, the consensus reality of the group • Institutions that provide order, stability and security for the people • Fear of change and resistance • Leaders and authority figures in positions of power, conglomerates, corporations, big business, regulations and controls • The Administration, the Cabinet and its executives, the Secretary of State • The conservative element, the 'old guard', the hierarchy; traditions of the culture; the elders • Attitudes towards ageing and the elderly • Conservatism and Cutbacks
When combining these two images we might imagine new laws or structures coming in to help regulate the media or education. Foreign policies and relations, as well as the portfolio of foreign affairs, could be emphasized. There might be fear and apprehension about new ideas or visions for social change, religious rigidity or racial and cultural intolerance. Try to combine the essence of each of these archetypes in terms of the collective.	

Here is the timing of these conjunctions which form their greater cycle through the elements. At the end of each passage through the elements there may be a conjunction in the next element*, but it reverts to the previous element at the next conjunction. Generally after this has occurred, the next conjunction will begin the series of conjunctions in the succeeding element.

Air	Water	Fire	Earth	Current Air Sequence
1226 ♒	1425 ♏	1663 ♐	1842 ♑	2020 ♒
1246 ♎	1444 ♋	1682–3 ♌	1861 ♍	2040 ♎
1265 ♊	1464 ♓	1702 ♈	1881 ♉	2060 ♊
1285 ♒	1484 ♏	1723 ♐	1901 ♑	2080 ♒
1305–6 ♎/♏	1504 ♋	1742 ♌	1921 ♍	2100 ♎
1325 ♊	1524 ♓	1762 ♈	1940–1 ♉	2119 ♊
1345 ♒	1544 ♏	1782 ♐	1961 ♑	2140 ♒
*1365 ♏	1563 ♋	*1802 ♍	*1980–1 ♎	*2159 ♏
1385 ♊	1583 ♓	1821 ♈	2000 ♉	2179 ♊
1405 ♒	*1603 ♐			2199 ♒
	*1623 ♌			
	1643 ♓			
10 conjunctions, approx. 200 years	12 conjunctions, approx. 240 years	9 conjunctions, approx. 180 years	9 conjunctions, approx. 180 years	= 40 conjunctions of approx. 800 years

The symmetry of the cycle is quite astonishing and another example of the regularity of astrological time reflected through recurrent patterns in the heavens. The new millennium was ushered in under the last of the conjunctions in the series of the Earth signs which had begun with the 1842 Capricorn conjunction. The current cycle in Air signs commenced at the next conjunction near the northern hemisphere's 2020 winter solstice, when Jupiter and Saturn were conjunct at 0♒29. Known as the Great Mutation, the new series of conjunctions in Air signs began December 21, 2020, ushering in a new aeon. The cycle continues in Air with its following conjunction on All Hallow's Eve 2040 at 17♎55.

Individually and together, the cycles of Jupiter and Saturn symbolize our education and maturation as we journey through life.

Now we turn to the outer planets, which initiate us into a broader and deeper experience of the soul through time.

7

AGENTS OF CHANGE
The Outer Planets' Timetable

Uranus, Neptune and Pluto were not known to the ancients. As archetypes of the modern era these planets symbolize dimensions beyond the certainty and materiality of Saturn. In 1977 Chiron was discovered between Saturn and the outer planets. Although astrologers did not classify it as a planet, they accepted its archetypal presence as being significant and revealing, embracing Chiron as part of the planetary pantheon. Being the channel to the trans-personal planets, Chiron is a symbol of initiation into outer realms that animate the new world of experience and consciousness beyond what has been known. These new worlds, whether they exist beyond, beside, behind or below the familiar, are marginal to the customs of the past. As initiatory archetypes, the situations that accompany these planetary transitions are often experienced as numinous or other-worldly. All four planetary archetypes are profound harbingers of transformation and consciousness.

Each outer planet transit is an invitation, a calling to confront the changes needed to live more fully in accord with the soul. The transiting planetary archetype may reveal itself in many ways, but generally it is experienced as an intrusion into our habitual world of security, family, work and relationships, often challenging what we have taken for granted. While we can choose to ignore the planetary god seeking our attention, it seems wiser that we honour the deity's presence, as over time its voice becomes louder and more persistent. When a transiting outer planet radically impinges upon an individual's horoscope, it is as if the qualities of that moment in time encroach upon the person's life; the god has an unsettling effect on the atmosphere and environment. The planetary energy that is arising and becoming more discernible encourages adjustments to be made to promote a more authentic way of being.

In ancient times the gods were thought to be the cause of our ills and difficulties. While we no longer believe that actual gods are the cause of our trials, in a contemporary context, the gods are metaphors of unconscious patterns that affect us. Therefore, like the ancients, it is wise to make a sacrifice to the summoning god: give back to the god what the god wants. In the past these may have been sacred objects, talismans or animal sacrifices. Today we are requested to be conscious of the archetype and participate in its genuine role in our individuation process. In psychological terms this could suggest altering one's direction, awakening a dormant aspect of the self, becoming more reliable or letting go of an outmoded way of being.

Astrologically, transits personify the gods who pursue us – the planet and house that is being transited distinguish psychological complexes and areas where transformation is possible. For instance, Uranus is the metaphor for awakening, separation and sudden change; therefore, its transits imply the need to honour these conditions. If Uranus is transiting Saturn, then astrologically we are alerted to the need to become conscious of our structures, routines and commitments, perhaps to disconnect from some of our duties and control. If Saturn is in the 4th house, then the home and family of origin are where these changes need to take place. These images arise from the logic and traditions of astrology, but how each individual will experience an outer planet transit is unique, dependant on many factors such as their temperament, consciousness, life stage, expectations and self-awareness.

Transits of the Outer Planets

Outer planet transits lead us into the exploration of the unknown, often triggered through unexpected or out-of-the-ordinary experiences or a confrontation with the unconscious, that is, the unidentified, repressed, missing or taboo aspects of the self. Here are some notes on ways of thinking about the nature of these transits. An outer planetary transit:

- May synchronize with events in the outer world that mirror and awaken psychic life

- Is a natural development on the life path, an initiatory process of individuation or an aspect of our destiny. While it may feel beyond our control, it becomes more manageable as we participate with the process

• Characterizes an encounter with the unconscious, summoning us to address the larger patterns and complex issues of life

• May be chaotic, as these transits evoke primeval and paradoxical aspects of the self. However, this is how creativity arises. To break through to this level of innate ingenuity, there is the necessity to break down defences and barriers. In addressing innate complexes and suffering, the denied life force has greater possibilities to awaken and transform

• Feels difficult and intense, but this is not as a precursor to anything negative, but more the nature of transition

• Assists us to discover our authenticity and reconnect to our soul's intention

• Epitomizes the struggle between the emerging self and its new intentions with the historical image of the self that we have come to accept as being who we truly are

• Encourages us to consciously cooperate in the transition, no matter how complex. It recommends that we collaborate with the intention of the transiting energy by heeding its energy and working in accord with its archetypal nature to ensure the optimum outcome

If what we desire or unconsciously seek is in conflict with parental and societal mores, then circumstances may arise that help us become more aware of our own needs and what is best suited for our personal development. Control during these transits is challenging; while we may not be able to control the event or the individual provoking the experience, we can manage our responses. Since 'bad' or random events belong to a complicated and enmeshed web, it is often impossible to see or know the fullness of any pattern's complexity; therefore it is not helpful to judge ourselves or our experiences. Physical and mental disorders may be symptomatic of what underpin the events that arise during the transit; therefore, images and symbols of these signs are clues to the psychological structure of what is endeavouring to express itself.

To delineate the nature of transits more effectively it is important to respect our natural human reactions like denial, anger, depression and bargaining, which are the felt experiences that occur during the journey towards our acceptance of change.[59] Often these processes along with grief, loss, suffering and pain are avoided by severing, rationalizing, judging or triumphantly managing this upheaval. Without genuine feeling and its accompanying pain, no transforming experience can occur. The complex is left frozen and unresolved. To recognize the stages and phases that are consistent with major transits, it is important to develop an in-depth understanding of the planetary archetype. This can be done through myth, symbol and metaphor, learning to deepen the process, so as the astrologer you do not get bogged down in the literal, outer and pragmatic manifestations of the transit.

The transits of the outer planets are experienced personally when they aspect natal configurations in the horoscope. Each transit will be unique to every individual; however, there are some archetypal themes and symbols that we can consider for each planet. When reflecting on the possibilities inherent in each transit, it is necessary to listen and place the transit in the context of the individual's stage of life, their experience and their conscious awareness.

Following are some images for each planet's rite of passage. Use these as a beginning to expand your own insight and accumulate experiences of these transits. Develop the table by adding your own impressions, insights and experiences.

Planet	Transiting Task and Rite of Passage
⚷ Chiron	• Spiritual awakening • A healing crisis whose symptoms express the soul • The heroic urge to heal the self • Acknowledging the inevitability of human suffering and mortality • Questing for the imaginative and restorative place where both physical and spiritual ways of being are acknowledged and integrated • Accepting the wound of being marginal • Discovering where sparks of life may still be ignited Symptoms of disease and illness during this period engage us in self-acceptance and an encounter with deeper personal issues, which provide opportunities for meaningful healing to take place on a soul level
♅ Uranus	• To take the road less travelled • To adventure into the unknown • To explore the unlived life and seek what could be possible • To risk being open to the possibilities inherent in life • To recognize choices • To know the difference between separation and severance; the distinction between detachment and disinterest • To be independent, but not disconnected • To become aware of opportunities that present themselves and knowing which ones to follow • To claim your own space, not push others away to gain or sustain your freedom Physiologically, the nervous system is heightened; therefore apprehension, anxiety and difficulties in resting and sleeping are often reported during this transit. The body needs to find ways to be more effective at grounding the influx of energies during this time

♆ Neptune	• Liminality and the experience of drifting between two fixed points • Pulling up anchor and floating; going with the tides of life • One step at a time • Being conscious of maintaining daily rituals by being aware of what the body needs – restful sleep, time out, a nurturing diet, quiet time and relaxing exercise • The task of creativity • Dreaming the impossible dream • Imagining • Finding what was lost Physiologically, one's sense of vitality is lowered; therefore, feeling alert, focused and able to be active can be impaired during this time
♇ Pluto	• To journey to the depths of the underworld to locate and redeem what has been buried alive • To be more authentic with one's feelings • To become more honest about one's intentions, being true to oneself • To let go of outworn attachments and find the integrity of emotional sincerity • To confront the ghosts and shades of one's familial past • To leave behind what is no longer valid or appropriate • To embrace the night, the dark of the Moon and spirits of the past • To re-member The individual may feel that their best skills and talents are inadequate at this time. A sense of melancholy may be accompanied by feelings of lethargy, depression, hopelessness, forgetfulness and despair. It is the acceptance and involvement with these feelings that allow any underlying trauma, guilt and shame to be released. A burden is lifted by allowing the feelings to live, promoting the exorcism of ghosts and shadows from the past

Timing the Transition

Because the outer planets travel slowly through the zodiac the impact of their transition will last much longer than the other planets. The time frame for the transit will depend upon the orbs assigned. Any orb is only a guide and not a matter of fact. Working with horoscopes through time, you become familiar with the subtle ways that transits can manifest. Astrological opinion varies on orbs of influence; I tend to see the heart of the transit occurring within a 1° orb. The following table suggests the approximate timing when using a 1° or a 5° orb. Due to Pluto's elliptical orbit the timing of this transit will not be consistent over time.

Planet	Approximate Time Using a 1° Orb	Approximate Time Using a 5° Orb
♅	15 to 22 months	42 months
♆	20 to 24 months	70 months
♇	22 to 24 months	70+ months

The Retrograde Sub-cycles

Another consideration is the forward and retrograde movement of the transiting outer planets, which advance, then retrograde and move forward again, passing over the same degree of the zodiac at least three and sometimes five times. This movement in itself creates a sub-cycle in planetary transition.

Imagine this sub-cycle as a process, like the pattern of Thesis, Antithesis and Synthesis. The first pass of the planet will be when it is direct, bringing the transitional passage and its issues to consciousness. The retrograde period is a time of internalization, reflection and consideration of the concerns and changes that are presented, while the final transit to the natal planet or angle suggests that understanding and acceptance of the inevitability of change leads to reconciling the transition.

Transit	Direction	Process		
1st 'hit'	Direct	Thesis	Separation	Consciousness
2nd 'hit'	Retrograde	Antithesis	Initation	Consideration
3rd 'hit'	Direct	Synthesis	Return	Change

If there are five exact passes of the transit, then there is an elongated phase of time in the transition, especially occurring around the separation and disconnection from old patterns.

The Rounds of the Outer Planets

Each outer planet has its own unique planetary cycle, which serendipitously equates to important timing in the human life cycle.

Neptune and Pluto cycles are far greater than an individual life cycle, focusing on major returns and cycles in a collective and ancestral context. Both Neptune and Pluto rule vast worlds: Neptune, the other-world and Pluto the underworld. Both their worlds are located in the unconscious terrain of the human psyche; therefore, their transits parallel journeys into the other- or underworld. Aspects to the natal chart formed in the Neptune and Pluto cycles are like psychological rites of passage, as the soul traverses the unfamiliar world of the unconscious.

Each critical aspect in the outer planet's cycle heralds an initiatory phase of the human life cycle. While I have used the Jupiter cycle of 12 years to define periods and phases of the life cycle, it is important to recognize the times when the outer planets mark important steps on the path of individuation as they form generic aspects to their natal positions. For instance, Uranus's waxing square to itself at the age of 21 announces the coming of age and the launching of the individual on their self-determining road of life, while its waning square at 63 prepares us for the journey that steers us away from the mundane world. Neptune's first square to itself at 41 occurs during the changing tides of midlife, while its opposition at 82 signals the shifting seas of old age.

Working astrologically with these cycles can also pinpoint recurring passages in an individual's life that link together certain times in the life cycle. A transit is not a 'one-off' experience, nor a series of events, but an unfolding process within the context of a larger cycle. Since an outer planet transits a house for a substantial period of time, its affect is more apparent when aspecting other planets. However, its first entry into a new house can often be highly significant. Let's turn to examining the outer planet's cycles, beginning with Chiron, the bridge to the transpersonal realm.

⚷ Chiron

Chiron does not move uniformly through the zodiac because its orbit is highly elliptical. It travels the slowest in Aries and the fastest in Libra. The astronomical detail of Chiron's slow movement through Aries is a reminder that Chiron's nature is to not follow the herd, preferring to remain outside the system. The following table shows the time it takes for Chiron to transit each sign, based on Chiron's last cycle through the zodiac.

Chiron Sign	No. of Years in Sign	Chiron Sign	No. of Years in Sign	Chiron Sign	No. of Years in Sign	No. of Years in Each Element
♈	8.3 years	♌	2.2 years	♐	2.6 years	Fire: 13.1 years
♉	6.9 years	♍	1.8 years	♑	3.6 years	Earth: 12.3 years
♊	4.5 years	♎	1.7 years	♒	5.5 years	Air: 11.7 years
♋	3.1 years	♏	2.0 years	♓	7.8 years	Water: 12.9 years
Total: 22.8 years spent in **personal signs**		Total: 7.7 years spent in **inter-personal signs**		Total: 19.5 years spent in **trans-personal signs**		**Total: 50 years**

Chiron is an orbit-crosser, like Pluto. While Chiron generally orbits between Saturn and Uranus, it will also cross over the path of Saturn. When transiting from Leo to Sagittarius, Chiron is mainly inside the track of Saturn, orbiting between Jupiter and Saturn.[60] Through the signs of Virgo, Libra and Scorpio, Chiron travels faster than Saturn. Chiron spends only 27% of its time between 0°♋ and 0°♑, whereas it spends 73% of its time transiting from 0°♑ to 0°♋. As evident in the table, Chiron spends most time in the first four personal signs.

Chiron, Saturn and Uranus
Chiron's relationship with Saturn and Uranus is noteworthy. As Chiron approaches Uranus's orbit it wanders through the zodiac at a similar speed to Uranus, and therefore stays in aspect with Uranus for extended periods of time. Between 1952 and 1989 there were nearly forty oppositions of Chiron and Uranus as Chiron transited between Capricorn to Cancer. There were no conjunctions of Uranus and Chiron in the 20th century and only twice were they in square aspect to each other (1943 and 1997). The next Chiron–Uranus conjunctions will occur in 2042–43. The Chiron–Uranus relationship emphasizes the opposition in natal horoscopes in the latter half of the 20th century. Saturn formed a series of oppositions with Chiron from 1986 to 1995 and again from 2003 to 2006. Chiron is conjunct Saturn only once in each of the 20th and 21st centuries: in 1966 and 2028.

The long series of oppositions from Chiron to Saturn and Uranus in the last half of the 20th century suggests that the universal wounds (Chiron) inherent in the principle of authority (Saturn) and the expression of individuality (Uranus) are embedded in all the horoscopes of these times. The preponderance of Chiron–Uranus and Chiron–Saturn oppositions symbolize the damage to individual freedoms and liberties (Uranus) within a dominating and hierarchical culture (Saturn). Chiron's emphasis, whilst personal in its passage through the signs, is also collective, leaving its imprint on generations born with Chiron in aspect to Saturn and the outer planets. Chiron's unique relationship to the outer planets made a stunning finale on the final days of the 20th century, commonly known as Y2K, when it conjoined Pluto in the sign of Sagittarius!

The Chiron Cycle

Chiron returns at about 50. Depending on its retrograde pattern this can occur any time between 49 and 51. Other crucial times in its cycle are its waning and waxing squares and opposition. The initiations depicted by Chiron's squares and oppositions take on a unique timing for each generation of Chiron signs. Unlike Uranus and Neptune, whose generic transits to their natal positions occur at predictable ages, Chiron's transits to its own natal position varies. The following table shows the age period when an individual will experience these crisis points, depending on their natal Chiron sign. Please note that this table shows an approximate age span. Because of the irregularity of Chiron's orbit and its retrograde pattern, these ages may vary.

Each Chiron generation has a different rhythm of time. Chiron makes its first square to its natal position when we are only 5 years old or not until we are 23. The opposition can occur anywhere from ages 12 to 37, while the final waning square occurs anywhere between the ages of 26 and 44. As with all transits, we must first understand the planet within the context of the natal horoscope to know its presence and nature in our personal life.

Chiron's cycle is an apt metaphor for the healing journey, the aspect of the individuation process that includes striving and working towards accepting the authenticity of the whole self. This Chironic journey embraces the encounter, remembrance and reconciliation with the pain and trauma of living. Key points in its cycle symbolize potential awareness into the process of becoming whole, including the acknowledgement and acceptance of anguish and suffering. At critical points in the Chiron cycle, emotional, psychological or spiritual wounds are reopened, often through a spiritual awakening or crisis that lends a hand in healing past trauma and distress. The archetypal nature of Chiron's cycle includes the interweaving of wounding and healing, like the two snakes on the Hermetic caduceus associated with the medical profession.

Natal Chiron Sign	% of Time in Sign	Waxing Square Occurs Between	Oppo- sition Occurs Between	Waning Square Occurs Between	Return at Age 50
♈	16.7%	Ages 14–19	Ages 20–26	Ages 28–33	Near the age of 50 a paradigm shift between the known world of substance and the unseen world of spirit occurs. Between the Saturn opposition at 44 and its return at 58–59 is a critical period of self-acceptance. It is a profound time post-midlife, before the entry into later life, for which Chiron prepares us.
♉	13.9%	Ages 9–14	Ages 15–20	Ages 26–28	
♊	8.9%	Ages 7–9	Ages 13–15	Ages 26–30	
♋	6.2%	Ages 5–7	Ages 12–13	Ages 30–35	
♌	4.5%	At age 5	Ages 13–17	Ages 35–40	
♍	3.7%	Ages 5–6	Ages 17–23	Ages 40–42	
♎	3.3%	Ages 6–8	Ages 23–29	Ages 42–44	
♏	3.9%	Ages 8–11	Ages 29–34	At age 44	
♐	5.2%	Ages 11–16	Ages 34–36	Ages 43–44	
♑	7.1%	Ages 16–21	Ages 36–37	Ages 41–43	
♒	10.9%	Ages 21–23	Ages 32–36	Ages 38–41	
♓	15.7%	Ages 19–23	Ages 26–32	Ages 33–38	

During important Chironic passages, instinctual and authentic responses that have been sacrificed for more acceptable and appropriate ones are evoked. Authentic feelings, unsanctioned or unapproved by family or society, arise to be integrated and accepted. Chiron symbolizes alienation from our own tribe, yet it also reveals how we collude in alienating ourselves through the choices we have made throughout our lives. Therefore at pivotal points in the life cycle, Chiron encourages the acceptance of one's mortality and humanness. At these crisis points the maverick theme of Chiron emerges in an effort to reconcile and redeem this wound.

'Maverick' was an original keyword used by Charles Kowal, the discoverer of Chiron, when describing Chiron's eccentric orbit. Our word 'maverick' suggests not having a brand, not being 'branded', and originates from Samuel Maverick, a cattle owner who did not brand his cattle. Mythological Chiron was not branded like the other Centaurs; astronomical Chiron also has a unique orbit and category. Chironic individuals are mavericks, outside the family, tribe or culture that they are raised in. This is why Chiron often signifies those who feel alienated, foreign or unwelcome, such as refugees, migrants or anyone living in a culture distinct from their heritage.

At Chironic turning points, we may face a healing crisis through physical or psychological injury. These times may also accompany a shamanistic experience of being called to something greater in ourselves through this suffering. A psychic shift is possible, bringing transpersonal realms into focus to experience something larger than our individual story or our own personal pain. We may struggle to resolve our instinctive nature, our desires, our sexuality or our authentic feelings. The times may feel as if we are alienated or cut adrift from our family and tribe, but Chiron embodies the alchemical amalgam of wounding and healing – when the wound is exposed, healing can occur. This is the gift of Chiron.

Clients at these crisis points describe their process as if they had crossed paths with an unpredictable alien or event, a painful experience which often ignited ancestral or familial wounds. For me, this resembles an encounter with a Centaur, the mythological wild man or wild woman. Centaurs were marginalized creatures: unpredictable and barbaric, brandishing tree trunks, boulders and firebrands as their weapons. They inhabited a threshold between the primitive past and emerging civilization, being creatures that lived on the margins, foreign to the city, rejecting the societal values and governmental laws of the times. They were hybrids, instinctual, intolerant of culture and disrespectful of its laws and customs. Even though Chiron was not part of the herd of Centaurs, archetypally he carries some of the shadow wildness associated with the unrefined instinctual life, which rises to meet us at transitional points in his cycle. This may literalize as an actual encounter with untapped and wild feelings projected onto actual individuals, or take the form of stormy feelings rising in and around us. This untamed instinct could manifest as an accident, illness or a loss, constellating deep layers of soul that erupt to begin the healing process.

In Greek myth the Centauromachy described the battle with the Centaurs, a mythic scene in statuary and literature that encapsulated the struggle with these barbaric forces. At transitional points in Chiron's cycle we experience the Centauromachy, battling wild and instinctual forces inside and outside our self. In these critical transitions we are called to reconcile our instinctual urges with our conscience that conforms to accepted patterns of moderation and restraint. When we reject these urges, we may harm ourselves. At other times, when consciously listening to the source of our frustration without judgement, acceptance arises.

At the waxing square we may experience being in-between two worlds. Clients have described this 'in-between' state sometimes as an illness, mental anguish, an out-of-body experience, a near-death experience, feeling marginalized, being dislocated or the loss of belonging, home and/or homeland. For the first time we may feel alienated from our true ancestry, an archetypal experience Freud wrote about in his essay 'Family Romances'.[61] The 'Family Romance' describes a child's fantasy of not belonging to his family of origin. To be liberated from identifying with siblings and/ or parents, the child romanticizes his origins as if he or she was adopted and the 'real' parents are more celebrated than the current ones. Or they are the only legitimate child and the siblings are born of mother's love affairs.[62] These common feelings of not belonging, being adopted and early experiences of being foreign or being excluded or dislocated often accompany the first square.

Equally, the first square could be the encounter with the wound through a physical illness or injury, emotional crisis or psychic upheaval. The first square represents the conscious experience of facing the Chironic wound in ourselves. At this first square, whether through accident, illness, self-injury or in an imaginal way, we feel foreign, even excommunicated or marginalized. While the experience may not be accessible consciously, this encounter with the wound of feeling marginal is psychically stored. At the first square our feelings of being overwhelmed by the experience of wounding or alienation may be rationalized or denied in the attempt to move forward.

The opposition confronts the wound once again; this time, more openly as the cyclical theme associated with wounding is re-encountered. This phase begins the healing, as we are confronted by and more conscious of the inevitability of this theme in our lives. It is a time when we realize the need for reconciliation and healing. Our quest begins as we discover ways to heal. From this place we become more conscious of our wounds and limitations. Although these feelings may be rejected or sublimated, they are closer to consciousness than before and will arise again in times of stress, anxiety and pain.

The waning square leads to an attempt to reconcile and accept the wound. This is not resignation, but a conscious effort to embrace the marginalized and wounded aspects of ourselves. We now recognize the need to fully accept that we cannot be whole in the way we once felt we should be. This is a time of reflection and contemplation, when we are more able to put our damaged feelings into context. While the physical or mental pain may still be difficult, at this point in the cycle the denial of the wound inflames the injury. Acceptance of the wound promotes the feeling of wholeness and encourages well-being. The Chiron thread weaves itself throughout these critical points of our life cycle. At its return, the Chironic themes of our lives are more recognizable and appreciated.

The return at fifty supplies an opportunity for integration. Unlived instincts can now be acknowledged, mourned, let go or even reintroduced back into life in an appropriate way. Our inner life and instinctual nature can be expressed through a mature ego perspective. Fifty designates a changing paradigm in human experience when the civilized aspects of our self no longer inhibit our spontaneous and instinctive expression; hence, this initiation symbolizes the beginning of liberating the imprisoned spirit. Potentially the return of Chiron frees the spirit, as we no longer need to carry the wounds that identified who we were. Hopefully we live more soulfully, attuned to the Self. Ageing and dying may preoccupy us throughout this transition. The bodily changes that occur throughout the forties become more apparent at fifty, pushing the individual into an encounter with their sense of mortality and the wound of incarnation. The two worlds of spirit and matter collide and a new myth is needed to embrace them both, one that honours opposites and tolerates the pain of being human. It is a time of acceptance and tolerance of our vulnerability and fragility.

At any of these stages we may experience painful transitions that eventually lead us to a greater understanding spiritually. We are forced to reconcile this empty place inside us where disease festers. These passages can accompany out-of-body experiences, lucid dreaming, periods of strong imagery through dreams or outer events, visions or spiritual experiences. In other words, our pain or illness may propel us into a dark place, the living symbol of Chiron's cave where initiation into the heroic act of healing can occur. Illness or critical events call us to the temple of healing where we re-encounter the inner psychic healer. At Asclepius's temple precincts in ancient Greece, pilgrims petitioned the god for healing, and their relief from suffering transpired through their contact with images of the divine. In contemporary experience this occurs through dreams and shamanistic experiences when we reconnect to psyche's healing images. The modern temple of Asclepius resides in the internal world of images. When we contact these potent symbols, they offer healing to the spirit.

♅ Uranus

Uranus's cycle is 84 years. Since all 12 signs are transited in 84 years, the 12th harmonic generic aspects of transiting Uranus to natal Uranus occur approximately every 7 years throughout the life cycle, as the following table illustrates.

The Waxing Half of the Cycle		The Waning Half of the Cycle	
⌄ Semi-sextile	At age 7	⊼ Quincunx	49
✶ Sextile	14	△ Trine	56
□ Square	21	□ Square	63
△ Trine	28	✶ Sextile	70
⊼ Quincunx	35	⌄ Semi-sextile	77
☍ Opposition	42	☌ Return	84

In the previous cycle Uranus spent approximately 7 years in each sign of the zodiac, but as evident in the following table it can stay between 6½ and 7½ years in a sign. This timing echoes the Saturn squares that occur every 7 to 8 years.

Uranus Sign	Time in Sign		Uranus Sign	Time in Sign		Uranus sign	Time in Sign	
	Years	Mths		Years	Mths		Years	Mths
♈	7	6	♌	6	5	♐	6	10
♉	7	3	♍	6	4	♑	7	1
♊	7	0	♎	6	5	♒	7	7
♋	6	10	♏	6	6	♓	7	6

Because of the difference in time, the critical phases of the squares and opposition may vary by a few years for each generation. For instance, the Uranus in Cancer generation will experience their waxing square between the ages of 19 and 20, their opposition between 39 and 40, and their waning square between 61 and 62 years. The Uranus in Capricorn generation will experience their waxing square between the ages 22 and 23, their opposition between 43 and 44, with their waning square occurring between 63 and 64 years of age.

While the exact times of the cycle vary slightly with each generation, the Uranus cycle follows the maturation course of the individuation process. In terms of the prototypical cycle it is relevant that the first critical period of the square is synchronous with the first nodal return and the waning Saturn square, initiating us into the post-adolescent decade of the twenties and into a world beyond the familiar. The opposition is an integral part of the midlife passage, while the waning square follows the Saturn and Jupiter returns, which initiate us into the decade of our sixties and an induction into later life. The Uranus cycle is a cosmic metaphor for the modern human life cycle.[63] In the waxing half of the cycle, which is the first 42 years, life is mostly directed into career, family, home and worldly identity, whereas, in the waning half of the cycle, psychic energy is more focused on self-knowledge.

Waxing Square Occurs Between Ages 19–23	Opposition Occurs Between Ages 38–44	Waning Square Occurs Between Ages 61–65	Return at Age 84

Uranus in Greek myth was the original Sky god, born from Gaia, the great Earth Mother. Due to his disconnection with the Earth and his suppressive and destructive relationship with his family, Uranus was overthrown by his own son Saturn. The mythic images that are imported into his astrological temperament are the characteristics of separateness, emotional disconnection and lack of attachment. This slender mythic profile has led to Uranus also being associated with the Titan Prometheus.[64] Prometheus reflects the astrological images of humanitarianism, inventiveness, rebellion, boundary-crossing and autonomy, and portrays a more dynamic and diverse archetype. Prometheus is punished for his insurgence, but freed when Chiron changes places with him in the underworld, thereby allying the two archetypes. Being mavericks and marginal, Chiron and Prometheus/Uranus are allied in myth and astrology.

One of the radical features of the Uranus archetype is its urge for freedom, individuality and reform. This is generally embodied through the desire to be separate and follow a unique and innovative course. Its archetypal nature is not inclined to follow in the footsteps of others, nor be conventional. From this perspective its planetary initiation throughout the life cycle is self-determination, promoting independence and autonomy. While the spirit of Uranus seeks equality and democracy, at times it can be contrary and rebellious. Temperamentally, Uranus seeks objectivity and non- attachment, yet in essence the archetype is often unpredictable, located on the fringes of the establishment. As in myth, Saturn's character is often hostile to Uranus, yet in essence they create a dynamic psychic tension between conformity and divergence. Uranus's unpredictability and risk-taking challenges Saturn's proclivity for predictability and control. Therefore, at critical times in the Uranus cycle the urge arises to break free from the past, disconnect from what is established or separate from what is familiar. Uranus's transitions challenge our prevailing attitudes, question our routines and confront our ways of being in the world, inviting us to be experimental and risk-takers.

The Uranus Cycle

This cycle symbolizes opportunity: a door opens, an unexpected encounter occurs or a new pathway is revealed. In my experience Uranus transits synchronize with the emergence of numerous opportunities. Timing is of the essence, because while all opportunities are possibilities, they may not all be the right ones. Uranus opens many doors but not all may be entered; therefore, its nature includes accepting that which cannot be lived out, the road not taken. Periods coloured by Uranus are exciting and liberating, often uncharacteristic and out of the ordinary. Each one is a step towards individuality and autonomy.

The first square occurs as the decade of the twenties opens. New relational, educational and vocational experiences are possible. The canvas of the Self is ready to be painted and it is time to take a chance. Like the Fool in the Tarot journey, often equated with Uranus,[65] we are ready to take a leap into the unknown to see where it takes us. The spirit of adventure is strong. At the opposition two decades later, we stand on the landscape of midlife, reflecting on what has not happened and what is still possible. It is a period of setting ourselves adrift from what no longer nurtures, supports or sustains us, so we can find the harbours that can shelter our passion and creativity. The opposition presents the opportunities to take a chance on ourselves and create the lifestyle we have been striving towards. At the final square we have just entered our seventh decade (the 60s) and the adventurous task of creating our final chapters of life in our own way is on the horizon. The opportunity and possibility of freedom and exploration presents itself in a new way.

Uranian transitions will always challenge our self-image. 'I am never going to marry,' said a client. But when Uranus transited her Descendant, she did. Another client once said she would never travel overseas as she was afraid of planes. At her Uranus opposition she won a trip to London and took the 32-hour flight from Melbourne to Heathrow! When transiting Uranus opposed a client's Moon in the 12th house, her relinquished son contacted her. Uranus transitions are filled with the unexpected and we are called to be adventurous, to challenge the assumptions we have made and take a chance on life and all its possibilities.

♆ Neptune

Based on the previous cycle, Neptune has spent just under 14 years in each sign of the zodiac. Because of its circular orbit its journey through the zodiac is more proportioned than the other planets, as the following table demonstrates.

Neptune Sign	Time in Sign Years	Time in Sign Mths	Neptune Sign	Time in Sign Years	Time in Sign Mths	Neptune sign	Time in Sign Years	Time in Sign Mths
♈	13	5	♌	13	8	♐	13	11
♉	13	7	♍	14	0	♑	13	10
♊	13	5	♎	13	7	♒	13	8
♋	13	6	♏	13	10	♓	13	10

Neptune's cycle of 165 years does not return in one lifetime; however, the first half of its cycle marks particular critical ages. As it travels through each sign approximately every 14 years, it also synchronizes with the timing of 7 years in the Saturn and Uranus cycles. The following table lists the aspects in its cycle including the semi-square and the sesquisquare at 21 and 62 respectively, which resonate with the two Uranus squares at 21 and 63. Other cycles harmonize with the Neptune cycle, as in the following table.

The Waxing Half of the Cycle		Synchronous Times in Other Cycles
⚺ Semi-sextile	At age 14	Approximately the first progressed Moon opposition, and first Saturn opposition by transit
∠ Semi-square	21	Approximately the Saturn waning and Uranus waxing squares by transit
✶ Sextile	28	Between the first progressed New Moon and the first Saturn return by transit
□ Square	41	Approximately the second progressed Moon opposition
△ Trine	55	Approximately the second progressed Moon return, and third nodal return by transit
⬚ Sesquisquare	62	Near the waning Uranus square by transit
⚻ Quincunx	69	
☍ Opposition	82	The third progressed Moon return

Of all the planetary archetypes, Neptune seems to be the most difficult to incarnate, contain or embody. Temperamentally, Neptune is fluid and porous, evading limits and restraints, preferring to be boundless, without borders or boundaries. Illusive, it favours invisibility and imagination rather than literality. Its nature is other-worldly and ethereal, and its effect is to disarm, dissolve and disorientate. Therefore, it initiates us into a world beyond literal form or real definition.

Its passage of 14 years per sign symbolizes a generation's dreams and ideals. For the Neptune in Libra generation, their expectations and ideals, yet also their disappointments, are focused on relationships while the Neptune in Scorpio generation idealizes intimate, darker, even taboo aspects of life. Neptune in Sagittarius encompassed a time of spiritual and religious ideals, while political and governmental ideologies rose to the forefront during the Neptune in Capricorn era. If born during these times, the prevailing atmosphere and ethos is internalized. In their twenties, these generations' values and principles are challenged by the transit of Pluto conjoining their Neptune.

For nearly 100 years Pluto and Neptune travel their zodiacal journey in sextile. There have been 49 exact sextiles between 1948, when they first were within a 1° orb, and 2033 when they are last within a 1° orb. Although the distance between them increases and decreases over this time, nearly everyone born between 1940 and 2040 will have a Neptune–Pluto sextile in their natal charts. Neptune will be two signs after Pluto in these years; therefore, Pluto will transit Neptune for each individual at some point in the first half of life. This could be described as a confrontation with inherited ideals, dreams and fantasies. Each generation will experience this at different times due to Pluto's irregular travel through the zodiac. Over the course of my consulting practice I have observed this transit to be of particular note. Often it is a dramatic encounter with the sustainability of our ideals that exposes our self-deception. The following table lists the generations that have the Neptune–Pluto sextiles and the approximate age when Pluto will conjoin their Neptune.

Neptune Generation	Years (includes retrograde back into sign)	Corresponding Pluto Generation	Years (includes retrograde back into sign)	Ages at Which Pluto Transits Natal Neptune
Libra	1942–1957	Leo	1937–1958	23–29
Scorpio	1955–1970	Virgo	1956–1972	28–29
Sagittarius	1970–1984	Libra	1971–1984	27–29
Capricorn	1984–1998	Scorpio	1983–1995	25–28
Aquarius	1998–2012	Sagittarius	1995–2008	24–25
Pisces	2011–2026	Capricorn	2008–2024	24–26
Aries	2025–2039	Aquarius	2023–2044	25–32
Taurus	2038–2052	Pisces	2043–2058	32–42

Like the transits of the other outer planets, Neptune impacts the deepest layers of psyche. Neptune evades literal forms and initiates us into the transcendent, mystical and imaginative aspects of life. Therefore its transits can be disorientating when we continue to use logical and rational constructs to understand what is taking place. It is a time when misdiagnosis, misunderstanding and confusion are liable to continue if we remain focused on logical outcomes. During Neptune transitions it often feels as if we are in a fog, drifting or lost. Those intent on controlling and structuring the process may find themselves forgetting what it is they were meant to do, feeling lethargic and without ambition. To make the transition to the next phase of life, an immersion into uncertainty and vagueness is demanded. It is a time of faith and trust in the soul and the spiritual aspects of our self that are demanding attention. Neptune initiates us into the other-world where material values are no longer dominant and worldly status is not that important. It is a world where identity is not separate or singular, but merged and collective.

Neptune transits reconnect us once again to soul and its values that may have been lost or covered over on the pedestrian walkways of our lives. Therefore it is often a time of heightened interest in spirituality and personal growth or a phase of creativity and self-exploration. The archetypal urge of Neptune is to transcend. When in its grip there is a loss of connection to the habitual rituals that ground and secure us. Therefore one of the important aspects of this transit is to be mindful of proper nourishment and food, maintaining regular sleeping habits, self-care and the continuity of physical routines. Clients undergoing this transition have often told me of losing their appetite, an inability to sleep or wake up, of feeling lethargic, unable to be active, as well as craving more alcohol, drugs and rest. It takes a conscious attempt to remain embodied and pursue activities that support the process.

My experience has been that it is hard to imagine where one is headed or what is in store during Neptune transits. With the insight of time we can look back and recognize how the process unfolded, but we can also appreciate how we could never have imagined planning this or even conceiving of it. Something incredible has occurred and we appreciate the unseen hand of the divine in helping to shape the outcome.

Neptune was shaped from the Greek Poseidon, god of the seas. Poseidon was not always connected to the seas, being known originally as the 'Earth-Shaker' and the god of horses. He became regent of the vast oceans, their stormy and turbulent waters and their shape-shifting inhabitants, when he was paired with Amphitrite, a goddess of the seas. His astrological temperament inherits this aspect of watery or emotional disquiet and unease. Neptune is also associated with Dionysus, the god of wine and the intoxication of the grape, who also was the embodiment of theatre, poetry, dance, spirituality, wandering, abandon and loosening, all aspects of this astrological archetype.

Astrological Neptune's domains are the vast seas and tides of human affairs, bittersweet feeling, fantasy, the longing to be complete, surrender, lack of inhibition and restraint, heartache and the yearning for the divine. Its other-worldly essence leaves a feeling of something missing or not yet completed that often leads an individual into a spiritual search, a sense of surrender or a period of feeling let down. It accompanies a deeper connection to and reverence for the sacred.

The Cycle of Neptune

The first critical aspect in the cycle is the waxing square near age 41, one of the potent aspects of the midlife passage. While each generation experiences this in the context of the times, one of the main elements at this time of life is the profound awareness of what is missing, what has not happened and the sense of something still unfulfilled. It may be a disappointment where life has led or the bittersweet longing for something or someone else. We feel lost, at sea; aware of the life we have constructed due to the life choices we have made. Neptune symbolizes the dreams we have harboured, the promises we have made and the hopes we have held. At this square they are challenged and measured against what has really happened. It may feel disheartening, yet the reality is quite the opposite. It is a soulful time and what might feel despairing is actually reconnecting us to soul. We feel lost, so we can find our way again; disappointed, so we might rework the agenda we have set; and confused because something creative and mystical is trying to present itself. There comes a point in every passage and on every voyage when we need to take stock. This is the time to explore what we still creatively and soulfully would like to accomplish in our life. It is a time of assessing where we have gone off-course.

While the first square may be experienced despondently, the irony is that it awakens the soul to unlived aspects of the creative and spiritual life, calling us to provide more meaning, more creativity and more imagination in our lives. At this time it is important to question and reflect; our declarations that everything is wonderful may in part be denial. Therefore, I always try to illustrate this time to clients as a reconnection to soul and creativity, to the authentic essences of self.

In our mid-fifties, Neptune trines itself and, in a way, rewards the work done in the last fourteen years towards steering the ship on a path aligned with soul. It is an age for recognizing that our spiritual life is what will sustain us in the future. It is a gathering time, a time of remembering and a time when many decisions are beginning to be shaped unconsciously. While we may not be aware of it, we are instinctively planning the next phase of life with the help of inner images and invisible forces.

In its transits to the planets and angles, Neptune draws down what often seems like a haze, a time when it is misty and unclear. Yet what is happening is a profound state of change, one that we cannot fathom with our intellect or mind. During a Neptune transition we are asked to trust in the process, relinquish control and follow the prompts. The signs are all around; we only have to be still, quiet and sensitive to what is taking place in order to make the transition into the next phase. In the ancient world, disorientation through a labyrinthine initiatory process prepared pilgrims to enter a more receptive and spiritual state. In a similar process, the confusion and uncertainty of a Neptune transit are often the clues that the personality is in flux and entering a new plane of spiritual growth.

♀ Pluto

Pluto does not move steadily through the zodiac due to its elliptical orbit, spending the greatest amount of time in Taurus and the least in Scorpio. Both being orbit-crossers, Chiron and Pluto have been classified as belonging to the Kuiper Belt; therefore they share a marginal quality by not fully fitting into the solar system like other planets. This was the same situation mythologically. While Chiron and Pluto were both sons of Saturn, they were not classified as Olympians. Astrologers still classify Pluto as part of the planetary pantheon but in 2006 the International Astronomical Union demoted Pluto to the status of a 'dwarf' planet as it did not conform to features set down for planetary status. Symbolically, however, Pluto is just as powerful and commanding as before.

Pluto Generations
The following table, from the current cycle of Pluto through the zodiac, shows the difference in timing per sign. Pluto crossed inside the orbit of Neptune in February 1979 in the sign of Libra and crossed back over Neptune's orbit in February 1999 in the sign of Sagittarius; therefore, the full transit of Scorpio is spent while inside Neptune's realm. During this twenty-year period Pluto is closer to the Sun than Neptune.

Pluto Sign	Number of Years in Sign	Pluto Sign	Number of Years in Sign	Pluto sign	Number of Years in Sign	Number of Years in Each Element
♈	29.3 years	♌	18.8 years	♐	13 years	Fire: 61.1 years
♉	31.5 years	♍	14.7 years	♑	15.6 years	Earth: 61.8 years
♊	30.1 years	♎	12.2 years	♒	19.6 years	Air: 61.9 years
♋	25 years	♏	11.5 years	♓	24.1 years	Water: 60.6 years

With Pluto's slower speed through the zodiac, the only critical phase that each Pluto generation may experience is the waxing square. For instance, individuals born with Pluto in Taurus during the 19th century received their waxing square in their 70s and 80s. Sigmund Freud, born with Pluto in Taurus, died in his 84th year while his first Pluto square was coming into orb, along with his Uranus return and his 7th Jupiter return. For the Pluto in Virgo generation, the waxing square came as early as 35, heralding a succession of cycles synchronous with the midlife passage. Some of the Pluto in Cancer, Leo and Virgo generations may experience their Pluto oppositions, as these take place during their 80s, along with the Uranus return and Neptune opposition. Here are the approximate ages of the waxing square for each Pluto generation.

Natal Sign Pluto	% of Time in Sign	Waxing Square Occurs Between	Natal Sign Pluto	% of Time in Sign	Waxing Square Occurs Between
♈	11.9%	Ages 86–91	♎	5.0%	Ages 36–42
♉	12.8%	Ages 73–86	♏	4.7%	Ages 42–49
♊	12.2%	Ages 58–73	♐	5.3%	Ages 49–59
♋	10.2%	Ages 45–58	♑	6.4%	Ages 59–73
♌	7.7%	Ages 38–45	♒	8.0%	Ages 73–85
♍	6.0%	Ages 35–38	♓	9.8%	Ages 85–91

When studying the effects of planetary cycles and transits I find it helpful to amplify the myths associated with the relevant planetary deity. In the mythic narrative are archetypal images and patterns that help us to understand the archetypal qualities and feelings constellated during the transition. In Greek myth, Hades is not only the personification of the underworld god Pluto but also refers to his extensive underworld kingdom. Mythological tradition and epic differentiate the underworld locale from the god Hades, who is regent of this place. The topography and atmosphere of this mythological netherworld is metaphoric of the subterranean feelings encountered during a Pluto transit.

Pluto's passage through each sign impresses each generation with a different experience of the underworld. For the Pluto in Cancer generation, the fear of the underworld is the dread of loss of attachment; for Pluto in Leo it is the anxiety of loss of youth and creativity; for the Virgo generation the fear of dis-order and chaos is high; for Pluto in Libra, it is the terror of the demise of relating; and for the Pluto in Scorpio generation their nightmares confront being out of control.

Pluto Passages

Journeys to the underworld are a common motif mythologically. The journey to the underworld is a vivid metaphor for the therapeutic descent into the repressed, taboo and unknown aspects of self. Carl Jung suggested that the journey into the Self was akin to this mythic descent to Hades,[66] a journey he personally described in his autobiography. At the age of 38, Jung experienced his own descent. He said that 'the ground literally gave way beneath my feet and I plunged down into the dark depths.'[67] In surveying 2,500 years of attitudes towards melancholia and depression, an historian recently concluded that two images consistently recurred in these states: 'being in a state of darkness and being weighed down'[68] like the descent into Hades. During Jung's descent he encountered the shades and guides of his own underworld. At the time Pluto, still undiscovered, had just ingressed into Cancer, the midpoint of his natal Moon–Uranus square. Hence transiting Pluto had semi-squared both the Moon and Uranus. Familiarizing ourselves with the terrain of Pluto helps us to psychologically appreciate the realm we are drawn into during depression, disillusionment and periods of existential doubt or major transitions in the life cycle. As astrologers it amplifies our understanding of Pluto and the process taking place during its transits.

As the lord of death and rebirth, Pluto is the silent and invisible brother who removes himself from the affairs of the Olympian family, yet governs much of the family fate. As the guardian of shades, Pluto is given the caretaking role for what remains repressed in both the individual and the family: secrets, shame, buried passions, unexpressed grief and loss, severed attachments, unresolved endings, negative and toxic feelings. Pluto rarely ventures above ground, choosing to remain in the underworld.[69] Pluto's mythic realms are also internal, interior and introverted as few images or altars survive to remind us of his worship or importance in cult. Virtually no temples were erected to Pluto. Rarely is the god represented in art, sculpture or vase painting. Pluto has been re-placed and dis-placed, potent clues to what we have culturally and psychologically done with this archetype. Having no specific temples or altars and being underground, his worshippers summoned Pluto by striking the earth with their hands. Pluto symbolizes the darker aspects of psychic life, once accessible and underhand: negative and dark feelings, loss, rage, jealousy, grief and death are his aspects of psyche.

Pluto is from *Plutus*, meaning 'wealth'. This title of the 'rich man' or the 'wealthy one' suggests the treasures beneath the earth, a reminder of the rich internal psychic world. Pluto symbolizes the immense resources hidden in the interior of the earth or metaphorically in the underworld of the psyche. Subjectivity is Pluto's realm and, when honoured, the richness of the interior world is tapped through dreams, images and symbols. Dreams appear in the stillness of sleep when the extroverted world becomes invisible and consciousness yields to unconsciousness. This world of shades and shadow is a resourceful place, the transformational aspect of the astrological Pluto.

The outcome of a Pluto transit is dependent on our motives and intent. Pluto demands that something is relinquished so new life may be conceived, and the success of this process depends on our attitudes to honouring the darker realms of life. Pluto transits to the angles or in a harsh aspect to one of the personal planets are times when we are most likely to experience the mythic themes of the underworld. An ending is inevitable. The call to relinquish outworn attachments and suspend activity in the outer world occurs. Suspension in the chrysalid period, between what is past and what may be, turns our familiar world upside down. Our orientation is now the underworld and the journey through its labyrinthine passages.

During the cycle of Pluto, the waxing square to its natal position is a time when we may find ourselves on the threshold of the underworld, seeking guidance on how to journey through this transition. Unexpressed grief, loss, shame or repressed memories may rise to the surface. This first Pluto square is a calling to descend, to be suspended, and to honour the deeper feelings stirring beneath the threshold of consciousness. This heralds an in-depth confrontation with our self, demanding honesty and integrity of our beliefs and lifestyle.

It seems unavoidable that an encounter with the personal and familial unconscious takes place at this time. Familial secrets emerging, the haunting feeling of what has been lost and may never be regained, depression and despair, a confrontation with mortality, sexual impropriety and regret, emotional outrage, an angst of aloneness and dislocation – all are experiences that clients have shared with me during this passage. Facing loss, mainly the loss of innocence, is the hallmark of Pluto's passage. Yet, alongside this pain, a process of healing is taking place.

To honour Pluto, prepare for the descent, be willing to be laid bare, be undefended and vulnerable. This attitude respects the underworld. A guide is necessary, but like Jung it may emerge out of one's own crisis like an internal priestess or *sibyl*. By letting go and no longer resisting the change we find the courage and inner strength to surrender to the process. Pluto's realm is the transformative place we could not see before we began the journey. Pluto's transforming power dissipates the dread of the transit as we engage and participate with its calling.

8

THE MARRIAGE OF THE SUN AND MOON
Lunations, Nodal Cycles and Eclipses

The Sun and Moon are perpetual timepieces. Although not considered planets from an astronomical perspective, in an astrological context they are catalogued as the key archetypes within the planetary pantheon. The ancients saw both as essential to character and nature. As luminaries, they are the lamps of heaven: the Sun shines during the day while the Moon reflects solar light at night. When the Moon is visible we read in her face the phase she is at with her partner, the Sun. This astrology has been part of mythology, human history and science forever.

Their rhythmic dance in the heavens yields many cycles. Foremost is the monthly cycle of waxing and waning, from New to Full Moon and back again. This cycle has been used effectively agriculturally, from planting to harvesting, in medical procedures, mundane tasks and rituals. This 29.5-day synodic cycle of the Sun and Moon also has a grand cycle of 19 years. Every 19 years the New Moon occurs near the same day within 1° of orb. This is known as the Metonic cycle named for Meton, a Greek astronomer who demonstrated that New Moons repeat every 19 years.

Another important timepiece is formed due to the intersection of the Moon's orbit with the Sun's. These two crossing points on the ecliptic are the lunar nodes, which retrograde through the zodiac every 18.6 years. When the Sun is near the Moon's North or South Node, an eclipse season occurs. During this time, at the New Moon, a solar eclipse takes place. Solar eclipses happen at least twice annually – once when the Sun is near the North Node and again when close to the South Node. Solar eclipses also form cycles through the zodiac, repeating approximately every 18 years. The marriage of the Sun and Moon creates three interconnected 18–19-year cycles, all of interest astrologically.

Cycle	Timing	Notes
Nodal Cycle	18.6 years	One complete retrograde cycle of the lunar nodes through the zodiac takes approximately 18.6 years
Saros Cycle	18 years, 10–11 days	There are at least two solar eclipses a year. Some years there are more, with a maximum of five annually. Each eclipse repeats after 18 years and 10–11 days (223 lunations) in a series known as the Saros Cycle
Metonic Cycle	19 years	The reoccurrence of New Moons every 19 years within one day and a 1° orb

Before we look at the marriage of the Sun and Moon, let's look at the bride and groom separately.

The Solar Cycle

The ingress of the Sun into each cardinal sign marks four transitional points on the wheel of the year, ushering in each season. These calendar points are determined by declination – the number of degrees that the Sun is north or south of the celestial equator. At the Aries equinox the Sun crosses the celestial equator moving north. Being on the celestial equator, its declination is 0°. As it reaches its northern pinnacle, it is at its maximum declination of +23°26'. This is the Cancer ingress marking the solstice, when the Sun 'stands still' at its highest point above the celestial equator. It marks the season of summer in the northern hemisphere and the season of winter in the southern hemisphere. Slowly the Sun turns to start its descent towards the equator. At the Libra equinox it crosses the celestial equator moving southward until it reaches its maximum southerly declination at the Capricorn solstice – a declination of -23°26'. Slowly the Sun turns and begins to rise towards the celestial equator once again. As it crosses the celestial equator the Sun's passage through all four seasons and all twelve signs of the zodiac is renewed. From a symbolic perspective the annual passage of the Sun's rising and setting across the celestial equator defines the seasons. Each one of the four seasons contains three signs, which reflect stages of an archetypal journey, metaphors for phases and passages of life; therefore, each sign represents its own unique quality of time.

The solar cycle reveals our personal high and low points during the year. Every year the transiting Sun passes through the houses of the horoscope at the same time, visiting for about a month, creating a personal timepiece that replicates itself annually. For instance, the house/s that contains Aries is transited by the Sun from the third week in March to the third week in April each year. The Sun returns each year on our birthday to its natal house, designating a new solar cycle for the year. Halfway through the year, the transiting Sun is in the opposite house to its natal position, marking the midpoint of our personal solar year. I have found great value in creating my own personal seasonal markers using these times of the year when the Sun transits through the houses.

Here are approximate dates when the Sun ingresses into each sign of the zodiac. Because the Earth's orbit is elliptical, the Sun does not travel evenly through the zodiac, spending approximately 31 days in Cancer, yet only 29 days in Capricorn. Become familiar with the annual path that the Sun travels through your horoscope by marking the approximate date, which varies slightly year to year, when it enters each house.

Sun Ingress into	Approximate Dates in Sign
Aquarius	20 January to 18 February
Pisces	19 February to 20 March
Aries	21 March to 19 April
Taurus	20 April to 20 May
Gemini	21 May to 20 June
Cancer	21 June to 22 July
Leo	23 July to 22 August
Virgo	23 August to 22 September
Libra	23 September to 22 October
Scorpio	23 October to 21 November
Sagittarius	22 November to 21 December
Capricorn	22 December to 19 January

Anniversaries are also etched in time by the passage of the Sun through the zodiac. Along with personal anniversaries, such as your wedding date or children's birthdays, are collective ones such as Armistice Day or '9/11'. The Sun's passage defines religious and social ceremonies including Christmas, Hanukkah, Kwanzaa and Thanksgiving. Anniversaries are psychic reminders that evoke celebration, remembrance and gratitude for life. The Sun's transit through the zodiac identifies these times, bringing them to consciousness to be honoured and remembered. In this way the Sun is comforting, as its rituals of rising and setting are dependable and instinctively known to each human being.

The Sun also rises and sets each day across the horizon, the line where earth meets heaven and divides what is visible from what is invisible. We mark time by the daily rhythm of the Sun as it ascends and descends through the houses. Hours of the day represent the Sun's movement, as approximately every two hours the Sun occupies another house. As the Sun climbs above the horizon, the night world cedes to the day as Eos, the dawn goddess, brings the first light. As it rises we awaken in the 12th house, the first house of the day. After it culminates near noon, we enter 9th house territory. As the Sun starts to descend it passes through the 8th house in mid-afternoon. At its set it crosses the Descendant, entering the hearth of the 6th house.

The nocturnal solar journey is metaphoric of the hero's descent, which astrology maps though the six houses underfoot. The setting place is the western horizon, the Descendant, where we descend into the night and the dream. From setting to approximately two hours after sunset, the Sun inhabits the 6th house, where the rituals of life are focused on the change from the day world to the night and the preparation for eventide. It is the place where we clear the day, let go and reorient ourselves to the dark. At midnight the Sun reaches the nadir of its journey and crosses the meridian that astrologically separates self and other. As it enters the 3rd house the Sun turns away from otherness to face its self and prepare for its ascent through the shady world of the dreamtime. This is the quadrant that focuses on infancy; therefore, the Sun's ascent through this area may connect with phantoms of the past. When the Sun reaches the horizon once again, it rises into view, dispelling the shades of night. Dawn heralds the day world and the diurnal cycle begins again.

The cycle of the Sun rising across the eastern horizon to begin the day is an image that helps us to understand that the Ascendant marks the visible beginning of all cycles – perhaps the birth of each new cycle. However, the IC also represents the seminal moment of all cycles; for instance, our clocks measure the beginning of the day at midnight. This is the subjective beginning of the cycle, not yet visible, still in the dark. In a personal sense the Ascendant is a reliable starting point, especially when studying the transits of planets through the houses.

The Lunar Cycle

The monthly cycle of the Moon can be measured in latitude, which is the distance north or south of the ecliptic.[70] When the Moon is on the ecliptic it is conjunct its node, as the nodes are defined by the crossing of the Moon's orbit and the ecliptic. After the Moon conjoins its North Node, it rises above the ecliptic to its maximum latitude. After approximately six to seven days, or one quarter of its cycle, it is at its highest point north of the ecliptic and 90° from its nodes. This period in the cycle is known to traditional astrologers as the 'bending' since the Moon is at its maximum height and ready to change direction, similar to the Cancer solstice of the Sun.[71] Another six to seven days later, the Moon will again be conjunct the ecliptic, yet this time moving southward below the ecliptic. Here the Moon conjuncts its South Node. Six to seven days later it will be at its southerly bending, squaring the nodal axis, before it turns to rise again and begin a new cycle. This is the Moon's latitude cycle of 27.3 days.

The more familiar sidereal cycle of the Moon is measured in longitude as it traverses the zodiac, spending just over two days in each sign. Being synonymous with moods, the Moon is a barometer of the emotional climate. Its passage through each sign illustrates emotional qualities and nuances, while its transit through the houses indicates where these feelings and impressions are located. Since the Moon moves so quickly, many reactions and feelings are unconscious, being stored subliminally and reawakened later through reflection, creative pastimes or dreams. While the transits of the Moon may not appear significant, they are often highlighted in a chart cast for a dream or a memorable event. Like the Sun that maps anniversaries, the Moon records and memorizes significant emotional and psychological episodes.

The movement of the Moon symbolizes emotional tides. Lunar time is measured by its quality of feeling, documenting a diary of our felt experiences. Moon diaries are a helpful way to track the lunar ebb and flow with our moods, feelings, humour and heart. I recommend following the Moon through the signs of the zodiac and houses of your horoscope for the next year, being alert for emotional patterns. For instance, if your natal Moon is in the element of Air, the period every nine days when the Moon moves through the Water Element may feel very different from when it transits the Fire signs. You might notice the difference energetically between when the Moon transits your 5th house as distinct from when it is in your 12th. Take note of the position of the Moon when you schedule social engagements, time off work or start a new course or project. Being aware of the Moon helps us to become more attentive to our emotional rhythms and feeling states, not so we can change or control them, but so we can learn how to participate with them to feel more secure and centred.

The Marriage of the Sun and Moon

As presented in Chapter 4, the synodic cycle of the Sun and Moon is 29.5 days and is divided into phases which can be used as a prototype for all cycles, no matter their length. The lunation phases mark the chapters of the month. Each one of the eight phases can be used as a timer for certain rituals and projects or to reflect on the stage of a process that we are undergoing. The dance of the Sun and Moon creates this eternally visible timepiece that reflects back the qualities of the time we are passing through. In subtle ways the relationship between the Sun and Moon creates other frames of reference that astrologically differentiate how to read the times.

The Cycles of the Lunar Nodes

The lunar nodes take approximately 18.6 years to complete one revolution through the zodiac. Their cycle maps out 4 to 5 distinct periods in the life cycle approximately every 19 years. The lunar nodes retrograde through the horoscope in the opposite direction to the planets, spending between 18 and 19 months in one sign or approximately in one house of the horoscope.

Nodal Cycle	Ages	Age of Opposition	Age of Conjunction (Return)
1st	Birth to 18.6	9	19
2nd	18.6 to 37	28	37
3rd	37–56	47	56
4th	56–74	65	74
5th	74–93	84	93

The retrograde transit of the nodes is an important image to consider, as their cyclical task and purpose is not sequential development, nor physical or material achievements. Nodal growth is concerned with the integration of the spiritual life, which often pulls us in another direction. Its cycle encourages how the soul's calling might be best practised and appreciated. While the cycles of everyday life immerse us in physical and emotional attachments, nodal transits awaken other values. Therefore each nodal return is a reconfirmation of our spiritual nature, a calling that emerges from the depth of soul. As the nodes transit our horoscope they address the personal and private areas of life that are being stimulated morally and spiritually.

The house position of the transiting North Node draws our attention to the environment that needs conscious attention. The transiting South Node, in the opposite house, emphasizes the sphere of life where past resources and experiences can be drawn on to assist in our spiritual development. Eclipses will occur near the transiting node. Approximately three to four eclipses will occur in a house polarity, accentuating this astrological environment. Take notice of the transits of the North and South Nodes over planets in the natal chart, also noting when the nodes change houses.[72]

There are two different geocentric nodal positions: one is the True Node, the other is the Mean Node. The Mean Node is the average position based on the daily movement of its 18.6-year cycle, which is about 3 seconds per day. The True Node is the specific position of the Node on the ecliptic. Until the early 1980s the True Node could not be calculated accurately, so the Mean Node was used. With the advent of computers the True Node can now be measured, but the Mean Node still remains in common usage.

The Mean Node has a harmonic that helps us to remember its approximate movement through the zodiac.

- The cycle of the nodes through the zodiac takes approximately 18 to 19 years
- The transit of the nodes through one sign takes approximately 18 to 19 months
- The transit of the nodes through one degree takes approximately 18 to 19 days
- In one year the nodes move approximately 18 to 19 degrees

Of interest to me is that the Moon and the Sun cards in the Major Arcana of the Tarot are numbered 18 and 19.

The True Node's direction is retrograde but at times it will also be direct. The True Node has a serpentine movement through the zodiac, slithering backwards for about four months, then reaching a plateau near the same degree for two to three months before it slips backwards to repeat its movement. This elongates the nodal transit over particular degrees of the zodiac. I differentiate the two nodes in terms of how they best can be utilized: the Mean Node gives a view of the overall cycle and its critical times whereas the True Node corresponds with personal transits through the horoscope.

The house that the transiting North Node is passing through is where more conscious understanding and spiritual development is arising. This is an area of intake and assimilation where soul development and growth occurs. The transiting South Node highlights issues and concerns from the past that need to be resolved and disseminated towards the new focus emerging at the North Node. This is a place of release where the experiences of the past, insight and instinctive responses can activate the growth indicated by the North Node.

Here are some keys to understanding the personal transit of the nodes through the houses. Imagine this cycle begins with the North Node transiting the Ascendant. Since the North Node retrogrades through the zodiac, the first house it transits is the 12th. At the same time the South Node transits the 6th. One way to imagine this is to consider the South Node as the task of release and dissemination while the North Node has a mission to develop and grow in this area.

Transiting Nodes	The North Node's Mission	The South Node's Task
☊ in 12th ☋ in 6th	*Understanding* To delve deeply into understanding our hidden motives and compulsions. To make peace with the spirits of the past	*Routine* To utilize the rituals and routines of our life to develop understanding. Work and health play an important role in the wider schema of our lives
☊ in 11th ☋ in 5th	*Communal Participation* To find our place within our circle of friends and colleagues so we know we are part of an eclectic community	*Creative Self-expression* To unleash our innate creativity and self- expression to become more present and willing to participate in life's parade
☊ in 10th ☋ in 4th	*Career-focused* To continue to forge our role in the world, striving to follow the course of our vocation	*Belonging/Settling* To be secure and settled in order to support our place in the world
☊ in 9th ☋ in 3rd	*Searching for the Truth* To quest for meaning, search for understanding, and explore beyond our familial and cultural boundaries	*Becoming Mindful* To let go of detail and rational considerations to feel free enough to move, explore unfamiliar neighbourhoods and question our beliefs
☊ in 8th ☋ in 2nd	*Honouring the Depth of Self* To become involved in speaking the truth, being honest about our feelings and vigilant about our integrity	*Reaping Past Rewards* To free up our resources and talents to be able to engage with others in trustworthy projects and more intimate adventures
☊ in 7th ☋ in 1st	*Respecting Relationships* To feel an equal and active part of all our relationships; to discover what is important in ourselves to be present with others	*Relinquishing the Focus on Self* To let go of the focus on independence and being self-reliant in order to be in relationships where we depend on others for support
☊ in 6th ☋ in 12th	*A Health Regimen* To concentrate on our daily routines, work and to strive towards well-being and health	*Secure in the Divine* To have confidence in letting life flow, secure in the faith that divine help and guidance is at hand

☊ in 5th ☋ in 11th	*Aspiration and Applause* To audition and perform, creating ways that align with our creativity and self-expression	*The Support of Friends and Loved Ones* Letting ourselves receive and feel love, acknowledgement and attention from others
☊ in 4th ☋ in 10th	*Building A Nest* To create emotional security through focusing on home and family	*Acknowledgement* To acknowledge the work that we do well and develop maturity and authority in the world
☊ in 3rd ☋ in 9th	*Expression and Communication* To develop our ideas, communicate our feelings and present our beliefs	*Educating Others* To share our innate wisdom, disseminate our beliefs and support the integrity of human values
☊ in 2nd ☋ in 8th	*Banking our Resources* To strive to value and appreciate who we are, building a healthy sense of self-esteem, personal resources and assets	*Intimacy and Involvement* Recognizing and celebrating the emotional resources of our life and paying tribute to our emotional connections
☊ in 1st ☋ in 7th	*Self-focus* Shining the light on the self, encouraging independence, space and freedom by knowing what we want and when to act	*Social and Relating Skills* To become more conscious of our social and relational skills in order to feel independent and free enough of others' expectations

The Saros Cycle

Eclipses accompany the transiting nodes through the zodiac, forming a cycle known as the Saros cycle. The word *saros* originates from the Greek, meaning 'repetition', and describes the recurrent and predictable nature of eclipses. Cidenas, an astronomer from the 4th century BCE, recognized that eclipses returned after 223 lunations. In the 10th century CE this phenomenon became referred to as the Saros cycle.

Eclipses occur at foreseeable times and are visible at predictable places. Each eclipse belongs to a particular group or series that contain between 70 and 72 eclipses. The length of each Saros series averages about 1,280 years. Each eclipse in its specific series occurs in a sequence, which starts at either the North or South Pole. The next eclipse in the series occurs 120° west of the previous one at a latitude closer to the equator. This is repeated by each successive eclipse in the series. The cycle reaches its midpoint near the equator and ends at the opposite pole from where the series began. The Earth is enwrapped by these chains of eclipses like a celestial ouroboros, the ancient image depicting a serpent encircling the world egg. The ouroboros, or serpent biting its own tail, symbolizes the eternal round of birth, death and rebirth.

These Saros groups are cycles of eclipses, often described as a family and numbered 1–19. If the inaugural eclipse occurs near the North Pole the series is labelled North; similarly, if the initial eclipse occurs near the South Pole, the series is categorized South. There are 38 series in total: 19 being North and 19 being South Saros cycles. Each eclipse in the series occurs at an interval of 18 years, 10–11 days; therefore, the longitude of the following eclipse in the series moves forward in the zodiac by about 10–11°. Once a series ends, then a new one will begin using the same Saros series number. As the eclipses approach the equator, they are near the nodes and adjust from partial to total eclipses. The closer the eclipse is to the equator, the more total it is.

Because of the cyclical nature of eclipses, they are important indicators of astrological time. Each Saros cycle has its unique individual life force and nature, which is influenced by the maiden eclipse at the inception of its cycle. The repetitive nature of the 18-year cycle of eclipses is important in light of the nodal transits and their returns. Since the eclipses occur near the nodes, a house polarity is emphasized; therefore when analysing the transits of the lunar nodes through the houses it is important to consider the eclipses that accompany the transiting node.

On average, the North and South Nodes each transit a house of the horoscope every 18–19 months. This transit will be accompanied by approximately three or four eclipses across the same house polarity. Therefore these two opposite houses will be in the spotlight, especially at times when eclipses take place. The following table demonstrates the ingress of the North Node into the signs from Gemini to Capricorn and the solar eclipses that occur during this transit. Note that during the nodal transit of Pisces, no eclipses fall in this sign. This is often the case: during a complete cycle of the nodes, eclipses often skip one sign.

True ☊ Enters Sign	Date of Entry Universal Time (UT)	Date Solar Eclipses Occur	North or South Node Eclipse	Solar Eclipse Degree
♊ Gemini	5 May 2020	21 Jun 2020	☊ North Node	00♋21
		14 Dec 2020	☋ South Node	23♐08
		10 Jun 2021	☊ North Node	19♊47
		4 Dec 2021	☋ South Node	12♐22
♉ Taurus	18 Jan 2022	30 Apr 2022	☊ North Node	10♉28
		25 Oct 2022	☋ South Node	02♏00
		20 Apr 2023	☊ North Node	29♈50
♈ Aries	17 Jul 2023	14 Oct 2023	☋ South Node	21♎07
		8 Apr 2024	☊ North Node	19♈24
		2 Oct 2024	☋ South Node	10♎03
♓ Pisces	11 Jan 2025	29 Mar 2025	☊ North Node	09♈00
		21 Sep 2025	☋ South Node	29♍05
		17 Feb 2026	☊ North Node	28♒49
		Note: No solar eclipses occur in Pisces		
♒ Aquarius	27 Jul 2026	12 Aug 2026	☋ South Node	20♌02
		6 Feb 2027	☊ North Node	17♒37
		2 Aug 2027	☋ South Node	09♌55
		26 Jan 2028	☊ North Node	06♒10
♑ Capricorn	26 Mar 2028	22 Jul 2028	☋ South Node	29♋50
		14 Jan 2029	☊ North Node	24♑50
		12 Jun 2029	☋ South Node	21♊29
		11 Jul 2929	☋ South Node	19♋37
		5 Dec 2029	☊ North Node	13♐45

The Metonic Cycle

In the Metonic cycle New Moons repeat within 1° every 19 years, an important consideration for astrologers. This repetitive nature is noteworthy, because if a New Moon is eclipsed, there is a 75% chance that the next New Moon 19 years later will also be eclipsed. The following table shows 16 of the 22 eclipses repeating within 1° after 19 years.

The table also shows the repetition of eclipses in both the Saros and Metonic cycles. Note that the Saros cycle repeats after 10–11 days or 10–11° of the zodiac, while the Metonic repeats within one day and 1°. Embedded in each eclipse is an 18–19-year timing that connects these times together: times when our understanding of the integration of the emotional and rational worlds – the marriage of the Moon and Sun – is heightened.

Current Eclipse		Previous Eclipse Saros Cycle		Previous Eclipse Metonic Cycle	
Eclipse Date	Eclipse Degree	Previous Eclipse Date	Previous Eclipse Degree	Previous Eclipse Date	Previous Eclipse Degree
21 Jun 2020	00♋21	10 Jun 2002	19♊54	21 Jun 2001	00♋10
14 Dec 2020	23♐08	4 Dec 2002	11♐58	14 Dec 2001	22♐56
10 Jun 2021	19♊47	31 May 2003	09♊20	10 Jun 2002	19♊54
04 Dec 2021	12♐22	23 Nov 2003	01♐14	04 Dec 2002	11♐58
30 Apr 2022	10♉28	19 Apr 2004	29♈49	*Eclipse did not occur at 1 May 2003 New Moon*	
25 Oct 2022	02♏00	14 Oct 2004	21♎06	*Eclipse did not occur at 25 Oct 2003 New Moon*	
20 Apr 2023	29♈50	09 Apr 2005	19♈06	19 Apr 2004	29♈49
14 Oct 2023	21♎07	03 Oct 2005	10♎19	14 Oct 2004	21♎06
08 Apr 2024	19♈24	29 Mar 2006	08♈35	08 Apr 2005	19♈06
02 Oct 2024	10♎03	22 Sep 2006	29♍20	03 Oct 2005	10♎19
29 Mar 2025	09♈00	19 Mar 2007	28♓07	29 Mar 2006	08♈35
21 Sep 2025	29♍05	11 Sep 2007	18♍25	22 Sep 2006	29♍20
17 Feb 2026	28♒49	07 Feb 2008	17♒44	*Eclipse did not occur at 17 Feb 2007 New Moon*	
12 Aug 2026	20♌02	01 Aug 2008	09♌32	*Eclipse did not occur at 12 Aug 2007 New Moon*	
06 Feb 2027	17♒37	26 Jan 2009	06♒30	07 Feb 2008	17♒44
02 Aug 2027	09♌55	22 Jul 2009	29♋27	01 Aug 2008	09♌32
26 Jan 2028	06♒10	15 Jan 2010	25♑01	26 Jan 2009	06♒30
22 Jul 2028	29♋50	11 Jul 2010	19♋24	22 Jul 2009	29♋27
14 Jan 2029	24♑50	04 Jan 2011	13♑39	15 Jan 2010	25♑01
12 Jun 2029	21♊29	01 Jun 2011	11♊02	*Eclipse did not occur at 12 Jun 2010 New Moon*	
11 Jul 2029	19♋37	01 Jul 2011	09♋12	11 Jul 2010	19♋24
05 Dec 2029	13♐45	25 Nov 2011	02♐37	*Eclipse did not occur at 5 Dec 2011 New Moon*	

Eclipses

In Vedic mythology the North Node is personified as Rahu, while the South Node is Ketu, a dragon-serpent severed in two. Eclipses occur within proximity of Rahu and Ketu, who wait on the ecliptic, ready to swallow the Sun.

To understand the separate nature of Rahu and Ketu let's imagine each one swallowing the Sun. When Ketu or the belly of the dragon swallows the Sun the hero becomes lodged in the abdomen, or the tail of the dragon. To be released he must be expelled. Hence at the South Node it is important to empty out the past, as its contents help us to become conscious of our present predicament. Other mythological motifs depict heroes emerging from the jaws of a serpent, like Jason being expelled from the dragon or Jonah being disgorged from the belly of the whale. At the South Node there is accumulated wisdom that needs to be disseminated.

When Rahu or the dragon's head swallows the Sun, it passes quickly through its severed throat. There is an insight, a realization, a heroic impulse, but it is hard to hold or sustain. Therefore at the North Node there is perception and passion, but it passes quickly and is often difficult to maintain. What follows is often disappointment and an urge to regress. When the South Node understanding is brought out, it provides the process with sustenance and encouragement.

Solar eclipses occur at least twice a year. In the annual course of the Sun's journey it will be swallowed by Rahu and Ketu, suggesting that these are the periods when we enter into the shadow lands, the spheres of our life where we may encounter the dragon. The North and South Node transits are pointers to where the head and tail of the dragon will attempt to swallow the heroic identity. The transiting nodes' house positions are important to track as it is in these spheres where the metaphoric encounter with the dragon takes place, casting a shadow across this area of the chart. Consider what the solar eclipses may be unearthing or eclipsing when they fall in the houses. Reflect on past eclipses and what you feel they may have brought to light in your life.

Eclipses Falling in Houses	The Solar Eclipses in these Houses could Highlight
12–6	Time to balance the daily rituals of work and well-being with the spiritual life, taking note of the areas of life that require order as well as unplanned activity
11–5	Time to recognize the tension between involvement with friends and community and the need to develop our own creativity and self-expression
10–4	Time to be mindful that the delicate equilibrium between attention to our public career and quality time spent with our private self and family might need refocusing
9–3	Time to integrate our ideas with our beliefs, becoming aware of how to educate ourselves in a way that supports the dissemination and communication of our ideas
8–2	Time to take an inventory of our material and emotional resources, reflecting on the way we provide these for ourselves and share them with others
7–1	Time to consider situations between us and others; where we are not feeling equal or identified so that we can participate more freely and openly in our partnerships

Eclipses as Transits

Solar eclipses occur every six months and may be either preceded or followed by a lunar eclipse. Eclipses are cyclic; therefore, they can be linked to previous times when they fell at the same degree of the horoscope in the Metonic cycle or were part of the same familial series in the Saros Cycle. Therefore, we can consider eclipses as a personal transit or part of the generic life cycle.

The astrological nature of an eclipse has always been significant. Before we knew how eclipses occurred, we considered them to be ominous and supernatural phenomena that portended disaster. Later, they became associated with important events concerning the king, sovereign, tribal leader or head of state. The disappearance of the Sun in the sky was interpreted as an omen for the waning of the ruling class, as a dark forecast for an upcoming battle or the death of a leader. Yet, on the other hand, eclipses could often herald a great event or the birth of a great leader, as is suggested with the birth of Alexander the Great. The eclipse before his birth swept through his birthplace of Macedonia and the countries he was to later conquer. Being born under an eclipse is to be born under its spell, sensitizing the individual to the intensity, unpredictability and providence that eclipse cycles represent. If the North or South Node is near the Sun in a natal horoscope, that individual was born during the eclipse season. In these cases I am alert to this individual's eclipse cycles throughout their life. Eclipses interrupt the instinctual circadian rhythm of animals, which often confuses them; hence we might argue that eclipses have an unsettling and disorientating effect. Astrologers often consider the path of an eclipse and the global regions where the umbra falls as highlighting areas of global concern and change.

The timing of eclipses is debated by astrologers; for instance, one theory is that their effect lasts for as many years as the eclipse lasts in minutes, much like a progression. Therefore, an eclipse of seven minutes would affect seven years of life. In my experience, because the eclipses are so regular and sweep the house polarities in a retrograde cycle, I work with the time frame of six months, that is, until the next eclipse occurs. I have witnessed their impact as being felt most strongly from 24 hours before to 12 hours after the exact time of the eclipse. About one week before the solar eclipse the energy builds, crescendos around the eclipse and tapers off over the following few weeks.

To interpret the impact of an eclipse I take into account its house position. Using an orb of 5°, I keep in mind any natal planets that are conjunct or opposing the eclipse. If the aspect is dramatic I am alert to the 18–19-year patterns that could be repeating. My focus is the transit of the house and the aspects that the eclipse makes. Of course, if the eclipse aspects outer planets, a whole generation will be experiencing this and its impact is more collective or global. Nonetheless, the eclipse can also be personal due to its house location.

By their very nature, eclipses are unpredictable, like a wild card. During a solar eclipse the Moon obscures the Sun, suggesting that the rational, controlled and objective nature is eclipsed by feelings. Therefore, if the eclipse is highlighted in the horoscope, it may trigger the release of psychological or emotional repressions. Eclipses can also energize and intensify the area of the chart they aspect, bringing hidden issues to the forefront. Not all eclipses impact the individual; however, in my experience when there are highly emotive and charged situations that are unresolved the eclipse triggers their release. Because eclipses are intimately connected with the movement of the nodes through the horoscope, I regard them as destined, a powerful marker of becoming conscious of one's direction and authenticity.

In *From the Moment We Met* I discussed the eclipse patterns that were synchronous with Princess Diana's marriage, separation and death.[73] She was born with the South Node conjunct the Moon in Aquarius when the eclipses were in the polarity of ♌ and ♒, the intercepted polarity of her 2nd and 8th houses.[74] The total solar eclipse before her birth was on 15 February 1961 at 26♒25, within 2° of her natal Moon. The eclipse after her birth was on 11 August 1961 at 18♌31. She married Prince Charles on 29 July 1981, two days before a solar eclipse occurring at 7♌51.

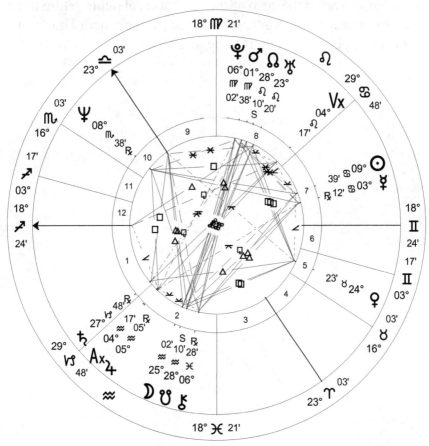

Diana, Princess of Wales
1 July 1961, 7.45 p.m. GMT, Sandringham, England, UK

Diana is the Roman name for the goddess of the Moon. The eclipse before her marriage of 7♌51 fell on her husband Charles's Ascendant: in so many ways he was eclipsed by her. Diana, the Moon, had obscured the future king (the Sun). During 1992 their marriage was in great turmoil. That same year, Diana's 7th house Sun in Cancer was eclipsed on 30 June (8♋57), the day before her birthday. Later that year, on 9 December, the Prime Minister formally announced the separation of Prince Charles and Princess Diana. That was the day of a lunar eclipse. The degree of the eclipse was 18♊10: the Sun was at 18♐10 and the Moon at 18♊10, exactly on her Descendant, the 7th house cusp of marriage. Diana now was obscured by the light of the Sun.

Diana died (31 August 1997) under an eclipse which occurred at 9♍34, close to her natal Pluto in the 8th house. The transiting North Node was on the cusp of the 9th house, about to return to her natal 8th house North Node, which was conjunct both Uranus and Mars and opposite her South Node and Moon.

9

WHAT TO DO UNTIL THE TRANSIT IS OVER
Rituals for Transition

Clients often ask what they could do to improve their understanding and experience when undergoing a major transit. Foremost is participating with the transition as consciously as possible, but this is not always an easy task. Honouring the transiting planetary archetypes is a good beginning.

Generally, it is the slower-moving planets that script the major storylines of the transitional experience. Psychological and spiritual models can help to reframe the narratives of these transitions allegorically. For example, one outline I have found helpful in framing the emotional and psychological states of transition is Dr Kübler-Ross's five stages of grief developed through her work with terminally ill patients. These stages of denial, anger, bargaining, depression and acceptance are listed sequentially, but are interchangeable during the course of major life transitions. I find value in recognizing and reflecting on the multifaceted stages in the process of major astrological transits; therefore encourage students and clients to find stories, metaphors, images, theories and other ways of thinking that help to picture their major transitions.

Metaphorically, transitions are like the alchemical process when primal matter is transmuted into gold. Like alchemical work, there are stages in the transitional process. After the initial struggles that accompany the changes, there is an interval when self-doubt, anxiety and despair surface. Yet, it is during this phase of anguish that the seeds of the new cycle are planted. As they take root, there is hope for the future. In the final phases the process becomes grounded in the material world, where it takes shape and has substance. The process of a transit, like alchemical work, is transforming as we move through its stages.

Generic transits are time passages constelled around life stages and ageing. In ancient societies, communal rituals and rites of passage helped the individual to navigate these life-cycle transitions. While graduation, marriage and retirement ceremonies mark important life events, they often do not address the deeper psychological and spiritual resources needed to successfully pilot this passage of time.

Major transits of the social and outer planets often equate with periods of enormous personal change, crisis and instability. Emotional and painful transitions can be assisted by the rituals and reflections that astrology helps us consider. When we are aware which archetype stirs beneath the surface, it can be acknowledged and encouraged through conscious intention and ritual. Astrology assists in negotiating this terrain, as it offers images and symbols to reflect and respect the transiting energy. When ritualized, the planetary god becomes honoured; in an ancient way of thinking this brought a sacred process into being.

Draw on your own experiences of what has or has not been helpful when you have experienced major life changes. Reflect on therapeutic, counselling and healing modalities that have been effective; courses and activities that have helped you move forward, or other activities or ways of being that have facilitated more consciousness and self-awareness. There is no manual for what each individual specifically needs, but astrology and our own creativity are reliable guides.

It is beneficial for an individual to feel there are ways they can engage and participate with the transit without feeling overwhelmed or victimized. Many clients feel that doing something different would be useful and meaningful. Ironically, it is the involvement with their current life process, and working through the transitional stages and troubles, that is often most helpful. Being in the moment, aware of the processes taking place, completing tasks and engaging in self-discovery and disclosure through ritual can all be highly effective and evocative.

Rituals are psychological processes that create a space for overwhelming feelings to be contained and modified. Through conscious intention and participation, the painful feelings connected with transition can be refocused. With the release of these tensions there is a renewal of faith and optimism as well as a wellspring of creative energies to propel us forward. In a modern context a ritual is a mindful practice that settles, focuses and utilizes the transitional energies in a constructive and creative way, such as enrolling in a course of study, pursuing a passion, being occupied with an engaging hobby, craft or creative activity, travel, volunteering, sports or other physical activities, therapies, healing techniques, consciousness-raising – the list is endless.

It is apparent that many of these practices resonate closely with certain planetary archetypes. A catalogue of helpful remedies for each transiting planet – whether therapies, courses, hobbies, sports, activities or some form of healing modality – can be compiled as a resource inventory for each transit. It is important not to be too rigid about defining what modality is best suited for a particular transit because each individual's experience will be unique. For any practice to be effective, it needs to suit the person's temperament, personality and stage of life.

Planetary Rituals

There is magic to astrology. We could look at this in two ways: organized or formal magic and spontaneous magic. Astrology has an historical association with magic. But while the tradition may have flirted with organized magic, in itself astrology is magical, not because of any technique, spell, chant, convention or ritual, but through an authentic participation in and sensitivity to its symbols.

Magic arises through spontaneous and participatory work with astrological symbols. Astrological magic is not manipulated, but works through us when we engage, honour and participate with its images in an intelligent and respectful way. When we engage with the transiting symbol through contemplation or action, we are involved with its process; in a way we are working with the gods of the moment. This is the concept of theurgy. The word 'theurgy' is from the ancient Greek words *theos*, god, and *ergos*, work, suggesting 'divine working' or working with the gods. Theurgy engages us in a process that invokes a divine presence. So in a contemporary way, to appeal to the archetypal energy assists in participating in our self-development symbolized by the transit.

In the ancient world invocations, rituals and operations were employed to connect with the divine. In our modern age we can imagine the symbol of the transiting planet as a call to participate with the archetype. We do not really need to fully understand the nature of magic or the *participation mystique* in order for the process to be effective. We do need to honour the archetypal energy and there is a variety of ways to do this.

Before we consider devising a list of potential rituals for each transiting planet, it is helpful to contemplate the planet's nature, such as whether it is more active or reflective, public or private, etc. Then we can begin to imagine some rituals that might be effective during major transits of the social and outer planets. Expand this list with your own experience and suggestions.

♃ Jupiter

Jupiter's urge is to learn more and to travel wider in its quest to venture beyond what is known. Its nature is to investigate, to lead an expedition beyond the coherent boundaries of the present. Its temperament is active; it believes in positivity and abundance; therefore, being cautious about overdoing or overcompensating is recommended. It is a time of possibilities and movement as well as a time of hope for the future.

During a Jupiter transit an individual is encouraged to stretch themselves. Consider the following suggestions of courses, activities and sports:

- A study of literature, philosophy, ethics or cross-cultural studies, such as a course in the classics, ancient civilizations, religions or foreign languages

- Activities that venture into nature and explore the outdoors, like bush walking, camping, hiking, white-water rafting and horse riding

- Jupiter is associated with travel and pilgrimage; therefore, adventure tours, travel to foreign and exotic places, a tour of mythological, historical or religious sites, revisiting places you have loved, or returning to your homeland or ancestral home may be of interest during this period. Visiting an ashram, a mosque, a church, a temple or experiencing prayer, meditation or other spiritual practices

- Becoming involved in different activities such as community work, coaching kids, volunteering for social work such as teaching refugees English as a second language, or community

emergency work like fire-fighting or the SES (special
emergency services)

• Becoming involved in a team sport or communal activity

♄ Saturn

By transit Saturn confronts an individual to become more
authentic, to acknowledge their calling, to manage their time and
resources better and to become more responsible and self-aware
in their everyday life. It is a time of maturing, stepping up, or a
promotion or movement into another level of being responsible.
While the individual may feel under pressure or over-committed, it
is important to complete any current obligations or contracts before
considering how any new structures can be employed. It is a time
of grounding, reorganizing and reforming so that a step forward can
be taken. Saturn's urge is to master; therefore, its transiting location
in the horoscope suggests an area under construction, improvement
and development.

There are many ways that an individual under a Saturn transit
could work with this energy:

• In terms of becoming more autonomous at work, a study of
  economics, management skills, time management or running
  your own business may be of interest. Writing or rewriting
  your CV, strategic business planning

• Hobbies that may be interesting and/or constructive that are
  also grounding, such as gardening, rock collecting, building
  projects, furniture repair

• Activities that help to organize your time, including keeping a
  diary, journal keeping, budgeting, scheduling

• Games of strategy where planning is necessary and choices
  and consequences are evident – perhaps backgammon, bridge,
  chess or Scrabble

• Activities that support us to be more flexible, poised and
  stable in the body such as yoga; ones that strengthen the spine

and lower back, for instance weight training; or exercise regimes that help improve fitness and focus, leisurely and focused exercise like golf

- Focusing on mental well-being using such techniques as mindfulness as well as physical well-being utilizing massage, Feldenkrais, etc.

- Following a chiropractic or osteopathic course to improve posture and heal back or shoulder pain

- Being aware and actively supportive of everyday rituals that help to maintain a healthy and balanced lifestyle such as a suitable diet, appropriate sleep, adequate water intake, a daily walk, meditation, etc

⚷ Chiron

Under major Chiron transits an individual may be involved in a 'healing crisis'. Whether this is a physical, mental, psychological or spiritual emergency, it marks out a time of personal growth and acceptance. What arises through the pain of living is an awareness of what is not being lived out authentically. These times invite participation with the crisis, not fixing or fighting it but accepting the limitations by listening to the voices of our symptoms. A Chiron transit can often be an encounter with a wild Centaur, a holy man, a healer, an illness or trauma that becomes our teacher and guide to helping us help ourselves.

Chiron's call returns us to an inner sanctuary to explore what the soul needs to feel fulfilled. It is a time of healing constellated through accepting the marginal aspects of self. Therefore, activities encouraging the inner world of symbol and image will be a healing balm.

- Chiron is the courage to heal. Therefore, this transition is soul-searching for the emotional and psychological trauma that underpins the symptom. Dream work and astrological counselling to promote healing through the understanding of symbols, symptoms and images of our life

- There are various healing modalities that resonate with Chiron, such as flower essences, homeopathic treatments, visualization and guided imagery, meditation, active imagination, absent and spiritual healing

- Chironic interventions are more inclined to be from complementary or alternative medicine; therefore, treatments like acupuncture, Ayurveda, Qigong and Reiki resonate with this passage of time. The name 'Chiron' is derived from the Greek word, *cheir* or 'hand'; therefore, we think of Chiron as handy; consequently, the laying on of hands, remedial massage and chiropractic treatments evoke the soulful essence of Chiron

- Alternative or ancient healing techniques such as naturopathy, natural remedies, herbs, Chinese and Oriental medicine also ritualize the archetype

- Biofeedback and hypnosis are consistent with Chiron's healing traditions

- Whether portrayed as animal and human, heaven and earth or secular and sacred, Chiron is the space between the worlds; therefore, processes like shamanistic training, crisis counselling and chthonic healing are appropriate at this time

- Vision quests and sweat lodges

- Chiron symbolizes the disenfranchised; therefore, volunteering to work with the handicapped, the underprivileged, the homeless, refugees or displaced people will be a way to focus the energy of the transit

♅ Uranus

Uranus jolts us into awareness; therefore, Uranus transits can feel equally invigorating and unstable. Its intention is change; often long-term change. Insights received during this period are often omens for our future, messages well ahead of 'real time'. During a Uranus transit the margins of time are breached; therefore, images and symbols in the future can often feel as if they are imminent rather than distant. It is a time of experimentation, even risk-taking, as the road less travelled and the unknown beckon. We are called to change our routines and disengage from what no longer sustains us. Since many opportunities present themselves during the period, discernment of choice is necessary. Not all can be taken; therefore, the passage of time feels as if the individual is at a crossroads with alternative or possible selves.

To become more centred during this period and embrace the Uranian archetype, an individual may benefit from the following:

- A therapeutic experience or training, such as Gestalt therapy, Voice Dialogue, group therapy or an individually orientated psychotherapy, which helps us to become more aware of our sub-personalities and conflicting parts of the self

- Uranus is future-orientated, so courses that focus on future studies, information technology, political reforms, etc., may be of interest

- Other studies that deal with understanding, developing and improving the human mind such as an archetypal or humanistic-based approach to psychology or comparative studies in sociology or astrology

- Human resources or social concerns

- Unique and distinctive activities that the individual may be attracted to can be encouraged during this time. Interests that clients have pursued during major Uranus transits have proved to be very helpful. These unusual or personal pastimes have included hobbies such as philately, glass blowing, bird watching and collecting feathers, and adventure activities including rock climbing, abseiling and white-water rafting

- Making a difference in the local community through volunteering, whether that is for the emergency services, a humanitarian project like Greenpeace, Big Brothers, World

Vision or a local animal refuge, the library, hospital or retirement home

- A physical training programme to help decrease anxiety, burn off the calories and reduce stress

♆ Neptune

The conspiracy with a Neptune transit is to be awakened from our multi-layered dreams to bring us closer to what is humanly possible. Under a Neptune transit the veil between the worlds is thinner than at any other time; therefore, feeling simultaneously vulnerable and inspired is common. It is a time of drifting, being anchorless and offshore. The 'real' world no longer seems as real as it did before. It is as if we are in a dream state; that is, we do not know the next scene or the plot at present, as we are moving through a different dimension. To a pragmatist this will sound fanciful; in essence it is, as during the Neptune transition we cannot even picture the possibilities. We have our dreams, our goals and our life path, but now a more divine architect is smoothing down the rough edges of our character. It is a creative time, a period of colour and full of imaginative episodes that bring us closer to the soul.

Therefore, to enter into the process of Neptune during a major transit, the individual could consider:

- Any imaginative therapies that give a voice to the soul and the inner life, such as Jungian analysis, dream work or a soul-centred psychotherapy

- Any study that awakens the power of symbols through imagery such as the Tarot, mythology or literature

- Any artistic pursuit that activates the creative sensibilities and imagination, such as painting, sketching, singing, playing music, etc.

- Forms of movement that help to centre and bring peace and relaxation, such as Tai Chi, yoga or other types of elegant movement. Self-expression and enjoyment through dance is always effective and many clients during a transit of Neptune have benefitted from dance classes

• Physical movements and sports that focus on balance, stretching, grace and symmetry; perhaps fencing to bring out the graceful warrior

• Other activities such as walking meditations, which might include walking the dog or taking time out to relax the mind. During a Neptune transit it is important to value and create times of solitude and times of centring

• Beautifying the physical space to create a healing space using subtle and vibrational effects through music, colour, art or design. Using essential oils, aromatherapy, candles or flower essences evoke the spirit of Neptune

• Being immersed in water, the elixir of life, during this time is renewing and a symbol of baptism into the spiritual side of life. Visiting the sea, swimming, floatation tanks, spas and baths could be invigorating

♇ Pluto

Transits of Pluto turn off the lights in our life so we can be accustomed to seeing in the dark. Therefore, under this passage we become aware of what is hidden, buried and ignored in the basement of our selves. It is a time of descent, a natural turning away from the busy life to see what has been left unattended and unmet. Therefore it often feels as if it is a time of loss, of grief, of depression. These feelings belong to the soul; during the Pluto transit they have an opportunity to be acknowledged, mourned, accepted and integrated. Pluto encourages us to look deep and celebrate the intensity and integrity of the soul. It is a time of facing some of the demons in the dark, speaking the shame and forgiving the self. When consciousness infiltrates these areas of our lives, the light returns. Mythopoetically this transition is illustrated as the hero's descent into the underworld to return with gifts that benefit himself and his community on his forward journey.

Some activities that could guide or be a companion during this descent into the abyss might be:

- Therapies that honour and value the darker feeling life and assist in reintegrating and accepting feelings of shame and guilt, such as in-depth psychotherapy, sex therapy or psychoanalysis

- Finding a way to acknowledge negative feelings and responses without self-blame or injury

- Primal therapy and other forms of healing like re-birthing that assist with birth or early trauma; any other form of recommended and well-established trauma counselling

- Any activity that is regenerative or transformative, such as renovating the bathroom or kitchen, cultivating and replanting a garden that has become overgrown, restoring a loved piece of old furniture or redecorating the bedroom or private part of the home

- Starting a physical training programme that helps to lose weight and improve body image. A makeover, cutting hair, change of presentation and dress

- During passages of Pluto there are often episodes of loss and grief. While seemingly located in the present the affect may be originating in the past; therefore, I have often found grief and loss counselling to be very beneficial during this period

- Trauma from the past may often be embedded or stuck in the body, especially the muscles and joints; hence healing modalities like deep tissue massage and Rolfing are effective in releasing the pain

- Pluto is about release, especially release of toxins and waste; therefore, some activities like fasting, detoxification and even colonic irrigation may be appropriate. Of course, this also needs to be balanced with a transformation in diet and awareness of bodily rituals such as cleanliness, drinking enough water, getting enough sleep, etc.

• During the Pluto passage there is a need to retreat from the world, experience periods of silence and aloneness; therefore, it is often valuable to consciously take time for retreat and time out to be alone. There is little time to waste on banalities and superficialities

Be the Change You Wish to See in the World
Like other wise individuals, Mahatma Gandhi suggested we change ourselves first and this will be reflected in our world. Rumi expressed it this way: 'Yesterday I was clever, so I wanted to change the world. Today I am wise, so I am changing myself.'[75]

From an astrological point of view, major transits symbolize times when we are invited to mature; perhaps best expressed as discovering an aspect of the authentic self and revealing that to the world. We have mused on the rituals of the transiting planets, but what part of the self is being drawn out? As already discussed, this is represented by the parts of the chart influenced by the transit. To summarize:

• First locate the house where the transit is happening. This is the environment that is reshaped during the transition, so hold in your mind the symbols of this house. If it is a Jupiter or Saturn transit, then recognize that this environment is significant to self-development and experience at this time. If it is an outer planet transit then the influence is more subtle and probably not as evident as when the planet first entered the house.
  – Note the sign on the cusp of the house and its ruler and reflect on their symbolic influence
  – Note the time frame of the transit through this house

• What is the planet or planetary aspect that is being transited? This is where the development of the character is being focused. Reflect on this archetype in your horoscope and what it means to you and how you can be more authentic and true to its instinctual nature.

– Which house/s does the planet being transited rule?
– Where is the focus of change in the environment and in the Self?

A transit does not happen to you; it is this moment that invites you to be present in time. This is not an easy task, as often the times are stressful, uncertain, painful or full of anguish. Archetypal energy is part of the soul and through participation and ritual we create the chance to be conscious of the change we want to be.

The Art of Not Giving Advice

Astrology is a perceptive tool. In skilled hands the horoscope, along with the openness of the individual whose chart you are reading, reveals core dynamics highlighting the root of the dilemma or the cause of the concern. Clients have often expressed that the chart has felt like a mirror being held up to their soul. Therefore, it is natural for their questions to arise as you engage with their horoscope: 'What should I do?'; 'What do you recommend?'; 'What would you do in my situation?'

I have always respected astrology as a healing tool and it is my experience that most astrologers and astrological students want to help their clients, family and friends by sharing insights they have gleaned through their astrological experiences. At any moment of time, in any location and for any circumstance, a horoscope can be highly beneficial. As an astrologer it is instinctual to want to help others solve their problems and we often see helpful keys to resolving the quandary. I have always felt my task was to encourage self-knowledge and assist the client in making choices by offering insight and reflection without offering advice. We may never know the whole picture, so it is wise to support self-determination in making decisions.

Not giving advice is an art form, especially when the answer seems so apparent. A major practice of the art is asking the right questions, which help your clients or friends open up about their feelings. Ask questions which help the individual to identify what is important to them. Setting boundaries is a priority so that you are not drawn into giving advice. If you are, then it is important to mention that you do not have all the details and cannot make the decision for them.

The horoscope can guide us in highlighting the positive qualities which assist in making decisions. Suggesting options and being optimistic when pointing out constructive characteristics supports the other person to build confidence in their decision-making. The horoscope also helps to open up different perspectives, create a time line and propose alternative pathways. A major part of the art of not giving advice is story-telling. The horoscope symbols are animated through story, myth, metaphor, image and symbol. Focusing on the areas and archetypes involved will help you to construct a story that offers another way of thinking about the current situation. A mythic narrative, a similar story from an anonymous client, a storyline from a novel, a film or a television series might just be the story that needs to be told.

Perhaps one of the greatest skills, yet one of the most overlooked in astrological guidance, is the art of listening. The opportunity to be heard is healing in itself, but when you pay attention to the individual while also looking at the images and symbols of their horoscope, it is as if you are listening on a soul level. That combination is highly therapeutic, even though it may not be apparent or articulated.

Transits are times of transition. By its very nature, transitions are in-between, liminal, an interval. We are between times: the times we have left and the times to come. And in this intervening time, we may desire certainty and advice, but resolution is born out of uncertainty and reflection. For our clients, our friends, our family, our acquaintances and ourselves it is important to participate in and ritualize the mystery of transition without always reaching for certitudes and assurances.

PART III

SECONDARY PROGRESSIONS

The Soul's Diary

Alice: How long is forever?
White Rabbit: Sometimes, just one second.

Lewis Carroll

10

SECONDARY PROGRESSIONS
The Soul's Intention

Throughout my consulting practice I have consistently used secondary progressions, always including them when preparing my clients' horoscopes. I have also used solar arc directions to explore and research events in the context of specific time frames, which has always been revealing. Since solar arcs are also a useful timing technique, in the Bibliography I refer you to books that delineate this method effectively.[76] Over time I have developed my own methods of working with secondary progressions, and so this section focuses exclusively on these progressions.

This method is not as well articulated as transits in the astrological literature. I feel this is because secondary progressions are subtle and difficult to convey. It is a technique that speaks more to the soul than the intellect. Since secondary progressions embrace an atypical motif of time by using one order of time to give meaning to another, it can often be confusing for students. Although there are some rationales for the technique, the method defies logic, being imaginative and subjective. Secondary progressions belong to a dynamic approach to astrology, inviting us to be more creative with our astrological symbols and signatures and to think outside the square.

Secondary progressions use the cosmic imprint of one day after birth as a metaphor for the soul's development in the first year of life, the second day after birth for the second year of life, and so on. The process draws on all the planetary phenomena of one day to symbolize one year. The nuances of daily planetary time often go unnoticed, yet it is these traces of time that are taken into account by this technique. Secondary progressions encapsulate these subtle shades and faint tones through time. Like a time capsule, secondary progressions retain the virginal and instinctual responses to life. It is as if the atmosphere inhaled in the early months is revived during the subsequent lifetime.

These progressions stress the psychological importance of the earliest days of life, when every nuance and delicate change is imprinted upon the psyche. By their very nature, progressions tend to be more psychological, unlike transits that may be experienced as outer manifestations such as events, experiences or relationships acting upon the psyche. Secondary progressions are unique to each individual horoscope and are genetically embedded within the horoscope since they are derived from natural planetary cycles. The unfoldment of each planetary progression is dependent upon the individual's birth moment, unlike transits, which happen to us, rather than being inborn. Secondary progressions are *the genes of the horoscope*, akin to dreams, as they arise from the soul.

Secondary progressions use one clock to symbolize another timeline. As discussed in the Introduction, time is relative and qualified and its measurement is open to interpretation. This is the timing of secondary progressions. Since we are linking a time already experienced early in life with a later period, the method distances us from sequential timing techniques. Secondary progressions are like soul imprints, having their own unique timing, inviting us to participate with imaginative and soulful qualities of time and encouraging us to deconstruct our inclination to understand time through events.

This technique has proved to be a valuable tool in contemplating psyche's time, or what I have come to identify as the soul's diary. Since we are acutely aware of time because of our ability for episodic recall or to remember past events, time is intimately entwined with events. Mostly, events are measured from a linear and objective perspective, yet there are many subjective factors in any particular time that do not conform to a clock: moods, sentiment, feelings, thoughts, senses, reactions and memories. For instance, the present is steeped in recollected time; that is, our experience of the present is altered by the subjectivity of the past and the way we re-collect that. What is occurring in the present has roots in the past. Secondary progressions represent the subtle underpinning of time and how we mature to meet these times. To me this is why transits and secondary progressions work well in tandem: transits encapsulate experiences while the Secondaries reveal organic development and growth that allow us to embrace change. When trying to articulate the difference between these systems in the classroom I would always point to the eucalyptus tree outside the second-floor classroom window of our centre on Johnston Street. One day a large truck swerved to miss a stalled car and rammed into the tree. This event was like a transit, as were drought and air pollution. The progression was similar to the tree's inner resilience and instinct to keep growing, shed its bark and ooze its resin.

Soul time is not clock time; therefore, it is best not to conceptualize soul timing, but to see it symbolically. Symbols are ambiguous and resist interpretation. They convey meaning beyond the limit of any definition that we could assign to them. In the same way, soul is a symbol that defies a limited view or fixed definition as it is fluid, porous, ephemeral and permeable. Soul is a perspective, a way of seeing or thinking, rather than a static point of view or belief.[77] Similarly, secondary progressions resist fixed interpretations and invite inquiry and reflection. When working with these progressions it is best to free yourself from connecting astrological time with literal events; rather, use astrological time as a mnemonic or symbol for contemplation.

Why Secondary?

When using secondary progressions, astrologers are not dealing with a current timing of a planetary cycle but with the cycle's secondary expression in time. What might this secondary expression of time be? Despite being related to a primary cycle, it will not be experienced or understood through the primary source. I imagine the secondary cycle of the progressions as being like a time of ripening and revelation, instinctive growth and maturation, conscience, as well as the developing ability of self-reflection and mindfulness about the passing of time.

The secondary movement of the Earth around the Sun epitomizes the technique.[78] Secondary progressions use the *rotation* of the Earth in one day to symbolically compare this to the annual orbit of the Earth around the Sun. In one day all twelve signs of the zodiac will rise over the eastern horizon, while in one year the Sun will pass through all twelve zodiacal signs. Two different journeys through all twelve signs of the zodiac are contrasted in secondary progressions: the Ascendant signs in 24 hours and the Sun signs in a year. In a way, the transience of daily life is contrasted with the faithful return of the Sun. On average, each sign rises across the

Ascendant every two hours, while the Sun spends about one month in each sign. In secondary time, then, two hours is equal to one month. The following table encompasses the two times.

Primary Time *in real time*	Secondary Time *by Secondary Progression*
1 day	1 year
24 hours	12 months
2 hours	1 month
1 hour	15 days
4 minutes	1 day
1 minute	6 hours

To begin to get a feel for secondary progressions let's use a wider lens to look at the territory. One of the first things to consider is that the zodiacal movement of most secondary progressed planets is slow, sometimes minimal, so we will need to differentiate how the planets can be used effectively.

For instance, the outer planets will move slowly over the course of a lifetime, so they are not generally used when considering aspects created by their progression. However, it does mean that the aspect that an outer planet forms in the natal chart remains in its progressed position for a major portion of the lifetime, thereby emphasizing this aspect. In this way the natal aspect is intensified. Symbolically, these planetary combinations are identified as priority aspects in the natal chart and take longer to be integrated; therefore, it is always of interest to reflect on the movement of a progressed outer planet in the context of its major aspect to an inner planet. If a slower-moving planet is near the cusp of a sign or house it may change signs or houses, and this is an evocative image. There is a high probability that one of the outer planets may change direction in the progressed chart, and in my experience this equates with an important change in the individual's relationship to the archetype.

Reflections on Planetary Progressions
Secondary progressions are the re-enactment of an earlier time previously impressed upon the psyche; therefore, they are not foreign or unfamiliar. Having been previously felt, they may be sensed like a 'déjà vu'. Any year of the life in a progressed horoscope

is a re-experiencing of the same planetary energies and aspects that occurred shortly after birth. The first exercise I encourage students to do is to photocopy the relevant ephemeris pages that signify their life progressions: their month of birth and the following two to three months. Only these three or four ephemeris pages will represent all your lifetime secondaries, and every piece of information on these pages, whether it be the phases of the Moon, lunar transits, planetary stations or ingresses, become secondary time. Study these pages: when did the Sun change signs for the first time after birth, when was the first New Moon after birth, what planet was the first to change direction, what was the first aspect the Moon made...?

Secondary progressions can often feel vague and indefinite; therefore, the technique is often eclipsed by clear-cut methods like transits and solar arc directions which outwardly reconstruct an individual's biography. Soul time is cyclical and repetitive; therefore, a valuable way to begin studying progressions is to reflect on the recurring nature of the planets. Consider the rhythm, cycle, design or pattern of the planet. To begin, consider the luminaries. These are the secondary progressions most utilized and researched. The secondary progressed Sun and the solar arc Sun are the same, so the progressed Sun is widely used in both systems. As core archetypal essences and primary planetary energies, their progressions in both sidereal and synodic cycles are highly revealing.

Illumination
The Secondary Progressed Moon circumnavigates the natal chart in 27.3 years, and is the only planet to complete the zodiacal round by secondary progression. Its full cycle is approximately two years less than the Saturn cycle, which also trisects the average life cycle. As the inner envoy of the outer Saturn cycle, it replicates its cycle three times in an average lifetime; the first round is youth, the second is adulthood and the third is eldership. It has both a generic and personal cycle: its critical aspects to the natal Moon characterize the life cycle, while its movement through the houses and aspects to other planets personifies the private and feeling life. As it repeats its journey through a house it re-members the previous cycle, not in terms of events, but as felt experiences. The Moon also progresses into a new sign every 2–2.5 years, thereby repeating a cycle of planetary aspects. The timing of the Moon's progressions is unique

to its placement in the natal horoscope. Its progression symbolizes our emotional development and maturation, our habitual responses, feelings and motivations.

The Secondary Progressed Sun moves approximately 1° a year; therefore, its cycle is more or less thirty years, when it returns to the degree of its birth position in the subsequent sign. It makes a 12th harmonic aspect to each planet in order of degree, repeating the sequence of aspects approximately thirty years later. Its movement through the signs and houses, as well as aspects to other planets, is a developmental record of the Self, growing in tolerance, confidence and character. Progressing by about 1° a year, the Sun will only progress through a quarter of the horoscope in a lifetime, advancing through its natal quadrant and into the next. Therefore, the progressed Sun crossing an angle is a potent symbol of evolution. Each natal Sun has its unique experience. For instance, a natal Sun in Fire progresses into Earth so that the fiery, intuitive, spontaneous urge for self-understanding may be harnessed, contained and brought down to earth. Earth Suns always progress into Air so that the pragmatic, sensate, realistic approach to selfhood becomes more varied, reflective and detached. Air Suns progress into Water so that the cerebral, thinking orientation to life can be more emotive, responsive and feeling. Water Suns progress into Fire, which aids the feeling, inner-orientated self to be expressed outwards into the world. While we retain our natal inclinations, progressions support a broader perspective, becoming more tolerant and mature, mindful that our natural inclinations are developing a larger worldview. The progressed Sun symbolizes ego development and the task of developing ego strength. It represents the growth of our identity and confidence in life by building a secure container to support our creativity and self-expression.

The progressions of the Sun and Moon form a profound life map. The **progressed lunation cycle** of 29.5 years can be divided into 8 phases that characterize the inner course of one's life from renewal to culmination, dissemination to recession to the end of the cycle, which regenerates at the following New Moon and brings the inception of another 29–30-year course which ensouls the phases of one's life.

Self-development with the Inner Planets

Reflect on the inner planets, Mercury, Venus and Mars, to imagine how each of these archetypes might develop and mature. Secondary progressions are vibrant and these faster-moving planets are metaphoric of the growth of character, be it intellectual development, the ripening of self-esteem or the emergent will. These progressions encourage the flowering of the authentic self. Each astronomical feature, whether it is oriental or occidental (rising or setting before or after the Sun, respectively), near a station, moving fast or slow, retrograde or direct, is technically of interest. Each of these distinctions may develop and change as the planet progresses through its cycle. Secondary progressions chronicle the years when the inner planets change signs, houses and direction and may even modify their point of reference to the Sun, changing from oriental to occidental or vice versa. In Mercury's case, this suggests that the planet changes sect.[79]

Mercury's speed of travel can vary from a minimal daily movement on the day it is stationing to over 2° per day near its superior conjunction. Mercury goes retrograde 3 times a year for approximately 3 weeks (20–24 years of progressed time). It is direct for between 13 and 14 weeks before it retrogrades. By progression, Mercury will travel anywhere between 0° and 2°15' per year, will probably change sect and may change direction during the course of a lifetime. If Mercury was retrograde at birth, then by the age of 24 it will have turned direct. If Mercury was direct at birth there is a high probability that it will turn retrograde by progression, unless born just after it had gone direct. Mercury by progression symbolizes the unfolding communication process, our learning capabilities and important stages in acquiring skills in speaking, reading, writing, and language. In my experience, progressed Mercury equates with major changes in education and the acquisition of knowledge and information. In essence, it traces the development of our Mercurial skills. When Mercury makes major aspects to natal planets or changes signs or direction, it signifies major developments in ways of thinking, ideas and comprehension.

Venus's daily speed can range from minimal in the days near its retrograde or direct stations to about 1°15' at its superior conjunction. Venus goes retrograde approximately every 19 months for a period of 6 weeks. If Venus was retrograde at birth, then it will have turned direct by the age of 43. Again, the importance of Venus by secondary progression will be the aspects it makes to the natal chart and the years when it changes signs, direction or orientation to the Sun (oriental or occidental). The secondary progressed Venus symbolizes the development of our sense of worth, value and self-esteem as well as our growing sense of personal taste and likes/dislikes. It also suggests the development and growth of relationships and interactions in our life.

Mars travels up to 1° per year by secondary progression. Its daily speed varies from negligible near its stationary periods up to nearly 1° a day. Mars turns retrograde every 25 months for a variable period of time between 58 and 81 days. By secondary progression, Mars is important in the aspects it makes to the natal horoscope and the years when it changes signs or direction. Progressed Mars describes the development of our personal will, the self-assurance to be assertive, to pursue what we want and champion our goals. It also embodies how we physically exert ourselves, our energy levels and output, how we set goals as well as our management and tolerance of volatile feelings, such as anger and frustration. We might think of progressed Mars as the active advocate for the expression of our passion and soulful needs.

Slow Cooking with the Social and Outer Planets
The movement of the social and outer planets is minimal; therefore, by secondary progression these planets linger in aspect to natal planets for longer, suggesting that these energies may be harder to shift, weighed down by the conditioning and experiences of the past. But they may station and change direction, highlighting consciousness being brought to bear on the functioning and experience of this planetary archetype. As the secondary perspective shifts, our perception of this planetary archetype and how we respond to its transits also shifts. Once a social or outer planet changes course, it will progress in this direction for the rest of the lifetime, suggesting that these directional changes are highly significant signposts.

I encourage you to consult the ephemeris for the few months after you were born to see which planets changed direction, then translate that to secondary time. Counting down the days after birth will approximate the years after birth in secondary progression. For instance, Oprah Winfrey was born on 29 January 1954 in

Mississippi. Looking in the ephemeris we can see that on 10 February, 12 days after birth, Jupiter turned direct, which was near age 12 by secondary progression. When she was 19, Saturn turned retrograde by secondary progression; when she was 22, Mercury turned retrograde, going direct at 44 while Uranus went direct at 57. From the viewpoint of secondary progressions, these are meaningful years when the archetypal perspective of these energies is heightened.

Jupiter's daily speed can vary between being negligible to its maximum speed of 0°15' a day. Therefore, by secondary progression its travel is slow, but during a lifetime it may progress by more than 20° in some cases, so there is the possibility that Jupiter may change signs in a lifetime. Because of its slow movement Jupiter will remain in aspect to natal planets for many years. Jupiter's progression describes the evolution of personal beliefs, ethics, morals, faith and the development of a life philosophy.

Saturn is slower by progression, and like Jupiter remains in aspect to natal planets for many years. Its effect is felt as it aspects planets over these years, bringing the theme of Saturn to bear upon that natal placement. Saturn's progression tells us of our unfolding autonomy, self-regulation and authority.

The progression of the outer planets is minimal in a lifetime; therefore, their natal aspects, particularly to the inner planets, are accentuated by their progression, becoming a potentially complex and recurring energy pattern. This is especially so when the outer planets are in an applying aspect to an inner planet or in a very close separating aspect. As the outer planets represent the archetypal forces beyond the systems of family and culture, their slow progression symbolizes the measured speed needed to recognize, understand and participate with their energies.

Because secondary progressions can be difficult to articulate, I encourage students to first examine the progressed Moon, the progressed Sun and their progressed lunation cycle by tracking their progressed Moon from birth, focusing on its movement through the houses; its oppositions at ages 13–14, at 41 and between 68 and 69, as well as its returns at ages 27–28, 55–56 and 82–83. When working with the progressed Moon over time, you begin to discover its deep archival content. The progressed Sun represents the strengthening of character, developing tolerance, self-acceptance and the illumination of the holistic self. Its repetitive aspects can be traced through the whole life while its progression into the next sign is always a potent shift in self-development. And, finally, the progressed lunation cycle epitomizes one of astrology's most outstanding cycles – the eight-phased 30-year soul mandala of life. We will assign a chapter to each of these important progressions.

To begin using secondary progressions, remember that you are working with a non-literal time system. Since the inner planets move more rapidly, these are the planets by secondary progression that concern us most; however, by implication the outer planets can also be potent as they remain by progression in the same zodiacal vicinity, stressing their instinctive archetypal dispositions, which are often experienced as dynamic, demanding and intense. Their slow movement symbolizes the time needed to assimilate their energies.

It is important to remember that secondary progressions are always compared to the natal chart. Although a progressed chart may be generated on its own, it should be read in the context of the natal chart to ascertain the development over time. Remember that secondary progressions are more akin to the inner life; therefore, we are not looking outwards for events or biographical hallmarks, but inwards towards the soul and character development. When progressions are married with transits of the social and outer planets, the constantly changing tides of life can be witnessed from both an inner and outer perspective.

11

THE PROGRESSED MOON
Emotional Maturation

The progressed Moon circumnavigates the natal chart three times in an average life span. Its cycle reflects both personal and familial development, as well as biological and emotional stages of the life cycle. As a measure of our emotional tides it is a constant barometer of our feeling life. As a symbol of emotional maturing, its progression through the horoscope remembers and records our reactions and feeling responses. Everything we have felt, wanted, tasted, desired and reacted to is registered, recorded and contained by the progressed Moon, a testament to our emotional history and a powerful metaphor for soulful and instinctual memory. As a returning cycle it assists us in tracing emotional attachments and sensations through time. The progressed Moon weaves feelings and memories into the tapestry of time. In subsequent cycles, as the Moon progresses through the same house, sign polarity or makes aspects to a natal planet once again, past feelings and memories can be linked through time. This is lunar time, invested with feeling, impressions, imagination and imagery.

The complete progressed lunar cycle is 27.3 years. The progressed Moon moves through a zodiac sign in 2–2.5 years. The daily Moon's travel is between 12° and 15°; therefore, the progressed Moon averages between 12° and 15° a year. As the only secondary progressed planet that will return to its natal position, the progressed Moon is a priority when studying the life cycle. Its passage through the houses and aspects to natal planets is of primary significance. In its generic cycle, the squares, oppositions and returns commemorate emotional stages of development which are also reflected in the stages of the family life cycle. Due to the threefold nature of the Moon I also note the significance of the trines that occur an average of nine years before and after the return.[80]

The progressed Moon is a herald and forerunner of the Saturn cycle throughout life.

Progressed Moon Cycle Approximate Ages	First Cycle Age	Second Cycle Age	Third Cycle Age
Age as the Cycle Begins	Birth	27.3	54
Age at the Waxing Square	6–7	34	61
Age at the Waxing Trine	9	36	63–4
Age at the Opposition	**13–14**	**41**	**68**
Age at the Waning Trine	18	45	72–3
Age at the Waning Square	20–21	47–8	75
Age at the Return	**27.3**	**54**	**82**

Subtle Sensitivities of the Lunar Cycle

In our early years the Moon is of prime importance, absorbing the family atmosphere, responding to the different attachment styles of primary caregivers, aware of the entrances and exits in family life. I consider the Moon to be symbolic of our felt experience *in utero* as well as any trauma before birth or perinatally that becomes part of our lunar memory. These sensations impact our earliest memories and compose the imagery embedded in the lunar vessel. Because these memories are pre-verbal, the content of the progressed Moon is not literal but feeling, sensory, imaginative and subjective.

Infants are particularly sensitive when the progressed Moon aspects an outer planet or enters a new sign. These changes are often reflected in the ambience of the family atmosphere – the child senses any emotional disturbances and distresses in the parental mood. These shifts might be registered as insecurity or danger, especially when the mother is unavailable or the familial routines are disrupted. In infancy the Moon may progress through emotional landscapes where issues of survival, dependency, safety, security, nurturing and helplessness are evoked. Later, in adulthood, these may be the issues triggered by the Moon's progression through similar territory in the horoscope. The progressed Moon evokes the aspects of our life that are pre-literate, sensual and unconscious. It is as if the progressed Moon is a continuing memorial to the soul. As it cycles through the horoscope, fragmented aspects of the self are evoked, remembered and re-collected. The remembered past cannot always be corroborated, as it may arise out of the familial or ancestral past, an image from the collective unconscious or a past life.

The progressed Moon is a gauge of what we can do as adults to feel more protected and secure or what we need to concentrate on emotionally. It measures the tides of the feeling life and is a powerful image that symbolizes the current emotional conditions. The Moon symbolizes habitual responses and instinctive motives that become clearer as we track its progression. It measures the appropriate time to break old habits or nurture ourselves. The Moon's changing rhythm religiously records, reflects and reveals each heartbeat, every breath and each nuance of primitive life. It is the protector of the menagerie of wild feelings, the guardian of treasured memoirs, the wise blood of the internal mentor. From New to Full to Dark again, it waxes and wanes, changing shape with each phase. The Moon has entranced and engaged us since conception.

The secondary progressed Moon is the most appropriate astrological calendar for recording the emotional maturation and evolution of an individual. The progressed Moon's movement registers the full spectrum of emotional reactions, the impact of the feeling life of the family and the climatic changes that occur in the familial atmosphere. As a cycle it measures the phases of family life from the birth of a sibling through to adolescence, leaving home and subsequently throughout adult and older phases until death. The progressed Moon operates systemically, responding and revealing phases in the family system, as well as changes to family members with whom we are emotionally attached. It is the record of the maturing, flowering and harvesting of our emotional life – our personal and experiential archives. As a continuous cycle of the loss and recovery of our emotional attachments, the progressed Moon symbolizes our continuous search to belong.

One of the keys to understanding the progressed Moon is in unravelling the ancient images and traditions that honoured her, becoming familiar with the goddesses who personified her. As previously mentioned, one of Luna's spheres is feeling memory. In Greek mythology, Mnemosyne, mother of the nine Muses, personifies lunar or instinctual memory. Art, music, poetry, dance and the heavens were her mnemonics. The progressed Moon weaves the disconnected fragments of our personal myth together through imagination, memory, sensation and feeling. While memories may be variable and whimsical, the recovery of feelings is one of the potent features of the progressed Moon. Fragments of memory that appear disconnected to our rational self are coherent language to our lunar side. The Moon encourages imagination as a tool for understanding. The progressed Moon flows through the horoscope, carrying the feeling memory of our life experience.

Honouring the Threefold Nature of the Moon

Matrilineal tradition separates the lunar cycle into three phases popularly symbolized by the maiden, the mother and the crone. For instance, Persephone as the maiden, Demeter as the mother and Hecate as the crone characterize this trinity. Hera is another example of these three phases, reflected by her epithets Pais, the maiden; Teleia, the fulfilled; and Chera, the solitary.

Lunar goddesses embrace the full round of life. Being threefold in nature, the first phase of the lunar cycle embodies the youthful and unattached maiden seen in the emerging crescent of the Moon, appearing out of the dark of the New Moon. The Full Moon personifies the woman of power, in all her brilliance as the benefactor of life, a mother and woman equal to all men. In the final phase the Moon comes to life as the crone, wise woman and elder, a guardian of the passages to the other world. The Moon embodies the three menstrual/lunar phases of womanhood: maidenhood, before she bleeds; menstruation, as the adult woman; and menopause, after bleeding ceases.

The triform nature of the lunar cycle amplifies the experience of the progressed Moon into three separate, yet interwoven, phases. Circling the horoscope three times in an average life span, the progressed Moon defines three distinct developmental stages: youth, adult and elder, charting important developments in the individual and family life cycle. During its first revolution from birth to 27.3 years old, the progressed Moon is absorbing, recording and gathering experiences, sensing and participating in the feeling life of the tribe. This is the maiden phase: the goddess Artemis reigning over this primal, wild, untamed and untethered time. The goddess was the 'mistress of animals', serving as the symbol for the protection of primitive instincts, the time when life is wild, undirected and virginal. This is the first round of the progressed Moon through the horoscope.

The Moon has no personal container in the early years; it is contained by mother and the family and participates freely in the feeling life of the family and tribe. Lunar boundaries are fluid. The child senses, absorbs and records the moods and feelings of the members within the family system. Aspects to the natal Moon help to indicate what impact the familial atmosphere had on the child. When the natal Moon is aspected by the outer planets, the child's feeling experience may have felt overwhelming. Lunar aspects also identify the child's attachment style, their experience of loss and grief and their ability to manage these feelings. The Moon registers and remembers the feelings in the family atmosphere as well as the emotional reaction to them. These remembrances become the record of the individual's feeling life, symbolized by the progressed Moon. During the first cycle, the progressed Moon experiences shape the individual feeling terrain.[81]

Emotional maturity is marked by the completion of the progressed Moon's first revolution at age 27. By then, every emotional experience available to us has been recorded. Its second journey through the horoscope, between the ages of 27 and 54, is when personal, emotional and adult attachments are formed. The life force is directed and creative. Giving birth literally, or to the creative self, initiates us into the new cycle when adult feelings co-exist with childlike ones. Remembering and reliving our earlier emotional experiences in an adult context begins. We have greater choice around our emotional responses and a greater ability to differentiate our feelings from those of others.

This second phase of life evokes the goddess Mnemosyne. She is the personification of memory, which is loosened during this time. Memory is not just about what happened in the past, but is an evocative and poignant way to describe our current feelings. Mnemosyne guides the progressed Moon's movement in this second phase, re-collecting the emotional experiences and memories from the first phase, bringing back psychic contents buried in our underworld.

Lunar memories are stored in psyche as images, symbols, feelings, impressions and instincts or imprinted upon the body. Lunar memory is not linear, memorizing dates and statistics, but is revealed through dreams and senses. Mnemosyne finds her voice in poetry; her memoirs are stored in fragments of a song, in verse, a story or a fairy tale, using poems, mantras or myth to preserve her remembrances. As the Moon progresses through the horoscope, she evokes dreams, images and lyrics which give continuity to our life narrative. Memory and imagination are woven together through Luna's progression.

Lunar memory is also stored in the body, in the adrenal and olfactory glands, the tension in the muscles, allergies and illnesses; therefore the progressed Moon synchronizes with health issues and is a measurement for well-being. The body remembers. Primal lunar responses may find their way into consciousness through particular eating habits, changeable moods, anxiety, obsessions and rituals or excessive fluids which misshape the body. The progressed Moon's movement during this stage evokes psyche's bodily souvenirs. Emotional patterns repeated throughout our adult relationships that are evoked by the progressed Moon may have their origins in early feeling responses. The Moon is habitual and through her steady progression of the horoscope we become conscious of the feeling life that underlies our emotional responses.

During this second phase of the progressed Moon through the horoscope, the same astrological territory is traversed as during the first phase, but this is no longer virgin territory. The progressed Moon remembers the images and impressions from the previous phase. During this second phase, it acts as a loosening agent, allowing buried complexes, taboo feelings and repressed memories to be felt again and to find some acknowledgment and acceptance. The astrological cycle provides a tool for connecting passages of time together. Links can be made back to times in the previous cycle, which allows space for the process of reflection and musing.

The third circuit of the progressed Moon between the ages 54 and 82 initiates us into the elder phase of life, symbolized by the wise woman, grandmother, tribal elder and crone. Emotional experiences are more anchored and directed, less reactive and instinctive. Our emotional attitudes become more integrated and embodied. The mysteries of the darkening Moon are being internalized. For women, the experience of menopause is a bodily symbol of this process of interiorization.

Hecate is evoked during this life stage. As the triple goddess she embraces the spheres of heaven (Selene), earth (Artemis) and underworld (Persephone). All three phases are in her; hence she is located at the crossroads. The Roman epithet for her was Trivia, *tri-via*, the three roads, and at this junction all three cycles converge into one. Both mother and child are memorialized and the cycle of the crone commences.

These three phases also correspond with the contemporary family life cycle of child, parent and grandparent, which the ancients saw as the maiden or child, the mother or bride, and the crone or widow. The three generations of the family are continually part of the progressed lunar cycle; therefore the movement of the progressed Moon can also describe atmospheric changes in the family, either the family of origin or the family of choice or both, specifically mother and children. Throughout the life cycle our progressed Moon continues to personify not only our moods and feelings but also the emotional atmosphere of those we are attached to.

The Circle Game
Imagery embedded in the houses of the horoscope is multi-faceted and rich. As the progressed Moon begins its second round, the horoscope terrain is somewhat familiar. Progressing through the same house again, the Moon recalls earlier experiences connected to that area of life. The Moon is the agent that loosens hardened complexes to reveal the richness of the authentic self. With the progressed Moon's passage through each house of the horoscope, we can link back to the primal, wild and virginal aspects of our self with an opportunity to recollect the disenfranchised aspects of the true self. Mnemosyne encourages remembering through images, dreams and feelings, which weave the narrative of our life together.

When the progressed Moon enters a new house, it evokes the complexes and issues within its jurisdiction, generally symbolized by the planets in that house. In the years when the Moon progresses through each house, the archetypal realm of the planets inhabiting this house is stimulated. This can begin as soon as the Moon crosses the cusp. A client with Pluto conjunct Venus in her 8th house had the progressed Moon within a few degrees of this conjunction when she made the appointment. The reason for the consultation, she said, was her feelings of rejection and abandonment, especially in relationship with her husband. As the 8th house conjunction spoke of this feeling and the progressed Moon was triggering this, I asked 'What happened 27 years ago in the previous cycle?' She responded 'That's when it all started.'

'When what started?' I responded. Her Venus–Pluto conjunction was also squaring the Moon in her 5th house. Twenty-seven years ago she fell pregnant with their first child and it was at this time that she first felt unwanted and undesired by her partner. The progressed Moon was excavating a major theme of her life which was her own ambivalence to her roles of mother and wife, intimacy and freedom. In exploring these themes, she recollected her father's affairs, which had destroyed her parent's marriage. Lurking in the basement of her own feeling life were memories of betrayal that now threatened the security and stability of her own marriage. After our discussion, she felt more empowered to confront her own feelings in the context of her marriage, having made a link to the memories of the past that were infiltrating the present.

The sign of the progressed Moon symbolizes the emotional hues of the times. As the progressed Moon accumulates emotional experiences over time, we grow more accustomed to the tides of our feelings. By the age of 7 the Moon has progressed through 3 differing modalities (cardinal, fixed and mutable); by the age of 9, it has progressed through 4 differing elements; and by the age of 27.3, through all 12 signs. Between 27 and 28, emotional maturity is forged from this full range of emotional experiences. The second cycle from 27 to 54 provides an opportunity to re-experience these feelings in an adult context, being more aware of our needs and how to nurture them. The third cycle, from approximately 54 to 82, allows us to re-experience these needs and feelings in more integrated and internal ways.

Each cycle personifies important interconnected stages in the family and personal life cycle. For instance, between 13 and 14 we experience the progressed Moon in opposition to itself for the first time, representing the conflicted feelings and experiences of early adolescence. This opposition recurs at 41 during the midlife passage when feeling awareness of being a dependable adult and reliable person are emotionally present. Yet we also have the memory and experience of what it was to be an adolescent. The third opposition occurs around the age of 68, as each individual becomes more established in being an elder of their community, drawing on the wisdom gained through living, specifically as an early adolescent and midlife adult.

	Youth	**Adult**	**Elder**
Familial Role	The Child	The Parent	The Grandparent
Goddess	Artemis	Mnemosyne	Hecate
Matriarchal Stage	Maiden	Mother	Crone
Keyword	Absorbing	Remembering	Feeling

Shifting Houses

The house that the Moon progresses through is a personal gauge of the emotional terrain over the next few years. Depending on the house's size, the Moon will spend an average of two to three years there. Its progression through the houses suggests which areas in our life need emotional focus and concern. The cycle begins at the Ascendant. As the Moon progresses from the 12th house of endings into the 1st house of life, the old cycle is emptied out and a new one begins. Generally, this movement synchronizes with feelings of 'coming out', an emotional watershed or images of new beginnings. It is a time of emotional reorientation, an interlude when we need to enter into the safety of the interior world. The 12th house phase of the progressed Moon prepares for the new cycle by clearing the past, signalling a time of withdrawal and retreat. We need to retreat to know what is no longer emotionally sustaining us; therefore, these years are often experienced as a time of isolation and aloneness, even when we are involved in a wide circle of family and friends. We may emotionally regress to re-experience the past, or parts of the past, in order to know what needs to be relinquished. It is a time of emotional preparation, a period of gestation in growing the space for new emotional structures and patterns. When discussing this 12th house phase with clients, many have spontaneously told me how they had been clearing out their cupboards and wardrobes, creating space for a new image of themselves.

The initiation of the progressed Moon crossing the Ascendant recognizes that the individual is ready to be more emotionally independent and less reliant on familiar forms of security. As the Moon progresses into the 1st house, feelings of new life are stirring, generating more comfort in ourselves. It is a time of beginnings and the emotional landscape is centred on our self. This may be translated into feeling more comfortable with ourselves in relation to the world and others, or at least identifying what it is that we want to emotionally change to feel this comfort. We may experience coming out of an insular period into more of an exchange with those around us. Since the 1st house is often visible in personality, feelings may arise to help us to feel more comfortable and emotionally available in the world. This begins the new cycle that will develop over the next 27 years.

The progressed Moon's movement through the horoscope helps to identify areas of life that are psychologically relevant as well as where to locate emotional security. As it traverses the psychic landscape of each house, we are confronted with old habits, feelings and reactions that have been interred. New rituals and ways to motivate emotional security are acquired. During the first cycle (from birth to 27.3 years old) the progressed Moon will be more reactionary, since unfamiliar feelings will be stirred as it passes through each house. In the second cycle (27 to 54) we re-experience these feelings and memories, developing a more mature perspective on each area of life. In the final cycle (54 to 82) our emotional experiences contribute to feeling at home in both our internal and external worlds. The following table summarizes the progressed Moon through the houses.

Reflect on the progressed Moon's passage through the houses being:

- The area of life which is emotionally sensitive and where we may feel vulnerable

- An area of life preoccupying our thoughts and feelings; where we may feel more emotionally engaged

- The activities or areas we need to pursue to make us feel comfortable

- An area of our lives where we are assimilating new psychological developments

- The area of our lives where we are becoming conscious of our attitudes, instincts, feelings, motives and responses

- An area of our life demanding more of our focus and attention

- The area of our life where we need to be nurturing of our self and others

- An area of our life where we recognize old habits and feel the need to change our outdated emotional patterns

- Memories and images from the past, which may be unconnected to the present, arise from a previous cycle, 27 or 54 years ago

As the progressed Moon moves through each house of the horoscope, reflect on the psychological task that needs attention and the emotional content that needs acknowledging:

1st House: Feelings of liberation, coming out emotionally, more comfort with self, new ways of being in the world, feeling more emotionally open

2nd House: Laying down emotional foundations, planning the future, providing more emotional and economic stability and consistency, sustainability

3rd House: Emotionally expressive, feeling nurtured through learning/reading/writing; emotional patterns with siblings

4th House: Emotional retreat into self, exploring family patterns, making a nest, remodelling the home, feeling more emotionally secure

5th House: Risking new emotional adventures, creative and playful time, pregnancy (symbolic and literal), expressing our needs, 'leaving home', experimentation in relationships

6th House: Focusing on what keeps us healthy, work habits, needing to purify and change habits, serving ourselves emotionally, review of dietary and health regimes

7th House: Sensitivity to others, needing to share, being emotionally involved in a one-to-one relationship, our patterns in relationship and the need to be emotionally secure in partnerships

8th House: Deep feelings emerging, feelings of loss/grief/ renewal, sense of aloneness, needing to purge and let go, vulnerability and an urge for more intimate relating

9th House: Needing to develop a sense of faith and belief, feeling comfortable pursuing study, travel or questing for greater understanding of life

10th House: Comfort with career goals, needing to be in the world, feeling a sense of achievement or attainment, being more comfortable in public and in the world

11th House: Needing to feel comfortable with a wider group of individuals, new social and group pursuits, close bonds with friends

12th House: The need to retreat from the world, feeling safe on one's own, exploring the imaginal depths, the dreamtime, preparation for more emotional understanding

Aspects to Other Planetary Archetypes
Since the Moon by progression will move by 1° to 1°15' a month, it will remain in aspect to a planet for nearly 2 to 2.5 months, using a 1° orb. It is helpful to tabulate the movement of the Moon in order to visualize when important aspects are being made to natal planets. We may be sensitive to many of the aspects of the Moon, so prioritize these aspects: the conjunction is the most significant, followed by the opposition, square, trine, sextile, quincunx and then the intermediate aspects.

When working with the progressed Moon's aspects, be mindful of the natal lunar aspects. When the progressed Moon aspects a planet that it also aspects natally, this releases and focuses innate complexes, feelings and moods. It may be a time to address some of our unconscious impulses represented by the planet, a time of heightened emotions around issues from the past. It is a time to be more emotionally and psychologically attuned to this planetary archetype.

The Moon's reactive energies may ignite issues that are ready to surface, especially if the planet receiving the progressed aspect from the Moon is also undergoing a major transit. When the progressed Moon mirrors a similar configuration that a transit is highlighting, emotional volatility might bring issues into the open through an emotional reaction, moodiness or intense feelings. The most dramatic instance is when the progressed Moon aspects an outer planet that is also aspecting the Moon by transit. For instance, a client's natal Moon in the 12th house is being transited by Saturn. At the same time, the progressed Moon is conjunct her Saturn in the 4th house. These months emphasize how the Moon–Saturn theme is brought to light in both the outer world (the transit of Saturn to the Moon) and the inner world (the lunar progression to Saturn). It feels as if the psyche cannot avoid the unfoldment of this complex or confrontation with the issues of spirituality and belonging, connected to the themes of ancestry (12th) and family (4th).

The progressed Moon by aspect reveals feelings, moods and needs connected to the planet it aspects. An emotional response may be triggered or a feeling of insecurity might be evoked. This helps us to be more aware of how this archetype can be better equipped to bring comfort and emotional security. Literally, lunar issues represent domesticity and home, the family of origin, mother and other attachment figures, those who are dependent on us, as well as all forms of emotional security; so keep these literal manifestations in mind when working with the progressed Moon. It brings awareness to these areas, often in unconscious ways such as dreams, feelings, responses, moods, etc.

Appendix 4 contains instructions on how to generate reports for the lifetime movement of the progressed Moon through the horoscope.

12

THE PROGRESSED SUN
Authority and Authenticity

The Earth's orbit around the Sun is elliptical, not circular; therefore the time it takes the Sun to transit each sign of the zodiac will be slightly different. When the Sun passes through Capricorn it is closest to the Earth and travelling its fastest; while in Cancer, the Sun is at its farthest distance from Earth, travelling its slowest. The average daily movement of the Sun, known as the Naibod arc, is 59'8.3". In Capricorn the Sun's daily movement averages 1°01'07", while in Cancer its daily movement averages 57'16". This is a minimal difference in our ephemeris, but when using the progressed Sun this variation accumulates throughout life. The following table summarizes the time the Sun spends in each sign (based on its 2020 ingresses). The final column reverts this time to secondary progressed time.

Solar Ingress Into Sign	Time Sun Spends in Each Sign (30°)			Using the formula of 1 day = 1 year, then:	Progressed Time 30 Years		
	Days	Hrs	Mins		Years	Mos	Days
♒	29	14	02	24 hours = 12 months or 2 hours = 1 month of progressed time	29	07	–
♓	29	22	53		29	11	13
♈	30	10	56		30	05	14
♉	30	23	03	2 hours = 1 month; 120 mins = 30 days or 4 minutes = 1 day of progressed time	30	11	16
♊	31	07	55		31	03	26
♋	31	10	53		31	05	13
♌	31	07	08		31	03	17
♍	30	09	46	Using this formula we can change ephemeris time into progressed time	30	04	27
♎	30	09	29		30	04	22
♏	29	21	40		29	10	25
♐	29	13	22		29	06	21
♑	29	10	38		29	05	10

If we use these figures to approximate how long the Sun would take to travel 60° or two signs by secondary progression, Gemini and Cancer Suns will take roughly 62.75 years to progress 60°, while Sagittarius and Capricorn Suns will take only 59 years. Perhaps there is some truth to the notion that Capricorns get younger as they age! Over time the variation accumulates, as the following table approximates:

Born with the Sun in	Progressed Sun's Time to Travel 60°	Born with the Sun in	Progressed Sun's Time to Travel 60°
♈	61 years, 5 months	♎	60 years, 3 months
♉	62 years, 3 months	♏	59 years, 5 months
♊	62 years, 9 months	♐	59 years
♋	62 years, 9 months	♑	59 years
♌	61 years, 8 months	♒	59 years, 6 months
♍	60 years, 9 months	♓	60 years, 4 months

The progressed Sun symbolizes the development of our identity and the growing sense of self-confidence. While the natal Sun embodies the vitality and creative potential of the Self, the progressed Sun reveals the emerging sense of identity and burgeoning self-assurance. Over time, the progressed Sun embraces different perspectives and modes of being. As the Sun progresses it forms new planetary aspects, changes signs and houses, offering new ways to identify and perceive the world. The progressed Sun assists us to become more tolerant, more informed and mindful of accepting differences in ourselves and others.

'Ego', the Latin word for 'I', is used in diverse ways and has different meanings depending on the context in which it is used. As a solar word it refers to our sense of self, especially our worth and appeal, but it is also used as a synonym for conceit. Ironically, when used to refer to self-importance or arrogance, the individual is generally lacking a sense of self or 'healthy' ego. Psychologically, the ego is related to our conscious decision-making process and is an arbitrator between our instincts and conscience, as well as a mediator between our urges and social norms. 'Ego' can also be used to evoke core identity or our unique personhood, akin to the conscious self and identity. Developmentally, a healthy ego supports us in handling the demands of life, emotional upheavals, internal and external stress while remaining true to our beliefs, ethics and desires.

The ego can be likened to many solar qualities such as light and illumination, creativity, the uniqueness of our personality, passion, drive and individuality. The progressed Sun is a key to healthy ego development along with the growing awareness of our self and the world at large. Its aspects to other planets by progression reveal images of soul growth and initiation. It is as if the progressed Sun is an inner clock that slowly and consistently times the developmental journey from self to Self: that is, the growth from a narrow world view to a greater awareness of self and other. It is of interest that the solar arc directed Sun and the secondary progressed Sun are identical. In terms of astrological techniques, the progressed and directed Suns are powerful symbols that identify psychological development, inner growth, consciousness and circumstances in the external life.

Change of Sign: I'm Not Who I Used to Be
The progressed Sun's change of sign is generally experienced as a gradual change over a period of time. The progressed Sun will generally change signs twice or three times in a lifetime, depending on the degree of the Sun at birth. The Sun progresses sequentially through the zodiac, so its first sign change is elementally antithetical to its natal sign. Other qualities and attributes are encountered. Characteristics that previously felt uncomfortable or unfamiliar challenge us to see new ways of being in the world. Our identity is confronted with the need to integrate alternative behaviours.

The Sun first progresses into an element that is psychologically opposed to its natal temperament. The ego becomes more conscious of a layer of shadow material and is invited to embrace this as part of its developing identity. Experientially, the individual faces different elements and essences of themselves, challenged to embrace and tolerate these new forms of being.

Fire progresses into Earth, learning to tolerate structure, routine, predictability and negativity:

• Aries progresses into Taurus, developing the capacity to use their leadership and adventurism in a resourceful, sustainable and valuable way

- Leo progresses into Virgo, growing in confidence through self-analysis, tolerating criticism and working with their creative potentials

- Sagittarius progresses into Capricorn, identifying the value in planning goals, committing to their ideals and taking direction from professionals

Earth progresses into Air, learning to acknowledge theories, ideas and acknowledging the intangible as a valuable resource:

- Taurus progresses into Gemini, finding value in new ideas and different ways to communicate, challenged with being more flexible and social

- Virgo progresses into Libra, feeling more comfortable with sharing feelings of insecurity; learning how to live with chaos and uncertainty

- Capricorn progresses into Aquarius, taking a risk to step outside the system, to explore the other side of being conventional, venturing out and stating their own opinion

Air progresses into Water, learning to accept feelings, moods, and uncertainty:

- Gemini progresses into Cancer, learning to settle and not feel smothered by attachments, developing the capacity to talk about their fears and feelings

- Libra progresses into Scorpio, recognizing that negative feelings can be shared in an intimate setting without rebuke; learning to be more forceful and passionate

- Aquarius progresses into Pisces, realizing that community is not just political and that human concern involves compassion and suffering

Water progresses into Fire, learning to tolerate insecurity, restlessness and spontaneity:

- Cancer progresses into Leo, to develop more confidence and self-assuredness by being original, creative and self-expressive, caring for themselves first

- Scorpio progresses into Sagittarius, to find ways of understanding their ethics and morals, learning constructive and therapeutic ways to identify and express their deeper feelings

- Pisces progresses into Aries, finding ways to assert their independence, differentiate when they are sacrificing the self for others, and taking a risk to be adventurous, even at the cost of being misunderstood

The progression into the sign that follows your natal Sun lasts approximately 30 years. Depending on the degree of your Sun this will happen in the first 30 years of life, so it is important to note the year when this occurred. I would use an orb of a few years to contemplate the subtle changes that began in the way you felt about yourself, your identity and your confidence in the world. As a quick guide, subtract the degree of your natal Sun from 30 and this will be the approximate age when the Sun progressed into the subsequent sign.

The second change of sign returns the progressed Sun to a compatible element, one which shares a similar polarity of Fire–Air or Earth–Water. While still distinct from the natal Sun, there is less reaction and more scope for self-reflection and understanding. Having identified many shadow elements over the past 30 years, these can now be integrated and utilized in a more authentic way. Astrologically, natal Fire will now progress into Air, while natal Air Sun signs progress into Fire. Similarly, with the feminine polarity, Earth signs progress into Water and vice versa. This progression will also last nearly 30 years and, depending on the degree of your Sun, will occur between the first and second Saturn returns, in the adult chapter of life: a fitting image for the maturing of one's self-identity. As a quick guide, add 30 to the age when your progressed Sun first changed signs.

In the third change of sign, the Sun again progresses into a sign not elementally compatible with the natal Sun sign. However, this time, over 60 years of living with the self have provided enough awareness and understanding to be able to use the tension to forge the final chapter of life, recognizing what is important to one's authenticity. The soul values the paradoxes of life and so as natal Fire progresses into Water, natal Earth into Fire, natal Air into Earth and natal Water into Air, the Sun has experienced all four elements. The alchemical round is completed; the self has been tempered by each element. This change marks a return to the natal modality of the Sun. Whether a cardinal, fixed or mutable Sun, it has experienced what it is like to shine through different lenses.

Progressions reference soul growth. While this embraces change, these changes are developmental in nature; therefore, the Sun does not change its disposition but matures through the forge of life, lightened and enlightened by its steady climb up the zodiacal steps. This progression develops the ability to tolerate and accept differences, shine steadily, create and build a more authentic and authoritative presence in the world.

Of interest is also when the Sun progresses into the next house. When using a system like Whole Sign Houses or Equal Houses, each change of house lasts 30 years. However, this time period varies for any unequal house system. When the progressed Sun progresses over a cusp it illuminates a different environment and our focus shifts to the new territory. The shift of perspective and focus is subtle, often evident earlier in the transition when the change in environment is more distinct.

Generally, the Sun illuminates one quadrant of the horoscope over the life span. Therefore, when it progresses across an angle, a new hemisphere of life is brought into consciousness. As the progressed Sun conjoins an angle one's identity is initiated into another direction, developing the expression of the self in the world and in relationships. Through the initiations provided by the progressed Sun we build a stronger sense of self-acceptance and tolerance for our self and others.

Developmental Aspects to Natal Planets
As the progressed Sun aspects a natal planet, it is time to identify and integrate this planetary archetype into our personality as much

as possible. Self-development is promoted, open-mindedness is cultivated and the ego is strengthened by acknowledging and accepting the presence of other archetypal forces and different ways of being. When the progressed Sun is in aspect to a natal planet it underlines the need to identify its presence to encourage a more conscious perspective. By nature, some planets are more antithetical to the Sun, which implies resistance to identifying these parts of the self. At these times we are confronted with shadow aspects of our self. Archetypes like Saturn, Uranus, Neptune and Pluto are more confronting and dangerous to identify; therefore, defence mechanisms are generally employed so we can remain unaware of their existence. The Sun in progressed aspect to these planets not only confirms the need to identify with this energy but suggests that the time is ripe and natural for these energies to be embraced as part of oneself.

Psychoanalytic theory classifies the strength of the ego in terms of its share of available psychic energy, which is increased when shadow energies are released into the light. One of the ways to think about the progressed Sun is that it illuminates the dark or shadow aspects of character, which strengthens the ego. The progressed Sun symbolizes character building through its identification, acceptance and assimilation of incompatible energies. By nature, the Sun is the giver of light; therefore the progressed Sun focuses light on any planet it aspects, illuminating its repressed or hidden aspects, releasing its shadow side into consciousness. When a progression synchronizes with a transit to the same planet, collusion between our inner and external worlds intensifies the identification with this archetypal aspect of our self.

In every horoscope Mercury and Venus are within a confined arc of the Sun. Because of their close proximity and cyclical relationships, Mercury, Venus and the Sun forge a planetary trinity, symbolizing conscious ego development. Mercury and Venus do not make any major difficult aspects with the Sun; therefore, they collaborate in forming our conscious identity and are of great significance in the progressed chart.

Take the synodic cycles of Mercury and Venus into account when working with progressions. If natal Mercury or Venus is before the Sun in zodiacal longitude, it rose before the Sun in the waxing phase of its cycle, moving from the inferior towards the superior conjunction. The planet progresses towards the natal Sun. If Mercury or Venus is later in zodiacal longitude than the Sun, it is between its superior and inferior conjunctions. In this situation, the Sun progresses towards the planet, making a conjunction with natal Mercury before age 28 and with natal Venus before age 48.

When the Sun progresses to natal Mercury we learn to identify our own thinking patterns, feel more confident about what we know, identify what we need to learn and communicate more effectively. When the Sun progresses to natal Venus we identify our sense of worth and value and are more conscious of what we need in relationship. This is a symbolic time of 'conjunctio', the identification with our personal worth and value, ultimately a time of self-love. This awareness may synchronize with an outer relationship unfolding in new ways or a re-engagement with our creativity. Thirty years later, the progressed Sun will aspect natal Mercury or Venus again, reinforcing these issues.

The Sun's progression to the other planets stresses the need to consciously identify and integrate their energies. When using a 12th harmonic aspect there will be a repetition of themes every 30 years. For instance, if the progressed Sun sextiles a planet, then in approximately another 30 years it will form an aspect to this planet again, either a square or semi-sextile, repeating the astrological theme.

What do we need to identify and integrate when the progressed Sun aspects different planets? This will depend first on our age. If the progressed Sun aspects Saturn or an outer planet early in life, there is not yet enough understanding to identify this as part of one's self and is referenced externally as belonging in the family system. Conscious integration depends on how the planet functions in the natal chart and how aware the individual is of this energy. How this planetary archetype is integrated or defended is contingent on the individual's accumulated experience of the planetary archetype. The progressed Sun highlights more awareness, more confidence in these areas and the necessity to identify shadow qualities associated with our experience of this planet.

Time Frames
When using secondary progressions, the standard orb of 1° applying to and separating from the aspect can be used. This equates to the

progressed Sun's period of influence being about two years. A way of reflecting on this process would be to consider that when the progressed Sun applies to another planet, a period of recognizing and reacting to this planetary archetype becomes conscious. As the progressed Sun's orb becomes minimal, the planetary archetype is in the spotlight. As it separates from the planet, integrating this energy becomes more possible.

I use the 12th harmonic aspects, or multiples of 30°, when working with the progressed Sun. My reasoning is that the progressed Sun's movement of 1° per year suggests it will aspect each planet in sequence and the same succession of planets will be aspected approximately 30° or 30 years later. As the pattern repeats, times can be linked together in the cycle. I am not excluding other aspects such as the semi-square or sesquisquare, but prefer using the 12th harmonic aspects because they create a cyclical process. When using the 12th harmonic, these are the aspects employed: conjunction, semi-sextile, sextile, square, trine, quincunx and opposition. While all of these aspects are significant, I prioritize them as to their impact: conjunction is the strongest as it represents the crossroads of the end of one process and the beginning of the next; then opposition, square, quincunx, trine, sextile and semi-sextile. This is only a guide, because the planet being aspected and its influence and condition in the natal chart is also highly significant.

Aspects of the Progressed Sun
As the Sun is the giver of light, it illuminates the planet it aspects. When the Sun is radiant and strong it casts shadows, revealing dark distortions of what is in the light. We start to recognize that we are casting these shadows and it is better to acknowledge them as part of ourselves, rather than as something dark and dangerous. Similarly, planetary shadows are exposed by the progressed Sun. Shadows of repressed and hidden aspects are brought into light by the Sun's progression to other planets. From a soul perspective, when what is unknown is illuminated, it can be meaningfully transformed. Soul embraces what is unidentified; therefore, what is dark and mysterious is soul territory.

The progressed Sun deepens our encounter with the Self, translating the events that happen to us into experiences, ensouling our world with meaning and insight. Let's reflect on what the progressed Sun in aspect to natal planets might identify.

☽ The Moon

I have progressed to the stage where I am more aware of my deeper feelings and soul urges and am more prepared to discover the revelations from my past which need to be identified.

- How can I become more conscious of nurturing myself in ways that support my true nature?

- How can I challenge my familial traditions about caring for others that are not authentic to my being?

- Can I be more attuned to where I belong and feel safe in the deepest part of my being? How can I be more comfortable with my darker feelings?

☿ Mercury

At this stage of my growth I am more conscious of my environment and the way I move in and out of this space. I identify my need to learn, to connect with others and communicate my ideas and thoughts in my own way.

- What do I need to learn, reflect upon or study in order to focus my thoughts and ideas on subjects that are important to me?

- Which developmental changes am I experiencing in my relationship with my siblings and my peer group?

- How can I become more mindful of the way I express myself and communicate with others?

♀ Venus

As I move forwards in my life I am more aware of my likes and dislikes, what I value, and what I appreciate in myself and others.

- How can I remain true to my own values and appreciate the depth of my inner resources?

- What are the qualities I am finding attractive in others and the world at large?

- How do I support my own sense of self-worth and self-love in significant relationships?

♂ Mars

At this phase of my life I need to become more identified with my goals and direction so I can support my passions and my aspirations. It is time to become more aware of my will, my deepest sense of self and what it desires.

- How might I be more conscious of my physical vitality and energy, my ability to assert myself to aim for what I want?

- Can I channel my frustrations and anger into service of the self? How can I accept my anger, be more tolerant of my frustrations and more patient with my shortcomings, realizing that these are all states of the soul?

- How can I become more independent and self-reliant?

♃ Jupiter

I am beginning to become more familiar with what I believe, challenging long-held assumptions and convictions. My sense of faith and the process of my life are becoming clearer. I am at the right time to begin to harness my abilities and find purpose in my life.

- How can I remind myself that I have faith in the future and am optimistic about life?

- What is the best way to pursue my beliefs and my urge to quest for answers?

- How can I seek to become more aligned with the spirit of life?

♄ Saturn

I am more conscious of a sense of autonomy and a need for structure in my life in order to support my life goals and ambitions. I can support this process by establishing firmer objectives and boundaries.

- Where can I become more self-reliant and develop more comfort with my sense of aloneness? How can I support the soul's urge to be alone and private?

- How can I be more aware of what I need to do that is innately authentic, not because it is socially acceptable or the norm, but because it is authentic to my nature?

- How might I develop more focus and self-discipline?

⚷ Chiron

I am more perceptive about the spiritual dimensions of life and the angst of being human. Being more attentive to this split I find I am more accepting of my feeling displaced and marginal. I am sensitive to the aspects of myself that feel unacceptable and forsaken and I am more willing to embrace and accept these parts of myself.

- How can I participate with the soul's urge to heal the facets of myself that feel insignificant and unworthy?

- How can I be more responsive to my symptoms and more aligned with my healing journey?

- How can I be more mindful of accepting the parts of self that feel marginal and outside the system?

♅ Uranus

I can identify the urge to break free of restrictive patterns. I am also aware of what patterns and habits I need to separate from in order to be true to myself. The awareness to take new risks needs to be supported in my life.

- How can I claim more space for myself, be independent and free to do my own thing?

- How can I be less attached to the outcome and more spontaneous in my choices? How might I encourage myself to take the road less travelled and explore the soul's urge for freedom?

- How can I support myself to take chances and risks that help me to attract opportunities?

♆ Neptune

I am more responsive to my inner life and its creative possibilities. I am aware that life is uncertain, filled with dreams and possibilities, but also fantasies and false hopes. I am sensitive to other realities and ways of being.

- How can I become discerning about my spiritual needs and more soulful in my feeling life?

- How can I be more informed about the co-dependent and addictive sides of my personality?

- Which rituals will help me be more attentive to my inner world, more in touch with my intuition, more aware of my dreams, more creative with my imagination and more perceptive with my feelings?

♇ Pluto

I am more conscious of the interplay of life and death and more accepting that death is a part of life, not something to fear or overcome. I recognize that negative feelings are part of the full spectrum of being human and I am more accommodating of them and those who express them. I am more comfortable with the shadow side of life and more understanding of my passions, desires and depths.

- How might I become more aware of my hidden motives and agendas, so that I can be more honest with myself and others?

- How can I acknowledge the losses that I have not grieved and feelings that remain unresolved so that I can cooperate with seeking closure by letting them go?

- Which darker feelings does the soul need to express in order to bring a more conscious perspective to my relationships and life?

As the progressed Sun aspects these planets, it encourages identification with the differing aspects of the self, becoming more multi-dimensional, open-minded and understanding. It is a time of questioning and identifying this aspect of the personality.

There is an order to the progressed Sun aspecting planets in your horoscope dependent on their degree. I refer to this as planetary order, as the progressed Sun will aspect the planets in this order when using the 12th harmonic aspects. The following section explores using this technique to trace the progressed Sun's aspects through your chart using the 12th harmonic aspects.

The Planetary Order

I am using the idiom *the planetary order* to characterize listing your natal planets from the lowest degree to the highest, with each zodiacal degree representing a rung on the planetary ladder. This is an interesting exercise in itself, as planets near the same degree will share a 12th harmonic aspect. In displaying the sequence of the planets by degree, we see at a glance which planets are being affected by transits. Instructions on how to generate the progressed Sun aspects for a lifetime on Solar Fire software, plus the planetary order worksheet, can be found in Appendices 4 and 5 respectively. Complete your own worksheet including the nodes, angles and any other points or celestial bodies that you use. By simply moving down each line you can approximate the movement of the progressed Sun during your lifetime. This approximate guide draws our attention to the important years when the progressed Sun aspects natal planets.

We will use this method to trace the progressed Sun's movement through the horoscope. Since the progressed Sun travels approximately 1° a year, it moves up one rung on the planetary ladder and so we can plot the age when the progressed Sun will make aspects to your planets. Thirty years on, it makes another aspect 30° later in the zodiac, following this sequence:

Waxing Aspects		Waning Aspects	
0°	♂	180°	☍
30°	⚺	210°	⚻
60°	✶	240°	✶
90°	□	270°	□
120°	△	300°	△
150°	⚻	330°	⚺

Here is an example of a worksheet for Carl Jung. I am using Carl Jung as an example because of his strong affinity to the symbolism of the Sun.[82]

Carl Jung
26 July 1875, 7.27 p.m. BMT, Kesswil, Switzerland

The Sun is at 3♌18, so place the Sun on the line between 3° and 3°59'. Note that Neptune is also in this degree at 3♉02; because they are on the same line note that there is an exact 12th harmonic aspect between them – the Sun square Neptune.

Place all the other planets, lunar nodes and angles on their respective lines. Since the progressed Sun will move approximately 1° a year, it will change lines every year. When there is a planet on this line the progressed Sun aspects this planet. For instance, Mercury is 10 lines after the Sun; therefore, the progressed Sun aspects Mercury at age 10. This aspect is a semi-sextile, as Mercury is in Cancer. Uranus is 11 lines down and the Moon is 12; therefore at age 11 the progressed Sun conjoins Uranus and at age 12 it squares the Moon. During these years the progressed Sun highlights the natal Moon–Uranus square. In his autobiography *Memories, Dreams, Reflections*, Jung states: 'My twelfth year was indeed a fateful one for me.'[83]

By adding 30 years we can ascertain immediately the next progressed Sun aspect to Uranus, which will be at age 41 and then 71. The progressed Sun at age 41 will be in Virgo, semi-sextiling Uranus, while at age 71 it will be sextiling from Libra. This exercise *approximates* the timeline of the progressed Sun. In Carl Jung's example, he is a Leo so the progressed Sun is travelling less than 1° a year and over 30 years it will lose nearly 1°. As it moves into Virgo and Libra it begins to travel closer to 1° per year. However, since we are using a degree orb which encompasses a 2-year period, the important developmental ages of the progressed Sun will still be highlighted.

What can be seen at a glance are the ages when the progressed Sun synchronizes with other major milestones. For instance, the progressed Sun repeats its aspects to Neptune in the years of Jung's first and second Saturn returns. During the Chiron return, the progressed Sun aspects Jupiter and Pluto.

While we tend to equate events with these times, it is important to see the underlying soul symbol. For instance, during Jung's first Saturn return while the progressed Sun was quincunx his Ascendant and trine Neptune, Sabrina Spielrein entered his life and the boundaries between doctor and patient were blurred. He was also appointed senior doctor and became a father for the first time. Outwardly the Saturn transit initiated him into new responsibilities in life, but the progressions reveal how these new solar identities of father and superior are naturally ready to ripen. The progressed Sun's aspect to Neptune replicated Jung's natal square. With natal Sun on the Descendant square Neptune, relational boundaries may become enmeshed or complex. The reiteration of the aspect in the progressed chart suggests this archetypal union is part of soul-making. When the progressed Sun squared Pluto and sextiled Jupiter at age 20, Jung's father died, while at age 80 as it trined Pluto and semi-sextiled Jupiter, his wife died. At each turning of the progressed Sun aspecting Pluto, Jung confronts the depth of loss to find meaning and reason in his life. These periods are painful, but profound. Remembering the soul sensibility underpinning the progressed Sun enriches our understanding of progressions and the powerful archetypes that the solar self encounters through life. The progressed Sun identifies and makes meaning of our life experiences.

Planetary order is also helpful when researching transits because the degree of any transiting planet can be tracked to see when it aspects degrees of the natal planets. However, in terms of the progressed Sun, it emphasizes its passage through the degrees of the zodiac, highlighting its 30- year passage though the signs of the zodiac which repeats its emphasis on each natal planet.

Planetary Order Worksheet for Carl Jung				
Degrees of a Sign	**Planet/ Node/ Angle**	**Approximate Age Progressed Sun Aspects Planet**		**Comments on Progression**
		1st cycle	**2nd cycle**	**3rd cycle**	
00°–00°59'					
01°–01°59'					
02°–02°59'	ASC/ DSC		29	59	The Sun on the Descendant is intimately entwined with
03°–03°59'	♆☉		30	60	Jung's search for Self and Other. Neptune makes an exact square to the Sun; therefore, it colours the nature of the progressed Sun throughout its cycle, suggesting that self- development is sustained through his imagination and understanding of the symbolic world
04°–04°59'					
05°–05°59'	Vertex		32	62	
06°–06°59'					
07°–07°59'					
08°–08°59'					
09°–09°59'					
10°–10°59'	☊☋	7	37	67	At age 67 the progressed Sun is conjunct the nodal axis: an awareness of the interface between the material and spiritual worlds
11°–11°59'					
12°–12°59'					
13°–13°59'	☿	10	40	70	Mercury is sextile the Moon which is square to Uranus; progressed Sun conjoins Uranus at age 11 and squares Moon at age 12. Throughout these years, innovative ways of thinking and feeling emerge to support the development of Self
14°–14°59'	♅	11	41	71	
15°–15°59'	☽	12	42	72	

16°–16°59'					
17°–17°59'	♀	14	44	74	Semi-sextile, sextile then square at 74: the developing Self engages with and values Other
18°–18°59'					
19°–19°59'					
20°–20°59'					
21°–21°59'	♂	18	48	78	At age 48, progressed Sun is square to Mars: Jung builds his tower at Bollingen
22°–22°59'					
23°–23°59'	♃♇	20	50	80	Jupiter is quincunx Pluto. At age 20, progressed Sun is square Pluto. Pluto is square Saturn, which is trine to Jupiter. At age 21, progressed Sun is opposite Saturn, a time of identifying and making meaning of loss, suffering and hardship
24°–24°59'	♄	21	51	81	
25°–25°59'					
26°–26°59'	⚷	23	53	83	At age 83, progressed Sun is opposite Chiron, a profound time of interior reflection and healing
27°–27°59'					
28°–28°59'					
29°–29°59'	MC/IC	26	56		
Progressed Sun Changes Sign		27	57		At age 27, the Sun progresses into the sign of ♍; and at 57, into ♎

13

THE PROGRESSED LUNATION CYCLE
Chapters of My Life

The progressed lunation cycle illustrates the phases formed by the aspects between the progressed Sun and the progressed Moon throughout their synodic cycle of 29.5 years. We are all born into a lunation cycle that began with the New Moon before our birth. Since the cycle was seeded while we were still in the womb it is deeply impressed upon our collective and familial unconscious. The New Moon after birth is the time marker for the beginning of the first progressed lunation chapter of our lives, an independent journey within the genus of the familial matrix, a soulful symbol of our initiation into our individuation process.

During the progressed lunation cycle the progressed Moon will make every possible aspect with the progressed Sun before it returns to inaugurate the next cycle. Synchronously, the duration of the progressed lunation cycle is the same time span as the Saturn cycle. While the Saturn cycle marks its return for everyone between the ages of 29 and 30, the progressed New Moon is personalized, entirely dependent on our Sun–Moon phase relationship at birth. What does happen near the first Saturn return is that the progressed Sun and the progressed Moon return to the same angular relationship and phase they had at birth, but now both are in the signs subsequent to their natal signs. With Saturn's return and the progressed lunation cycle phase return, the structure and substance of the personality is prepared to build and contain the next stage of life.

The first progressed lunation cycle begins with the conjunction of the progressed Moon and the progressed Sun. Those born in the waxing half of the lunation cycle will not experience their first progressed New Moon until adolescence or later. Since the seeds were planted at the New Moon before birth, the illumination at the first progressed Full Moon belongs to a past ancestral, cultural or karmic cycle, rather than to the current one. Those born in the waning half of the cycle will experience their first progressed New Moon before they are 15. The fact that 'waxing' individuals have a longer period before their first progressed New Moon implies that their ancestral or karmic past may be more firmly ingrained than for those born in the waning phases. The waxing or first half of the lunation cycle is more subjective, instinctual and reactive than the waning half.

The time at which we experience the progressed New Moon depends on the natal phase. For instance, if we are a New Moon person, our first progressed New Moon will occur between the ages of 26 and 29.5. Although we need to calculate the exact time of the progressed New Moon after birth, the following table shows the approximate ages when it occurs.

Natal Phase	1st New Moon	2nd New Moon	3rd New Moon
New Moon	26¼–30	56–60	86–90
Crescent	22½–26¼	52½–56	82½–86
First Quarter	18¾–22½	49–52½	79–82½
Gibbous	15–18¾	45–49	75–79
Full	11¼–15	41–45	71–75
Disseminating	7½–11¼	37½–41	67½–71
Last Quarter	3¾–7½	34–37½	64–67½
Balsamic	0–3¾	30–34	60–64

The progressed lunation cycle is 29.5 years, so each phase lasts approximately 3–4 years. Due to the fluctuating speed of the Moon, these phases will vary in length and should be calculated separately, especially the New, First Quarter, Full Moon and Last Quarter phases. The progressed Moon can travel between 12° and 15° degrees a year, building in speed and then decreasing. Therefore, the progressed phases will generally follow the same undulation – increasing in length and then decreasing. Here is an example of the length of each phase for Carl Jung's first cycle.

Progressed Phase	Time Span	Progressed Phase	Time Span
New	3 years, 4 months	Full Moon	3 years, 10 months
Crescent	3 years, 7 months	Disseminating	3 years, 7 months
First Quarter	4 years	Last Quarter	3 years, 7 months
Gibbous	4 years, 1 month	Balsamic	3 years, 5 months
Total: 29 years, 5 months			

Each complete cycle is like a book of our life and the phases can be seen as its chapters. All three cycles comprise the trilogy of our life, whether the cycle is completed or not.

When the progressed Sun and Moon return to the same phase as the natal phase, there is a sense of familiarity because the individual is back in phase. This occurs between ages 29 and 30, as well as between 58 and 60, contributing to Saturn's importance of 'coming into your own'. At the return, the person has experienced Saturn through all the houses and in every aspect to the other planets, as well as experiencing the progressed Moon in a complete cycle of relationships with the progressed Sun, which is a powerful image of maturation. Saturn symbolizes the initiation of structure, form and responsibility that supports life; it is the skin and bones of the life cycle. The progressed lunation cycle symbolizes content and meaning; it internalizes the essence and soulfulness of life.

It should be remembered that this is not an event-orientated cycle but more a soul-focused cycle. Outer events are not as apparent at the critical turning points in the progressed cycle as they are with transits. It is important to see the cycle as a whole, as a phase-orientated development of the life purpose. The transits and other progressions within these phases point to the events and psychological growth of that particular time. Each cycle builds on the past.

Phases of the Soul
Reflect on your natal lunation phase and how this image characterizes your instinctive response to life. Next, identify the zodiacal degree where the New Moon occurred before your birth, as this is the seeding degree of the cycle you were born into, and is sensitive to transits. The New Moon before birth occurs in the natal Sun sign or the sign before. If it is in the previous sign to the natal Sun, the qualities of this sign can shine through the personality for the remaining phases of the first cycle.

Born at a distinctive moment in the cycle between the Sun and Moon, you will experience your own unique passage through its progressed phases. Your first round begins at the New Moon after your birth; from this point you can map your astrological phases using the progressed lunation cycle. These cycles are a private and profound diary of your soul's passage, a simple and straightforward schema of the soul time of your life.

The Eight Phases of the Progressed Lunation Cycle
The progressed lunation cycle is a unique timetable for considering your individuation process. Progressing the lunation phases throughout life creates an individual developmental chart for your life. Unlike any other astrological cycle, the progressed lunation cycle contextualizes phases of life within a broader and deeper framework, making it one of the most profound of all astrological cycles. The following table summarizes these phases of development. Take note of the aspects that occur within each phase, as these suggest times during this phase when psychic activity may be more pronounced, being periods of reorientation and change.

Progressed Phase *Degrees Moon is Ahead of Sun*	Key Images for the Waxing Phases	Aspects Involved
New Moon 0°–44°59'	Emergence/Birth Projection/Beginning	Conjunction (0°) Semi-sextile (30°) Novile (40°)
Crescent 45°–89°59'	Expansion/Struggle/Effort Breaking Away	Semi-square (45°) Sextile (60°) Quintile (72°)
First Quarter 90°–134°59'	Action/Expression/ Engagement, 'Crisis in Action'	Square (90°) Trine (120°)
Gibbous 135°–179°59'	Growth/Analyse Evaluate/Overcome	Sesquisquare (135°) Bi-quintile (144°) Quincunx (150°)
	Key Images for the Waning Phases	
Full Moon 180°–224°59'	Perfection/Culmination Realization/Fulfilment	Opposition (180°) Quincunx (210°) Bi-quintile (216°)
Disseminating 225°–269°59'	Demonstration/Distribution/ Sharing/ Circulation of Ideas and Creativity	Sesquisquare (225°) Trine (240°)
Last Quarter 270°–314°59'	Revision/Reorientation/ Integration 'Crisis of Consciousness'	Square (90°) Quintile (288°) Sextile (300°)
Balsamic 315°–359°59'	Release/Preparation/Mutation Transformation/Commitment	Semi-square (315°) Novile (320°) Semi-sextile (330°)

Let's look at each progressed phase of development separately.

Progressed New Moon

The progressed New Moon phase commences at the conjunction of the progressed Moon and the progressed Sun and lasts until the progressed Moon is 45° ahead of the progressed Sun, between approximately 3.25 and 4 years later. The New Moon is the induction into a new cycle of life involvement, although we may not yet be consciously aware of it as such. It is the dark of the Moon, a subjective and confusing time as a subtle shift in life's direction is stirring. It is a time of re-orientation; a purpose and potential for the new cycle has been seeded. Solar forces are releasing a new purpose, fertilizing the unconscious with new images, impulses, ideas and projects. The sense of purpose and direction becomes more evident as the cycle progresses, especially after a few years when the first reflective light appears through a sliver of lunar light.

There is need for change. The past cycle remains strong; however, the new direction has taken root. The way is being prepared for new life developments, which will reach their crescendo at the Full Moon. There is a new force and momentum operating as this phase ushers in its 30-year round. The zodiacal sign of the progressed New Moon is either the Sun sign at birth or the following sign. Similarly, the house position is either the Sun's house at birth or, generally, the next house. The placement of this New Moon by sign and house suggests what we want to identify with over this next cycle. The Moon, during the next cycle, progresses through our whole horoscope, giving us a complete emotional experience of what we are striving to identify.

Progressed Crescent Moon

The progressed Crescent phase commences when the progressed Moon is 45° ahead of the progressed Sun and lasts until it squares the progressed Sun. At the semi-square, the challenge of the new direction and purpose, as represented by the Sun, conflicts with past and conditioned patterns. It is a time of crossroads between the past and the future. What is no longer valid must be relinquished; however, we may not yet feel strong or confident enough about the new direction to bring about the necessary changes. Hence, we struggle between forward movement and regressive forces. As we become less reactive and more conscious, an intense coming to terms with the new life path emerges. The Crescent phase characterizes the breaking away from the past and being instinctively pulled towards the new direction. Here we may experience major shifts in life, being uncertain and confused about why these changes are taking place.

The struggle between the urge to move forward and the urge to remain in the past dominates the landscape of this phase. However, at the sextile between the progressed Sun and Moon, opportunities may arise which allow the new cycle to open up, releasing the tension of the conflicted past. Opportunities can arise to sweep clean the past and to take a new direction.

Progressed First Quarter Moon

This 'crisis in action' phase lasts from the square until the progressed Moon is 135° ahead of the progressed Sun. The impetus and force of the new direction creates a critical turning point during this phase. This begins with the dynamic aspect of the square igniting the need and urge for change. Compelled to act upon the new energies, we make decisions that have an effect on the outcome of the new cycle. Because the past cycle has ceded to the new, the current cycle is underway. The momentum of the new cycle expresses itself through action and new commitments. At this point the urge to act and move forward is stronger than the pull to regress to the past. There may be no awareness as to why we feel driven to push forward, but action and movement feel necessary.

At the First Quarter square, we feel compelled to act upon these new impulses. The activity may lack conscious application; however, by the time the trine aspect unfolds, the focus emerges. Towards the end of the phase, productivity is centred on our goals and direction. During this phase there is lots of movement and change, allowing new developmental opportunities to emerge.

Progressed Gibbous Moon

This phase lasts from the sesquisquare until the opposition of the two progressed luminaries. New techniques and tools are developed during this phase in order to guarantee and support the effectiveness and success of the cycle. Productivity, hard work and perseverance are keys to perfecting the purpose. The cycle's direction is now more conscious and the impulse to act is directed towards a conscious goal. The life direction becomes established through preparation and planning. Adjustments to the direction are made at the quincunx phase in order to get ready for the culmination of the cycle at the Full Moon.

Life is full of meaning and purpose during this period and we are more open to possibilities, new methods and systems. Often this is accompanied by soul-searching and by spiritually embracing new beliefs and attitudes. Obstacles and challenges are recognized as part of the process necessary to be best prepared and equipped for the next stage. This is a phase of building and preparing, as we create a strong container to hold the developments that will come into bloom at the Full Moon.

Progressed Full Moon
The cycle is now at its peak. The Full Moon illuminates the successes and failures of the first half of the cycle, the past 14–15 years' work. An objective and conscious realization of our purpose comes to light and we are more aware of our role in the process. With a more defined purpose, it feels necessary to apply it to a larger sphere of life. A new course is beginning to take hold as we become more aware of our responsibilities and consciously participate with the process.

At the Full Moon, we have a heightened vision – one of inspiration and fulfilment. This stimulates a greater understanding; however, this realization also brings the failures and missed opportunities to light. This clarity of vision returns us to being more in tune with our authentic goals and purpose. Whatever is illuminated is best perceived in an objective and detached light. Becoming enmeshed or involved in emotional reactions diminishes the clarity available at the present time. As the Moon is in its most reflective period, mindfulness and contemplation are fundamental. By the time of the waning quincunx, we are ready to assimilate the experiences and make the adjustments necessary to shine in the world. At the peak of the cycle we need to be more aware of and in touch with the purpose and meaning of the life we lead.

The progressed Moon begins the second half, or waning part, of the cycle behind the progressed Sun and will repeat in reverse the aspects made to the Sun in the first half of the cycle. It is a time of balancing the relationship between our self and those who we love and partner.

Progressed Disseminating Moon

What was identified, understood, experienced and practised during the Full Moon phase needs to be shared. There is a reaching out and wider participation in life. The challenge of integrating and disseminating knowledge gleaned through the last 18–19 years, a nodal cycle, is the task of this phase. This is a time of outreach as we interact with the world, giving back what has inspired and transformed us, what we have learnt and created, as well as what we passionately know to be true.

The desire to demonstrate what has been illuminated is strong and the ability to do so is enhanced around the waning trine. Developing the faith and trust in our own convictions, integrity and truth is crucial, because it is from this firm foundation that the knowledge can be shared. This is a period of communication, writing, inspiring, publicizing, sharing – the dissemination of our creative self. This phase ends as the progressed Moon forms its waning square to the progressed Sun.

Progressed Last Quarter Moon

This 'crisis of consciousness' phase commences with the waning square, a critical period of determining what is obsolete and no longer of value. This is when we reap the true understanding and meaning from our experiences and are challenged to let go of what is no longer purposeful. It is the autumn of the cycle when there are deep urges to withdraw, yet paradoxically there is more that can be offered and produced. But the time is passing for building in the outer world, because the time has come to journey inward.

Whatever remains unconscious seeks awareness and possibly elimination. There is a feeling of transcendence as we are challenged to question old assumptions and go beyond them. Unlike the First Quarter phase when we may have instinctively taken action, at this point we need to consider what happened 15 years ago. The First Quarter crisis in action stage may now have its completion, revision or culmination.

As the Moon moves towards the waning sextile, the opportunity to let go of whatever is unnecessary arises. We are more imaginative and reflective during this phase, so our dreams and feeling life are animated and meaningful. During this phase the images and signs from the unconscious are strong guides and way-showers. This is the time for revision and remodelling. The phase ends as the progressed Moon semi-squares the progressed Sun, signalling the entry into the last phase of the cycle.

Progressed Balsamic Moon

As the Moon darkens, a period of inner reflection and withdrawal beckons. At this phase of life the old cycle is emptied out, so that new intentions and purposes might be germinated. It is a time of preparation for a new cycle by letting go of the old. The quality of consciousness and depth of understanding are allies in the preparatory work of letting go.

Internalizing the experiences, knowledge and wisdom born out of the previous cycle is the task of this time. The discoveries and experiences of the past are imprinted upon the psyche, so the essence of the past becomes a template for the future. We may find that the content of our lives, our creativity, our career and our close associations are being focused in a different direction. It may seem that we are withdrawing from many aspects of life; however, the preparation for the next cycle takes abundant internal energy. This is a time of retreat; the vision for the future intersects with the experiences of the past. It is not a time of outer manifestation, because the psychic energy becomes inwardly focused.

During this phase our attempts to push out into the world are often met with an equal force pushing us back into the inner world. Entering the Dark Moon phase suggests the withdrawal from outmoded aspects of self, no matter how uncomfortable, so that a fuller identity may flourish during the next cycle. During this final phase the essence of the previous cycle is distilled and the experiences of the past are digested and integrated. The distilled essences fertilize the emergent cycle. Psychic energy is directed internally, making it necessary to find the time and space for retreat. In this internal world the new vision for the future can be formed. This phase ends at the conjunction of the progressed Moon and Sun, heralding the appearance of the new cycle.

Another cycle begins by building on what has been developed, understood and integrated during the previous cycle. Like a spiral, each cycle brings us closer to the conscious realization of the Self, the goal of individuation. The new cycle starts in the next sign. The Sun has progressed approximately 30° of our chart, while the progressed Moon has progressed through the whole chart, plus one further sign. Their conjunction renews the cycle once again.

Journaling the Journey

In Chapter 4, the following mandala outlining the eight phases of the progressed lunation cycle was introduced. This can be used in your own creative way to mark the times when the phases occur and to note what you remember of those times. I prefer marking the season of year on the mandala, rather than the date, in order to highlight the natural progress of time. Events are the symbols of the ambience and soul time of each phase. Using a mandala pays homage to the passing of time.

My Progressed Lunation Cycle: The First Round

Using Appendix 6, you will be able to generate the progressed lunation phases of your lifetime using Solar Fire software. Once you have this report, you can detail your progressed phases through your lifetime. I always encourage students to buy a special journal dedicated to reflections on these phases of life. Dedicate a couple of pages in your journal to each phase. By following the development of these phases you begin to see the soul's unfolding patterns throughout life and the growth of consciousness as we age.

Here are Carl Jung's progressed phases from birth to death. I have listed each one separately, with the position of the progressed Sun and Moon at the opening of each phase.

Progressed Lunation Phase	Date	Season and Year	Degree of Progressed Sun	Degree of Progressed Moon
Birth – Last Quarter	26/07/1875		03♌18	15♉32
Balsamic	01/01/1878	Winter 1878	05♌38	20♊38
The Progressed Lunation Cycle – First Round:				
New	03/05/1881	Spring 1881	08♌50	08♌50
Crescent	05/12/1884	Autumn 1884	12♌16	27♏16
First Quarter	03/12/1888	Autumn 1888	16♌06	16♏06
Gibbous	05/01/1893	Winter 1893	20♌01	05♑01
Full Moon	03/11/1896	Autumn 1896	23♌42	23♒42
Disseminating	30/05/1900	Spring 1900	27♌08	12♈08
Last Quarter	06/11/1903	Autumn 1903	00♍27	00♊27
Balsamic	02/04/1907	Spring 1907	03♍44	18♋44
The Progressed Lunation Cycle – Second Round:				
New	07/10/1910	Autumn 1910	07♍08	07♍08
Crescent	01/08/1914	Summer 1914	10♍50	25♎50
First Quarter	06/09/1918	Summer 1918	14♍48	14♐48
Gibbous	03/09/1922	Summer 1922	18♍41	03♒41
Full Moon	23/04/1926	Spring 1926	22♍14	22♓14
Disseminating	03/09/1929	Summer 1929	25♍32	10♉32
Last Quarter	26/01/1933	Winter 1933	28♍50	28♊50
Balsamic	30/07/1936	Summer 1936	02♎17	17♌17
The Progressed Lunation Cycle – Third Round:				
New	25/04/1940	Spring 1940	05♎57	05♎57
Crescent	29/04/1944	Spring 1944	09♎54	24♏54
First Quarter	12/06/1948	Spring 1948	13♎58	13♑58
Gibbous	20/04/1952	Spring 1952	17♎47	02♓47
Full Moon	30/09/1955	Autumn 1955	21♎11	21♓11
Disseminating	01/01/1959	Winter 1959	24♎25	09♊25
Death	06/06/1961		26♎50	14♋38

You can use the mandalas provided in the Appendix to creatively present each cycle. These worksheets are for your own interest, to use in whichever way you feel works best for you – I like to feel free enough to write my ideas all over the page. This can be done with all three of Jung's progressed lunation cycles to reflect on his individuation throughout life. I will concentrate on Jung's second progressed lunation cycle, which lasted from 1910–40, placing it on the following progressed lunation cycle mandala worksheet.

I am using the second cycle of Carl Jung's adult life from ages 35–64. This period of his life illustrates his breaking away from an orthodox and established view of psychoanalysis through his personal psychic exploration and participation with the unconscious. This internal journey yielded the psychological theories and creative psychic insights which he shared in his voluminous writings. Jung's confrontation with the unconscious, as he called it, began after his split with Freud. During these years he described encountering 'this stream of lava and the heat of its fires reshaped my life. That was the primal stuff which compelled me to work upon it'.[84] It was during the years of his second progressed lunation cycle that his goal of a scientific psychology was confronted and his encounter with the prima material, the 'primal stuff', became his vocational call that gave birth to his lifework. He said:

> The years when I pursued the inner images were the most important time of my life – in them everything essential was decided. It all began then; the later details are only supplements and clarifications of the material that burst forth from the unconscious, and at first swamped me. It was the prima material for a lifetime's work.[85]

During the Balsamic phase of his first cycle, Jung met Sigmund Freud, the person whose psychological work he greatly admired. Freud was also the embodiment of the master and elder in unconscious studies, which dovetailed with Jung's vocational calling. Just before Jung's second progressed New Moon, Toni Woolf, his later muse and mistress, entered his life as a patient at his workplace, the Burghölzli Psychiatric Hospital. Seeds of the new cycle were being sown. Jung's next cycle began shortly after turning 35 in the advent of his third Jupiter return which was also being squared at the time by the Uranus–Neptune opposition. It was a major time of spiritual and psychic awakening.

The New Moon phase previewed many of the themes that wove their way through the next cycle and forged the soulful nature of Jung's life's work and purpose. The cycle allows us to stand back and see the unfolding of a significant period of life. I found it of great interest that Sigmund Freud entered Jung's life in the Balsamic phase of the first cycle and died in the Balsamic phase of Jung's second cycle. The second cycle began with Jung's breakaway from Freud and it ended with Freud's death. Freud was the intense personification of Jung's desire to be acknowledged and respected by the establishment.

Jung separated from his psychoanalytical colleagues as the new cycle began in order to discover his own vocational trail. During the New Moon phase his lifelong study of astrology began, one of the many symbolic systems he studied in depth. He published *Psychology of the Unconscious* that presented his independent position on psychology and activated the programme for the next few decades of his life. This manuscript was revised in the third cycle and retitled *Symbols of Transformation*, but it had its birth during the second progressed New Moon, a phase which produced fertile seeds for the subsequent cycles. During this phase he also had an overpowering vision of a 'frightful catastrophe',[86] a prophetic image of the coming war. Also during this phase, he had a feeling of falling – plunging 'down into the dark depths'.[87] Uranus was transiting his Ascendant and opposing his Sun, and this fall precipitated a breakdown, one he described as his 'confrontation with the unconscious'. It was this breakthrough that contributed to the discovery of a great deal of Jung's philosophy, which developed over the following years. This led him to resign as a university professor and as president of the International Psychoanalytic Association. The progressed Crescent phase approached and the seeds of the new cycle had been firmly planted. Now they would struggle to find their roots in the new soil.

Jung's progressed Crescent phase began two days after Germany declared war on France in August 1914. As Jung was in Scotland at the time he had to make his way back to Switzerland through the turmoil in Europe, metaphoric of his own soul's homecoming – his struggle to return home to his authentic nature. Ironically, his third progressed Crescent phase synchronized with the Second World War. These images serve as profound metaphors for this Crescent phase, which characterizes the struggle with the ghosts of the past. During the progressed First Quarter phase Jung travelled for the first time to North Africa, a place he longed to be, as it was far removed from the westernization of the psyche, again symbolic of the instinctual and undomesticated psychic aspects that captured his imagination. He also published *Psychological Types* in his effort to reconcile Freudian and Adlerian typologies. Unbeknownst to Jung it would become one of his most popular theories and books. Ironically, Jung's popularity increased as he mastered and guided his own course. During this time, through his travels and his work, he met others, such as Esther Harding, Herman Hesse and Richard Wilhelm, who would help steer his course to international recognition.

Jung's Gibbous phase was overshadowed by the death of his mother and characterized by the commencement and completion of erecting his tower at Bollingen, emblematic of building and preparing for the times to come. It also represented his necessity for psychic refuge and containment. The tower was illustrative of the Work, the alchemical opus that he would begin to study during his progressed Full Moon phase. The Full Moon brought astrology's sister science alchemy to light for Jung. Sown at the New Moon were seeds filled with symbols that would ripen and flourish through Jung's alchemical studies. Many lectures and presentations testify to Jung's illumined New Moon revelations, but none perhaps more so than his commentary on *The Secret of the Golden Flower*, written near the end of the phase. A synthesis of cross-cultural and inter-psychic symbols had been brought together. As the Full Moon phase ripened, transiting Saturn was approaching his MC, having spent the last two years tilling the rich philosophical ground of his 9th house. It would culminate on the MC during this phase, as Pluto was transiting his 6th house Mercury–Venus conjunction. Both Saturn and Pluto were allies in developing the vocational promise of the Full Moon phase.

After the ripening of the fruits of the Full Moon they can be disseminated during the next phase. As the progressed Disseminating phase arrived, more of Jung's writings were released in German and he began a seminar series in Switzerland and started to lecture in Germany. Compilations of his work and its dissemination through writing and lecturing continued into the Last Quarter. His Last Quarter phase began with his lectures in Cologne and Essen on 'The Meaning of Psychology for Modern Man', but now Jung was beginning to feel tired. His influence and attraction were growing as he found many opportunities in the English-speaking world to share his psychological philosophy. These concepts were born from insights carved out of his personal inner work.

The Balsamic phase was initiated by Jung's discovery of a dead snake with a dead fish protruding from its mouth. As progressions explore the landscape of the symbolic inner world, this synchronistic image on the cusp of the Balsamic phase is like a finishing touch to the cycle in which Jung explored his religious self through his profound inner journeys. He conceptualized the serpent as the embodiment of the pagan spirit, the snake, having devoured the Christian one, symbolized by the fish.[88] His alchemical work that came to light at the Full Moon continued throughout the waning half of the cycle. This influence inspired Jung to see this image as a reconciling symbol between his pagan and Christian spirits. At the end of the cycle, his pagan spirit had become identified and integrated.

His last trip to America was followed by a trip to India at the end of 1937. Storm clouds gathered over Europe and this cycle ended, not only with the death of his elder former colleague Sigmund Freud, but the declaration of war on Germany by Britain and France, twenty days before Freud's death. An era had ended – a new one was to begin.

The progressed lunation cycle is a potent image of an inner round; a cycle of Soul lived out in the world of our human experience. For Jung, these thirty years marked by the phases of the progressed lunation cycle became a way not to just honour the soul's intention but also to marvel at its unfolding. It is a potent cycle for each of us to honour; one way is by journaling our experiences. What follows is a mandala I like to use to visualize the unfolding of the cycle, followed by Jung's mandala for his second round.

Carl Jung Progressed Lunation Cycle for the Second Round

My Progressed Lunation Cycle
My Second Round

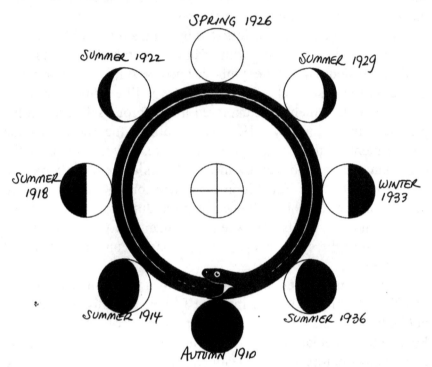

My Next Progressed New Moon is *SPRING 1940*

© **Astro*Synthesis**
designed by Emilie Llewellyn Simons

Carl Jung Progressed Lunation Cycle for the Second Round

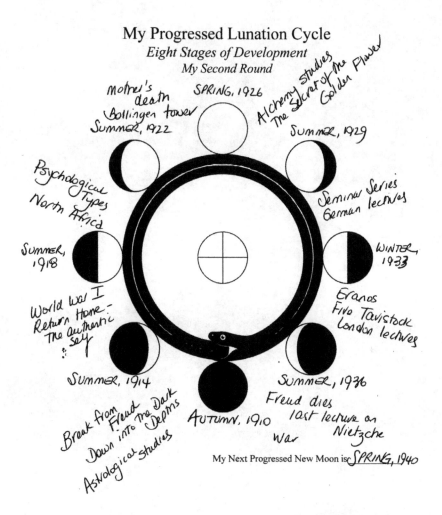

My Progressed Lunation Cycle
Eight Stages of Development
My Second Round

Mother's death
Bollingen tower
Summer, 1922

SPRING, 1926

Alchemy studies
The Secret of the Golden Flower

Summer, 1929

Psychological Types
North Africa

Seminar Series
German lectures

Summer, 1918

WINTER, 1933

World War I
Return Home -
The authentic self

Eranos
Five Tavistock
London lectures

Summer, 1914

Summer, 1936

Break from Freud
Down into the Dark Depths
Astrological studies

AUTUMN, 1910

War

Freud dies
last lecture on
Nietzsche

My Next Progressed New Moon is SPRING, 1940

© Astro*Synthesis
designed by Emilie Llewellyn Simons

14

INNER TIMING
Working with Secondary Progressions

Secondary time invites us to be reflective, less literal. Life events and experiences mark the times of our lives, but trying to fit life events into astrological time frames objectifies astrological symbols, rather than letting the symbols reveal their time. Working with secondary progressions returns us to a subjective examination of the times at hand. Although they are linked to actual clock time, they encourage us to be symbolic, focused on soul purpose, to be introspective. Hence, it is often difficult to articulate Secondaries and why metaphors, images, imaginings and stories suit their expression better.

In the previous three chapters we have focused on the progressed Sun, the progressed Moon and the progressed lunation cycle, all of which offer us abundant soul food. To begin working with the secondary progressions I highlight three tasks that I feel will be enormously helpful in facilitating your understanding of this technique.

1. Track the progressed Moon through the houses of your natal horoscope from birth until the present, being mindful of when the progressed Moon changes houses and especially when it crosses the angles of your chart. Reflect on these times of your life, writing your reflections and memories in a dedicated journal devoted to the timing of secondary progressions.

2. Complete the Planetary Order Worksheet (see Appendix 5) to track your progressed Sun's aspects to your natal planets. Note the years and the type of aspect the progressed Sun is making in order to consider these times of your life. Reflect on how the progressed Sun illuminates the planetary archetype that it is aspecting.

3. Use the progressed lunation cycle to determine the progressed phases of your personal cycle, starting with your first progressed New Moon after birth. Reflect on these phases of your life, first recalling the passage of time and which memories remain significant from this period, then reflect on each phase as a developmental stage and the building blocks that have forged the path you are now on. Use the journal you have dedicated to the timing of secondary progressions to record your reflections and observations.

While these three progressions are primary, there are other secondary considerations that are informative and revealing. Let's look at some of these.

The Progression of the Inner Planets: Developing Character
Unlike the Sun and Moon, the inner planets Mercury, Venus and Mars may change direction after birth, altering their natal course in the progressed chart. A change in the expression of this archetypal energy occurs when the planet turns retrograde or direct. Mapping the progressed inner planets assists in recognizing changes of direction, sign and house. All these changes reflect the growth of the planetary energy as it embraces new experiences. The change of house suggests the shifting topography, as if new rooms in our psychic house are being opened and explored.

Changing Direction
If you are born with **Mercury retrograde**, it will turn direct by progression by at least age 24, its maximum retrograde period. Since Mercury is retrograde on average for 22 days, or 22 years in progressed time, you can approximate the year when it will turn direct by knowing how many days have already elapsed in its cycle. Look in the ephemeris to ascertain when Mercury went retrograde before your birth. How many days before your birth did this happen?

If Mercury turned retrograde 0–11 days before your birth you were probably born when Mercury was in later zodiacal longitude than the Sun, thereby being the evening star, setting later than the Sun. It is the close of the cycle. In your secondary progressed horoscope you will experience the Sun–Mercury inferior conjunction by secondary progression early in life. At this time in your secondary progressed horoscope Mercury will change from the night to the day sect and begin to rise before the Sun. You will also experience the superior conjunction of Mercury and the Sun in your progressed horoscope about 48–60 years later – approximately one half of the synodic cycle.

If Mercury turned retrograde around 10 or 11 days before you were born, you were born near the inferior conjunction and the beginning of a new synodic cycle. If Mercury turned retrograde more than 10–11 days before you were born, Mercury rises before the Sun in its new cycle, having made its inferior conjunction before birth. By progression Mercury will change orientation to the Sun, aligning with the night sect at its superior conjunction about 36–48 years later.

The year when Mercury turns direct is significant because the way we communicate, express, learn, share ideas or are part of a system subtly alters. For instance, there may be more opportunities to externalize our thoughts and ideas. Movement and change allow new avenues of expression and communication. Our natural patterns of learning and connecting are being reshaped and refocused in step with the changing environment. The next significant time zone will be when progressed Mercury conjuncts its natal position after it turns direct. This suggests an alignment with our inner urge to communicate and express through the written and spoken word.

If you were born with **Mercury direct** there is a strong possibility that Mercury will station retrograde by progression in your lifetime. When Mercury turns retrograde by secondary progression it remains retrograde for 21–24 years; the natally externalized Mercurial function is deepening and becoming internally focused. This is often experienced as an ability to contain or hold onto thoughts rather than expressing them, to think more deeply, to prioritize important issues or to enhance our capacity for reflection, discrimination and listening.

Mercury changing direction suggests important years in education and interaction. All areas under Mercury's rulership, such as communication, exchange of ideas, learning, writing, school, siblings, travel and transportation, are emphasized when Mercury changes direction.

If you were born with **Venus retrograde**, then by the age of 43 it will have turned direct in your progressed chart. As with Mercury, the age at which it turned direct is dependent on where in the retrograde cycle you were born. If Venus turned retrograde less than 0–22 days before your birth, you were born when Venus was in later zodiacal longitude than the Sun. As the evening star, Venus was setting after the Sun at the close of its cycle. In your secondary progressed horoscope you will experience the Sun–Venus inferior conjunction by secondary progression somewhere in first two decades of life. In your secondary progressed horoscope Venus will change from being a western goddess as she sets after the Sun to her eastern counterpart as she now rises before the Sun. If Venus turned retrograde around 20–22 days before your birth, you were born near the inferior conjunction and the beginning of a new synodic cycle. If Venus turned retrograde more than 20–22 days before your birth, you were born with Venus rising before the Sun in a new cycle.

Perhaps the more inner-orientated, private retrograde Venus starts to turn out towards the world as it turns direct. The inhibited or aesthetic Venus may become inclined to project her sense of worth and value out into the world and participate more fully in the sphere of relationships. When progressed Venus conjuncts its natal position after it turns direct, the following years are important in reaffirming oneself, re-establishing a sense of worth and value and consolidating your assets. If Venus is direct and turns retrograde by progression, it will remain retrograde in the progressed chart for nearly 42 years. You could feel more private, insular or inner-orientated. Your resourcefulness may be withdrawn from social or other-directed concerns into an exploration of your own inner creativity. At the midpoint of this cycle the inferior conjunction will occur; in the progressed chart this signals progressed Venus now moving in front of the Sun. As a metaphor this might imply that your values, assets and worth are more perceptible. You may be more likely to demonstrate and share your deeper essence and inner beauty. These changes in Venus's direction can correspond to significant years in relationships, our sense of self-esteem as well as our values and personal worth. This also signifies a different orientation to our personal tastes, that which we may have previously valued and appreciated and what we now find attractive in others.

A **retrograde Mars** that turns direct by progression corresponds to a change in the expression of our aggressive instincts, our competitive urges and desire nature. The tendency to repress our anger, or not overtly go after what we want may shift, as we start feeling more comfortable with and capable of expressing our competitive urges and asserting our will more openly, becoming more identified with what we want. This may also suggest an increase in vitality and energy, as we become more direct and open.

Mars turning retrograde by progression signals times when we are more focused in supporting our innate will and sustaining enough stamina to accomplish what we want. A direct Mars that turns retrograde enhances the ability to maintain energy, to pace oneself and channel the aggressive instincts into positive outcomes. These changes of direction correspond with the way we handle our aggression, anger and will, signalling years of innovative enterprises. It is important to remember that this process is subtle and will occur over longer periods of time. Once Mars goes retrograde, it will remain retrograde anywhere from 58–81 years, which in many cases may be the rest of one's life.

Changing Signs and Signals
The progression of the inner planets into new signs and houses suggests maturation, acceptance and breadth of experience for this planetary archetype. When these progressed planets aspect natal planets, I recommend you use a similar approach to these aspects as we did with the progressed Sun.

Progressed **Mercury** symbolizes the development of our communication skills and learning capabilities. It represents the acquisition of information, education, the maturation of our ideas and comprehension. In its first sign change by progression it enters an incompatible element. The qualities of the new sign confront our programmed responses, fixed ideas, opinions and prejudices. We are on a steep learning curve, being exposed to new ways and qualities of thinking. The progression of Mercury develops our capacity to consider other people's ideas, cultivates the capacity to listen and reflects on ideas and initiatives that we may never have considered before. When progressed Mercury aspects natal planets, these years synchronize with important developments in education, learning or the gaining of new skills. During these years, we pursue new studies that are stimulating and exciting. Mercury's progression often parallels changes in schooling and personal interests, awakening our urge to be involved with ideas that inspire us. The progression of Mercury helps us to forge new viewpoints, concepts and ideas about ourselves so we are more skilled in dealing with the world.

Venus by progression symbolizes our growing sense of worth and value. It guides the development of our personal values, tastes and pleasures. Like a barometer, progressed Venus gauges how our unique style of expression is cultivated over time. It represents the continuing refinement of our relationship patterns and the changing prism of light that we are attracted to in others and ourselves. Ultimately, Venus's progression concerns our sense of self-love and appreciation and the way this translates into personal interactions and relationships; therefore, progressed Venus is a symbol of establishing harmony and balance within our lives and partnerships. It also illustrates the growing need to relate and interact with others, often signalling important years in the development of equal relationships. Progressed Venus is also the continuing development of our creative instincts and our fostering and appreciation of art and beauty. Therefore, as progressed Venus changes signs, our senses are opened up to new perceptions and pleasures. We are challenged to expand our appreciation of the things we value, explore new forms of creativity and be more tolerant of our differences with others, especially intimate friends and partners. As progressed Venus aspects planets it brings a new appreciation and feeling to the planetary archetype.

Mars by progression symbolizes the development of our will and power in asserting what we want. It describes the developmental ways our aggressive instincts and competitive nature are managed. When guided by progressed Mars, our instincts and urges can be channelled more effectively in service of the soul. Mars is associated with vitality and physical energy and its progression will show how we might best utilize our physical vigour and adrenalin. Progressed Mars directs the appropriate action; it displays the courage of our convictions. It aids in the struggle to be true to ourselves and to establish our personal territory. Its change of sign suggests that Mars's focus and motivation is being sharpened and challenged.

When aroused by desire or challenged by innovative possibilities, progressed Mars encourages a mature approach to becoming more skilful in our projects and more discerning of our time. Progressed Mars can encourage or enflame the planets it aspects; in terms of psychological development, this activation is designed to hearten, promote and animate the planet to its best expression.

When using all the planets by progression, I recommend a 1° orb for both applying and separating from the aspect. Therefore, these inner planets may be within orb for a couple of years or many more when they are near their stationary periods. Examine the part of the horoscope that they are influencing and ascertain what they are triggering and bringing into consciousness. They symbolize the growth, maturation and development of the personal self.

As mentioned in the preamble to secondary progressions, the social and outer planets have minimal movement in the secondary progressed chart, which highlights the importance of their aspects in the natal chart. Once they change direction in the secondary progressed chart they will continue in this direction for the rest of one's life. Therefore, I find their directional shift important in addressing a change of orientation in the experience of the planetary archetype in the individual's life.

The Progressed Angles: Developing the Directions of our Lives
There are many different methods of progressing the horoscope's angles. The most common method is to progress the Midheaven at the same rate as the Sun, using the solar arc, which is the degree of difference between the progressed and the natal Sun. This arc is added to the natal MC to get the progressed MC. The progressed Ascendant is derived from the progressed Midheaven, using a Table of Houses to find the corresponding progressed Ascendant.

The progressed **Ascendant** is the evolving archetype of the personality. It represents how we are presenting ourselves to the world, the maturation of our character and the growing ease of our interactions with others. The Ascendant symbolizes the image that we create in the world to form a bridge between our self and others. Therefore, the progressed Ascendant highlights this evolving image of the self, recognizable through our changes in style and appearance, the way we project ourselves, and the way we create our image and aura in the world. The progressed Ascendant symbolizes the development of personality and our capacity to authentically project ourselves into the world.

The progressed Ascendant will generally advance through the first quadrant of the horoscope while the progressed MC proceeds through the last quadrant. On average, they conjoin the next house cusp near age thirty, the following house cusp near age sixty and the subsequent angle near age ninety, but this is dependent on the size of the houses and whether the Ascendant is in a long or short ascending sign. These progressions divide the life cycle into three phases. When the progressed Ascendant conjuncts the 2nd house cusp, a greater capacity to value self and be valued by others ripens. We are more aware of the impact of our personality and how that operates and is received by others: we become more self-aware. At this time we are able to use our personality in tandem with our personal values to build self-esteem. As the progressed Ascendant enters the 3rd house, our personality is more at ease with our true self. Our identity and roles in the community and local environment are more reflective of how we feel about ourselves. The Ascendant progressing into the 2nd and 3rd houses signals a change in the way we relate to the world. When the progressed Ascendant aspects natal planets, this archetype is incorporated into the way we project ourselves into the world.

Changes in self-identification, behaviour, appearance and style are characteristic of the deeper changes that occur as we work to discover our authentic self. This is notable as the progressed Ascendant changes signs. It is as if the personality has a wider field in which to extend, explore and express itself. The first sign change is the most awkward, as the quality of the sign is dissimilar in temperament. Yet it is this tension that builds a greater awareness of the self and its resourcefulness. Often the progressed Ascendant's first change of sign also reflects the 2nd house cusp, which supports the personality in being more self-assured. Its aspects to natal planets acquaint the personality with the archetypal forces underpinning character.

The progressed **Midheaven** symbolizes the evolution of our role in the world, our public image and reputation, along with our professional quest. Its image centres on the development of authority and autonomy. As it progresses through the 10th house we become aware of these issues. As it progresses into the 11th house we begin the process of taking our profession into the community. As the progressed MC reaches the 12th house cusp, we are ready to withdraw from public life and internalize the successes of our work in the world to create an inner relationship with our professional self. As the progressed MC aspects natal planets, we experience their potentialities in the development of our profession and public image. Each aspect encounters the authority of the archetype and how it is best managed to support the career trajectory.

Reflect on the year when the progressed MC first changed signs and how the quality and sense of your vocation began to be more apparent. The first change of sign generally marks a step along the vocational path: perhaps a move, study, an encounter with a mentor or guide, a job or new passions and longings emerge that place you on your vocational trajectory.

In sync with the progressed Ascendant moving through the first quadrant, the progressed Descendant moves through the third quadrant of the horoscope. Similarly, while the progressed MC moves through the last quadrant, the progressed IC moves through the second quadrant. Over the course of a lifetime all four angles progress through the whole chart. Every direction of life as symbolized by the angles combines to reach out and enrich the experience of self in the world.

Preparing and Presenting Secondary Progressions
Generate the secondary progressed horoscope for the time in question. While you may progress the natal chart to today, or an important date in your life, remember that the progressed chart does not operate in the same time frequency as other charts, but represents the natural unfolding and outcome of the natal chart. Make a note of the progressed sign positions of all the inner planets, which natal house they are progressing through, whether they have changed direction and what aspects they are forming with inner planets. Be aware of all the progressed angles and their interaction with the natal chart. Take note of any planet that may have changed direction and, if so, in what year it changed direction by progression.

These progressions may become clearer as you generate a bi-wheel with the natal chart on the inside wheel and the secondary progressed chart on the outer one. For consultations, I place the current transits of the nodes, social and outer planets in blue on the outer rim of the horoscope, along with the current secondary progressions of the angles and inner planets in red, also on its outer rim. I note any progressed planetary change of direction and the year when this occurred, as well as notes to myself about any secondary movement that feels significant. Over time you will find your own way to present these progressed images.

Here is Carl Jung's secondary progressed chart for 3 March 1907, the day when he first met Sigmund Freud in person. There are many times in a life to choose, but I chose this one as this encounter was highly significant in forging Jung's vocational path and his search for his authentic self. I did not choose this as a case study to confirm secondary techniques, but to demonstrate a progressed chart in time. I have set this chart for 12 noon at his birthplace.

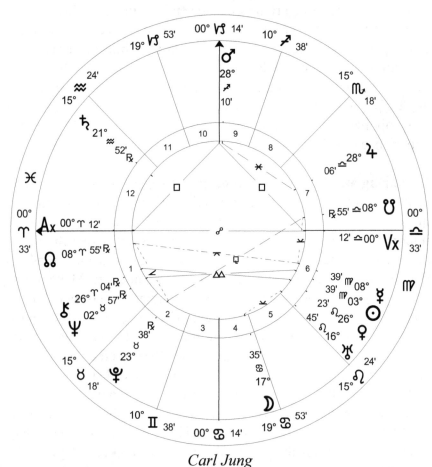

Carl Jung
Secondary Progressed Horoscope for 3 March 1907

The time does not alter the chart. On the following page a bi-wheel compares this progressed chart with Jung's natal chart.

With the progressed Moon in Jung's natal 6th house (see the following bi-wheel) there is a psychological focus on his sphere of work. Feelings and sentiments about his comfort and engagement with work are occupying him. The progressed Moon is conjunct his natal 6th house Venus, an image that speaks to me of an emotive rendezvous with someone who values and relates to work in a similar way. As the Moon had progressed over Mercury in the previous four months, Jung and Freud had been in contact by letter; in a way, the symbols of Mercury and Venus come alive in Jung's experience of a workmate, associate and partner. While meeting Freud is representative of this progression, inwardly it implies that Jung's growing sense of security and care for his own relationship to work is being deeply felt.

An outer connection to Freud is formed, yet the progression reveals the composition of Jung's soulful connection to his work.

Of interest to me is that at this time, synchronous with Jung's first meeting with Freud, the progressed MC had reached 0♑ and the Ascendant had progressed to 0♈, reflecting the natural wheel or what is often referred to as the horoscope of the *anima mundi*, the soul of the world. When 0♑ is on the MC, the Vertex is aligned with the Descendant, as in the progressed chart. While all the progressed angles reveal a powerful statement, what that is, or the feeling of what that might be, is difficult to articulate. However, it offers confidence that this time is the beginning of a potent stage of vocational mastery.

The natal chart ruler of the MC is Mars, and the natal chart ruler of the Ascendant is Saturn. Note that in the progressed charts the rulers have swapped positions, as Mars now rules the progressed Ascendant and Saturn rules the progressed MC. This image speaks to me of Carl Jung coming into his own sense of authority with his pioneering and innovative personal discoveries that were integrated into his profession.

Chiron, Neptune and Pluto are now all retrograde in Jung's progressed horoscope. Progressed Pluto had turned retrograde three years earlier, while Chiron turned retrograde by progression in Jung's fifth year; progressed Neptune had turned retrograde in his eleventh year. This triumvirate of powerful planets, familiar with

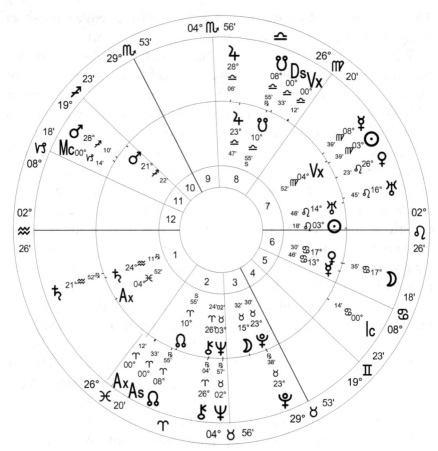

Inner Chart: Carl Jung – Natal Chart
Outer Chart: Jung's Secondary Progressions for 3 March 1907

the landscape of the psyche and underworld, are now more focused
and internalized, excavating deeper and darker archetypal realms.

Carl Jung was 31 when he first visited Freud at his home in Vienna.
Two powerful men in the psychoanalytic movement crossed paths
that day. Such destined appointments are often accompanied by
nodal points. By 'nodal' I also include the angles of the horoscope,
as these are crossing points and can also be referred to as nodal
points.[89] Since all nodes characterize the crossing of orbital planes,
they are potent symbols of destined encounters. The transiting
South Node had just conjoined Jung's natal Ascendant. In the
progressed chart, the progressed Sun is applying to a conjunction
with the Vertex, a point in time when potent encounters in our life
take place.[90]

Secondary progressions help to picture Jung's life's work and life experience from a developmental point of view. They can be integrated with transits to amplify the psychological perspective of the times. At the time of the meeting, Pluto was stationary at 21♊44, opposite Jung's Mars in Sagittarius, ruler of the MC, and in the 11th house of colleagues. Jupiter was in Cancer, poised to transit Mercury and Venus in the next few months, while Neptune, also in Cancer, would transit this planetary conjunction over the next few years. Uranus in Capricorn would be transiting in opposition to Mercury and Venus over the upcoming year. The themes of work, profession, colleagues, competition, interactive ideas, etc., are all indicated. These transits echo the progressed Moon's movement in the 6th house.

Planet/ Angle	Carl Jung Natal Positions	Notes on Transits for 3 March 1907
Ascendant	02♒26	The transiting South Node was at 1♒53, having just risen across the horizon; therefore, the transiting North Node had recently transited Jung's Sun on the Descendant. The transiting nodal axis was aligned with Jung's Ascendant–Descendant axis.
Mercury	13♋46	Jupiter was at 1♋02, having turned direct a week earlier, and was about to enter his 6th house and conjunct Mercury and Venus in June. Neptune was in his 6th house, about to turn direct and transit Mercury by the year's end. Uranus at 11♑50 would transit Mercury and Venus over the next few years; therefore, all three longer-range transits focused on the themes of work, connections and values.
Venus	17♋30	
Mars	21♐22	Pluto was stationing direct at 21♊44, exactly opposing Mars in Sagittarius. Pluto had been excavating Jung's Mars for the previous 2½ years and this meeting would ignite his individual philosophy and doctrines.

Working with secondary progressions is a valuable adjunct to transits. For me, they are perfect partners, as one faces towards the soul while the other looks towards the world. While we may not always be able to clearly articulate these progressions, they are deeply felt and instinctively sensed, and on that level they confirm the soul's evolutionary process.

Another potent astrological time period is marked by the return of the planet to its natal position. Since myths and stories of returns have always reflected the human longing for homecoming, astrological returns are vibrant metaphors that mark out times of initiation. We will now turn to exploring the impact of planetary returns through time.

PART IV

RETURNS

The Soul's Homecoming

Time is the womb of souls

Dane Rudhyar, *The Astrology of Personality*

15

THE ETERNAL RETURN
Reappearances Through Time

Eternal recurrence or the image of the perpetual return is a theme which has woven itself through the thinking of the ancient Egyptians and Hindu truth-seekers as well as Pythagorean and later Greek philosophers. Fundamental to various hypotheses on returns was the belief that a similar situation would repeat at some point in the cycle. Aristotle summarized it well when he said: 'The same opinions recur in rotation among men, not once or twice, but infinitely often.'[91] In the 19th century, Friedrich Nietzsche developed this premise of eternal recurrence in his writings, especially Thus Spoke Zarathustra. He characterized existence as an hourglass turned over and over, a similar concept to other writers and poets who have articulated this image over time.

Many symbols and natural images have been used to characterize the eternal return and its connection to renewal and rebirth; for instance, the Egyptians saw the dung beetle as a sign of the renewal of life. The circle, the spiral and the ouroboros also epitomize the eternal return. We encountered the image of the ouroboros in the Saros return cycle of eclipses as well as on our mandala for the progressed lunation cycle. This dragon-serpent swallowing its own tail embodies the recurrent nature of the cosmos and underpins the nature of cycles. It represents the alpha, the beginning or the head, and the omega, the ending or the tail, yet both are at the same point. The knot of time represents chronological time fashioned into an endless cycle. When two ends of a piece of rope become knotted together, the line becomes a circle, with the knot being both the start and the finish of the endless loop. The ouroboros symbolizes both the beginning and ending of the sacred circle. Head and tail are one and mark the nodal point where time ends and begins concurrently. Astrologically, this is the powerful concept that underpins the conjunction, the aspect where a cycle returns to begin again.

Creation emerges from the eternal cycle that revives itself at the conjunction. Life is renewed through the process of endings. At the node where the dragon-serpent devours its own tail, life is carried forward in a new form. Death and rebirth, creation and cessation, beginning and ending, heads and tails – all mark the eternal return, the never-ending cycle of regeneration.

A permanent image of the eternal return embedded in the human psyche is the re-emergence of the Sun every morning; the dawn threshold marks the point where day, the re-creation of light, devours the dark, like the dragon swallowing its tail. The Sun has daily and yearly returns, which are instinctual to all human experience. At its diurnal return the Sun reappears on the horizon, surfacing from its night's journey underfoot. Annually it rises across the celestial equator, increasing in light, and brings a new season of life: spring, being the re-emergence of life on the wheel of year.

Similarly, returns are natural to human experience, being deep-seated and inbred in the soul. While we may not be familiar with the philosophy of the eternal return, we know returns at an instinctual level. Astrologers make meaning of the eternal return through various charts and techniques, such as ingress charts, when the Sun returns to 0° of an equinox (Aries, Libra) or solstice (Cancer, Capricorn) sign, or a solar return horoscope when the Sun returns to its exact natal position. 'Many happy returns'[92] is the celebratory salutation when the Sun returns each year on our birthday. The solar return horoscope celebrates this phrase.

The Sun's planetary homecoming is the renewal of our personal annual cycle. A double meaning of 'return' can also be considered as a yield or profit on returns from our investments. While 'Many happy returns of the day' in the context of a birthday greeting acknowledges another year of life, it also can be used as a metaphor for the renewal of investing in our greatest asset, the Self. In this way the solar return horoscope is a remarkable tool for acknowledging the return to one's authentic self, as in this chart all the planets are in service to the solar pursuit. It is an annual reminder of the contract with soul, symbolized by our natal and secondary charts.

The Mythological Return

In Greek myth, return was an aspect of the hero's quest detailed in the great Homeric epic *The Odyssey*, which narrated the return of Odysseus from Troy to his homeland of Ithaca. *Nostoi* is the ancient Greek word for 'return' and implies a homecoming. The plural

Nostos refers to a collection of epic tales recounting the return home from Troy of Greek heroes like Agamemnon, Menelaus, Diomedes and Ajax. These returns epitomized homecoming, returning to the place where they had started from, yet now the hero returned with a full cycle of experience, understanding, conquest, challenges and wisdom.

Nostoi is the journey homeward, perhaps to a home we may never have known, but one authentic to our soul. At the time of return we are drawn forward into the future by our intuitive spirit while, at the same time, pulled back to our past by our feelings. Pushed, pulled and prodded, we return to a place we started from, yet now witness, understand and know more consciously.

The word 'nostalgia' is constructed from the ancient Greek words *nostoi* and *algos*, meaning 'pain' or 'suffering',[93] so nostalgia characterizes the pain of return. While nostalgia generally refers to sentimentality in regards to return, on a feeling level it implies grief about being powerless to go back – the pain of not being able to return to the way it once was. Return disappointments are aching echoes of unmet expectations. Therefore, the image of return is a powerful concept in the human psyche, a process that demands we become more mindful of the present so we may return to the places of our past consciously. *Nostoi* implied that homecoming, the return, was an epic journey.

From an astrological point of view, mythological returns can be useful as metaphors of planetary returns. Planets, like heroes, represent the archetypal nature of return to an authentic essence that underpins our birthright. Studying the mythic returns of heroes and heroines – such as Odysseus, Jason, Persephone and Psyche – amplifies the process of the solar return from an astrological context.

Archetypal Returns
The *return home* is a significant part of the heroic saga. In myth and ritual, the return marks the ending, yet also the beginning. Joseph Campbell, a much-admired scholar on the archetypal stages of the heroic journey, amplified the cycles associated with rites of passage as separation, initiation and return. Campbell constructed a format for the heroic biography that could be applied to the return of the planets. The return demarcated the ending of liminality and the beginning of a new phase. During the liminal period, fixed points

of reference are suspended; therefore, the time is opportunistic to meet the gods. Psychologically it is time when a deeper connection to the psyche can be realized, as the landscape travelled is home to the divine.

The road leading from the past and the road stretching into the future cross at the return. Like Janus, one face glimpses the past; the other looks forward to anticipate the future. The forward-looking spirit is influenced and shaped by its backward-looking counterpart. Returns are a time of transition and ending, yet, like all endings, seeds of the future distilled from the past cycle have been planted. Like all beginnings the time is subjective, unknown, anticipatory, hopeful and fearful.

Home is the inner anchor where we begin; hence where we return, in order to make reparations to begin anew. In Joseph Campbell's way of thinking, the heroic return brought blessings as well as responsibilities. The hero returned from his mysterious adventure with the power to bestow boons on his fellow man. The return marks a cycle of completion and, with it, freedom from past experiences. In reference to the planets, the return is the archetypal homecoming, reawakening the authentic purpose and potential of the natal planetary archetype. The previous cycle has brought consciousness, awareness and meaning to the planet, all of which can be taken into the new cycle. The return is the bridge between two cycles and two ways of being.

Astrological Returns

One way of thinking about how the horoscope continually renews itself is through planetary and nodal returns. Each return infuses the planetary archetype with experience and awareness that deepens and expands our understanding of this capacity of our self. Planetary returns occur at the end of their sidereal cycle after completing one full round of the zodiac. This time contains both alpha and omega; an ending, yet also a beginning, a period of completion, yet also a period of anticipation. At the crossroads of return, the past and the future intersect with the present.

Astrologically we can reflect on returns in two distinct ways. First, we can contemplate the planetary return by creating a horoscope for the precise moment the planet returns to its natal position. Each return horoscope is a tribute to the new cycle and highlights the conditions of the subsequent cycle. It is born at the crossroads when completion of the last cycle and commencement of the new one happens in the same instant. A return horoscope honours this moment of rebirth; in essence, it captures the image of the eternal return, symbolizing a renewal of life by regenerating the natal patterns. The return chart is a herald for the next planetary cycle as it can be read in context of how the planetary archetype is refreshed and revitalized for its next round. While this technique could be applied to all planets, return charts are mainly utilized for the inner planets, most prevalently the Sun and Moon.

Second, we can consider the planetary return as a homecoming: a coming back to an authentic aspect of the self. As we look back on the last cycle and forward into the next, the planetary symbol can be re-visioned in its movement through time. This is especially helpful for forward planning and scheduling, given that each planetary archetype has its own timetable. The synodic returns to the inferior conjunction of Mercury and Venus with the Sun are effective planning guides. The returns of Mars, the social planets Jupiter and Saturn, the lunar nodes and the progressed Moon outline the time frames that reconnect us to our authentic entrepreneurial, social, moral, vocational and emotional selves. Each return marks a milestone on the path of life.

Planetary returns are also very personal, highlighting initiatory stages in the life cycle. We have previously honoured each planetary cycle, but it is worthwhile recollecting these returns as significant time markers in the life cycle. Be creative in pondering how we can utilize their return from an astrological perspective. Reflect on each return:

Planet(s)/Point	The Return to and Renewal of:
The Sun	The true Self
The Moon	The feeling Self
Mercury, Venus and Mars	Connectivity, values and engagement
Jupiter	Hope
Saturn	Autonomy, containment and self-determination
The Lunar Nodes	Purpose
The Progressed Moon	Belonging
Chiron	Our authentic humanness
Uranus	The soul story

Jupiter and Saturn are the social storylines of our life. They outline our common initiations during the life cycle. Although each return occurs near the same age for each person, the experience of the passage is personalized. As we mature with these cycles, we have more freedom and autonomy in consciously responding to the times. Jupiter returns every 12 years and celebrates the beginning of a new horizon of life. Each return of Jupiter is an initiation into a broader perspective and recognition of life's possibilities. Saturn's return marks three distinct phases of the life cycle, each activating a new sphere of responsibility and maturity. The first return at 29 signals the maturation, self-responsibility and authority of an individual as they claim their place in the world, while the next return at 58–59 demarcates a shift away from the outer world to the internal world. Review the Jupiter and Saturn cycle, as discussed in Chapter 6:

Jupiter's 12-year Cycle	Return/Beginning of the Cycle	Life Phase
1st cycle (0–12)	Birth	Childhood
2nd cycle (12–24)	12	Adolescence
3rd cycle (24–36)	23–24	Young adulthood
4th cycle (36–48)	35–36	Midlife
5th cycle (48–60)	47–48	Middle age
6th cycle (60–72)	59–60	Seniority
7th cycle (72–84)	71–72	Eldership
	83–84	

Saturn's 29+ year Cycle	Return/Beginning of the Cycle	Life Phase
1st cycle (0 to 29–30)	Birth	Youth
2nd cycle (29–30 to 58–59)	29–30	Adult
3rd cycle (58–59 to 88–89)	58–59	Elder
	88–89	

Chiron's return at 50 reveals the authentic and spiritual aspects of the self that are stifled by the necessity to conform to parental, cultural and social paradigms that have not suited us. Planetary returns of Jupiter, Saturn and Chiron mark thresholds of a lifetime and specify important transitional periods.

We can look at planetary returns from a collective viewpoint as well. For instance, in 2010 we experienced Neptune's return to its discovery degree. On 23 September 1846 the planet was first sighted after it had eluded astronomers for some time. On this date Neptune entered the collective awareness at 25° Aquarius. As Neptune reached this degree in 2010, humanity had experienced one full cycle of Neptune. Theoretically, although not necessarily experientially, the human race was now conscious of the archetypal nature of Neptune. It is interesting to note the many ways that this archetype, the god of the seas and also known as the 'Earth Shaker', has manifested since its discovery. At this planetary return a new vision can be contemplated, questioning how to collectively participate with this archetype in the next 165 years, mindful of what we understood from Neptune's previous cycle.

Astrologically, a technique called a return chart can be constructed when a planet returns to its natal position. The return chart focuses on the nature of the returning planet, encapsulating its prominent energies during its coming cycle. The horoscope for the precise time that the planet returns to its natal position is a map outlining the next cycle. The Sun returns each year; therefore, a solar return horoscope can be constructed each year. The Moon returns each 27.3 days; therefore, the lunar return chart can be calculated at this time. There will be thirteen lunar return charts annually. Mercury and Venus also return annually, whereas Mars will come back to its natal position every two years. For Mercury, Venus and Mars, there is also the possibility of a series of three returns if the planet turns retrograde after its first return and tracks back and forth over its natal position.

The return chart most widely used is the horoscope that is constructed annually for the Sun's return to its natal position. This chart symbolizes the renewal of the Sun on its annual birthday and as such is used as a tool to explore the archetypal energies of the coming year.

The Solar Return: The Sun's Homecoming
Solar returns are an ancient concept, as attested to by Firmicus Maternus in the 4th century CE. In the Hellenistic system a technique called *profections* acknowledged the annual cycle. A solar return technique was also used by the medieval Arab astrologers,

although not in the same way we use it today. During the 17th century William Lily, in *Christian Astrology*, and John Gadbury both mentioned the technique. However, it was Jean-Baptiste Morin de Villefranche who wrote more extensively on solar revolutions in *Astrologica Gallica*. In the 20th century the French astrologer Alexander Volguine developed his system of solar returns from Morin's foundation stones. Throughout the 20th Century solar return horoscopes gained popularity as a timing technique. In *Today's Astrology* (1941), Clement Hay's article 'Business Astrology' used the technique of a business solar return chart. Both sidereal and tropical astrologers began experimenting with this technique again in the later 20th century. As solar returns became popular in the last quarter of the century, different methodologies were proposed.

Birthday festivities ritualize the return of the Sun and the renewal of the spirit of birth. Since the Sun represents vitality and the light of the self, it is an important archetype to honour. As a renewal of solar energy, the solar return is an annual rebirth of our distinctiveness and purposefulness. It not only maps the potentialities of the year ahead but restates the soul's intention – the deeper motives behind our life experiences and the unfolding of our individuation process. The birthday, or celebration of the Sun's annual return, is one of the few rituals still celebrated in our society and one that importantly honours and recognizes the renewal of spirit.

The timing of each annual solar return will be within 24 hours of our birth time. The Earth's sidereal cycle or the return of the Sun is 356.256 days. The Sun returns to its natal position within approximately 6 hours each year due to the extra quarter day, which equates to about 6 hours. The solar return is an initiation into self-development, identity and purpose, focusing on important themes during the coming year. Each solar return chart, in effect, runs from one birthday to the next.

Generating a Solar Return Chart
Your solar return horoscope is calculated for the precise moment when the Sun returns to its natal position. In order to work with the angles and houses of a solar return chart, a fairly exact time of birth is needed. If the time of birth is not accurate then each solar return will be calculated on an incorrect premise. Every four minutes the

MC shifts 1°; therefore, one hour will shift the MC of the natal chart by approximately 15° or half a sign. An incorrect birth time will compound the error in subsequent solar return charts. On the other hand, this preciseness could be of value in helping to rectify or consider a more precise time of birth.

There are two important points to consider when constructing the solar return chart, as these details influence the angles. Let's consider two features that change the dynamic of the solar return horoscope: the precession of the equinoxes and the location for the solar return in a particular year.

Timing the Solar Return: The Precession of the Equinoxes

When we take precession into account, the *actual* zodiacal degree, minute and second on the ecliptic at the time of the Sun's return is not the Sun's actual natal position. The precessional rate of 50.26 seconds per year amounts to 1° of precession in 72 years. In other words, if we were born with the Sun at 0° Aries, by the age of 72 the *actual* position of the solar return Sun, taking precession into account, would be 29° Pisces, as the Sun will have recessed by 1° over these years. What we call 0° Aries in the tropical zodiac today would actually be 1° Aries if we were born 72 years ago. This is the zodiacal difference between the tropical and the sidereal zodiacs.[94]

Most western astrologers work with the tropical zodiac, which is a moveable zodiac, not tied to the fixed stars. Calculating the return to the precessed position of the Sun creates a distortion in the actual timing of the return, altering the position of the angles. My resolution is to be consistent and not use precession to calculate the solar return, since we do not use precession to time transits or other techniques. By using the tropical position, we are not literalizing the position of the Sun, but keeping it symbolic and metaphoric. Since we are accustomed to using a tropically-based zodiac in delineating natal charts, we need to be consistent by not mixing metaphors.

The Location of the Solar Return

There are three possibilities when determining where to locate the solar return. The first is the *birthplace*. Of course, this will always be where we cast the chart if we still live at our birthplace.

To learn the nature of the cycles within the solar return chart, I recommend that you generate all the solar returns of your life using your natal place of birth. Since all secondary progressed charts are derived from our natal chart, this is a viable and realistic horoscope to use. Calculating all our solar returns for our birthplace illustrates how planetary cycles develop, as well as demonstrating how the Sun and angles move each year. This is the primary consideration for the location of the solar return, as the essence of our life experience is derived from the birth chart. Therefore, we might consider this birth location as the *potential* of the solar return chart, showing the underlying motives and energies underpinning our experiences.

If you have relocated from your birthplace, there is another possibility for locating the solar return, which is the *place of residency* or *domicile*. If an individual has relocated, I use this location to cast the solar return if I am focusing exclusively on that year. If I am using a one-off solar return and I am looking for particulars about this year in the context of environment, then this is a helpful chart. However, for students still learning how to work with this technique, I recommend using the natal location.

If I were studying many solar return charts in the context of each other I would revert to using the birthplace. However, I have discovered that when looking at just one solar return chart as a stand-alone chart, the relocated solar return is very effective. The relocated solar return chart shows the manifestation of the potential, the areas where current experience and environment reflect what is developing at a deeper level. Therefore, the natal and relocated solar returns can be of assistance when used together. The natal underscores the developmental themes and deeper issues, while the relocated chart offers insights into where these might manifest. Applying transits and progressions to the relocated solar return chart is also very helpful.

The third option is to cast the horoscope at the *place where the individual celebrated their birthday*. This suggests that the solar return chart is determined by the place where we are on our birthday. This may also be valid, but certainly not if we specifically arrange to be in a particular spot to influence the return chart. Some astrologers have speculated that you can change the outlook of the year by changing the location of your solar return. I am not in favour of manipulating the solar return by changing places, as this attitude assumes that the house positions of the planets determine the outcome. However, if we have visited a specific location on our birthday in the spirit of pilgrimage, then this chart could be valid. This chart could be used as an accompanying chart to the other solar return charts (set either for the birthplace or place of residence) to study the variances between the charts – a mini relocated chart for the birthday.[95]

The solar return is a valid chart to use on its own or in tandem with transits and progressions. The outer planets' placements are transits that will be in effect for the year. The solar return considers the conditions of the upcoming year and its goals, challenges, interests and successes. This chart can be presented on its own, but it becomes dynamic when contrasted with the natal chart. The year is then examined in the context of the individual's natal temperament and disposition. This is my preferred option as it demonstrates continuity with natal patterns and whether these are repeated, supported or stressed. When evaluated with the natal chart, the solar return can be considered as the annual stage upon which certain natal patterns unfold. The solar return horoscope should be placed on the outside of the natal chart so it is evident in which natal houses these planets are placed. Use different colours to highlight the distinction between the natal planets and the solar return planets. Compare the solar return planets to the natal planets and houses, using the solar return angles, and include the Vertex.

In the next two chapters we will examine the perceptive technique of solar returns.

16

MANY HAPPY RETURNS
Rebirth and Renewal

Since the Sun is fixed at its birth position in the solar return, its synodic cycle with each planet is embedded in every solar return horoscope. This arrangement creates patterns that return to repeat at certain ages. To become familiar with these patterns, generate the solar returns for your lifetime using your birthplace, as this ensures that the angular and planetary patternings are maintained. Appendix 7 gives instructions on how to generate these horoscopes for your lifetime.

With each annual chart you will observe the successive movement of the angles and the planetary cycles. Patterns involving the angles, planets and the houses are evident when the same location is used; hence why I recommend calculating the solar return at your birthplace to begin your study. Changing the location of the solar return horoscope alters these annual patterns. Major relocations in our lives restructure the rituals and habits that we are accustomed to, altering patterns that may have become rigid and tedious; therefore, relocating the solar return can be very revealing when reflecting on the adjustments that changing location generates. But first, let's familiarize ourselves with designs created by successive solar returns generated from the natal birthplace.

Every sidereal year or 365.25 days, the Sun returns to its natal position. This will be about 6 hours later each year within 24 hours of the birth time. Using the same location each year, the solar return Midheaven advances by about 3 signs, staying in the same modality for about 9–11 years. Like the Wheel of Fortune, the MC shifts, turning the wheel of the chart about one quarter of the zodiac.

Angular Patterns in the Solar Return
In every solar return, the Sun is at the same degree, minute and second of zodiacal longitude as in the natal horoscope. Although the Sun is consistently at the natal longitude, its relationship to the MC–IC axis alters each year because this axis is moving forward

by zodiacal longitude. The MC's movement varies each year, but mostly fluctuates between 87° and 93° in moderate latitudes. In latitudes farther away from the equator, the movement can vary between 80° and 90° or more. Over time the MC slips back through the degrees of the zodiac; in four years the MC will have regressed anywhere from about 6° to 18°. This annual movement moves the Sun clockwise into the next quadrant.

Here is an example of Carl Jung's solar return MC movement in the first eight years of his life. Note the MC's movement through the signs every four years: from 29♏53 to 13♏18 to 3♏18. Over time, the MC slips back through the modalities, favouring one mode before it moves back into the previous one. By the age of 33, or in some cases 29, the angles return to their natal positions within an orb of a few degrees and the journey starts again.

	Natal MC	MC Mode	MC advances	Quadrant of the Sun	Comments
Birth	29♏53	Fixed		☌ DSC – 3rd/2nd quadrant	Jung was born at 48°N, so the MC has a wide range of fluctuation as it slips back through the fixed signs. The Sun is moving clockwise through the quadrants. Due to the birth latitude, these quadrants vary in size. In years when the Sun conjoins an angle, it is between quadrants.
Age 1	20♒53	Fixed	81°	1st quadrant	
Age 2	23♉10	Fixed	92°	4th quadrant	
Age 3	13♌03	Fixed	80°	3rd quadrant	
Age 4	13♏18	Fixed	90°	3rd quadrant	
Age 5	07♒09	Fixed	84°	☌ IC – 1st quadrant	
Age 6	08♉42	Fixed	91°	4th quadrant	
Age 7	01♌20	Fixed	82°	☌ MC – 4th quadrant	
Age 8	03♏18	Fixed	92°	3rd quadrant	

The return of the solar return MC to its natal position occurs in the 29th or 33rd year. In the case of Carl Jung, his solar return MC at age of 29 was 1♐32, within 2° of his natal MC of 29♏53.[96] His natal Ascendant is 2♒26; at age 29, the solar return Ascendant was 4♒49.

The age of 33 is often mythologized as being a significant one; age 29 marks the first Saturn return. Check your own sequence of solar returns to see at which age your angles return to their natal position. Below are four horoscopes that demonstrate the ages of 29 and 33, when the solar return angles replicate the natal angles. Note that in Marilyn Monroe's case the angles return exactly to their natal position at the age of 29. Similarly, Diana, Princess of Wales's angles are closer to the natal position at age 29 rather than age 33. John F. Kennedy Jr and Prince Charles's angles at age 33 are closer to their natal degrees. This return will again repeat 29 or 33 years later in the solar returns, linking these ages together in the life cycle. The degrees for the solar return MC and Ascendant closest to their natal positions are shown in bold in the following table.

	Marilyn Monroe 1 June 1926 9.30 a.m. Los Angeles CA, USA	Diana Spencer 1 July 1961 7.45 p.m. Sandringham England	Prince Charles 14 Nov 1948 9.14 p.m. London England	John F. Kennedy Jr. 25 Nov 1960 12.22 a.m. Washington DC, USA
NATAL MC	**06♉01**	**23♎03**	**13♈18**	**09♊18**
Solar Return MC at 29	**06♉03**	**21♎12**	23♈18	20♊19
Solar Return MC at 33	25♈59	11♎07	**15♈12**	**07♊16**
NATAL ASC	**13♌05**	**18♐24**	**05♌25**	**11♍58**
Solar Return ASC at 29	**13♌07**	**17♐01**	12♌00	21♍30
Solar Return ASC at 33	05♌11	09♐48	**06♌39**	**10♍13**

The Ascendant

The solar return Ascendant is derived from the position of the Midheaven, so they are intimately involved. In a symbolic sense the meridian, or vocational and familial destiny, shapes the horizon of personality and relationships. Depending on latitude, each MC partners with its own unique Ascendant; therefore, each solar return Ascendant has its own special relationship with the Midheaven.

The solar return Ascendant has no perceptible cycle, except that, like the MC, it will return at ages 29 or 33, subsequently repeating its position in the following returns. Since the MC moves each year, the angular relationship between the MC and the Ascendant will also change, especially at latitudes farther from the equator, because latitude influences the relationship between the MC and Ascendant. When the latitude is quite far north or south of the equator, the size of the quadrants in unequal house systems is altered, emphasizing different quadrant sizes each year.

If using a quadrant-based house system, note the phenomena of long and short ascending signs. Certain signs rise faster or slower than others, shaping the horoscope's quadrants in a certain fashion. Relocating the solar return, especially when there are great changes in latitude from the natal chart, shifts the natal relationship between the MC and the Ascendant. The northern signs of long and short ascension are reversed in southern latitudes; therefore, the angular relationship between the natal MC and Ascendant is altered when changing hemispheres.

The signs of long ascension rise slower than the average of two hours per sign, whereas signs of short ascension rise faster. If 0♋ or 0♑ is on the MC, 0♎ or 0♈ will be on the Ascendant.

	Southern Hemisphere	Northern Hemisphere
Signs of Long Ascension	♑ ♒ ♓ ♈ ♉ ♊	♋ ♌ ♍ ♎ ♏ ♐
Signs of Short Ascension	♋ ♌ ♍ ♎ ♏ ♐	♑ ♒ ♓ ♈ ♉ ♊

Due to long and short ascension, some signs may not be on a house cusp and other signs may be duplicated on two consecutive house cusps. This phenomenon of intercepted and duplicated signs highlights these sign qualities in the context of the solar return houses for the year. Intercepted signs symbolize issues that are not readily accessible in the house environment during the year. Duplicated signs suggest the affairs of the two houses bound by the same sign are enmeshed and difficult to separate this year. When using Equal or Whole Sign house systems, this will not occur.

Due to variances in latitudes and house systems, there will be inconsistencies in the patterns that the Sun forms as it returns each year. The pattern is always there but may diverge in certain years, which is interesting in itself. It is informative and revealing when we contemplate these rhythmic patterns that the Sun creates as the craftsman of the solar return horoscope.

When the Sun Comes Back

The Sun adheres to its own unique path through successive solar returns, stressing one quadrant annually, following a trail through the angular, succedent and cadent houses. Over 29 or 33 years, the Sun will have occupied every house. Using the same location, the Sun spends between 9 and 11 years in the angular houses, then takes up residence in the succedent houses for approximately the same period, and finally the cadent houses for the next 9–11 years. This cycle is not always so precise because of differing house sizes, whether the Sun is near a house cusp or in an intercepted polarity. Nonetheless, this is the habitual patterning of the Sun in consecutive solar returns.

Obviously when there is a change of pattern from cadent to angular, angular to succedent, or succedent to cadent, this suggests a qualitative change in our environment. As the central key to the solar return, the Sun's house position represents an area that will be significant in the coming year. When the Sun is angular, these are years for self-development, identity and building confidence and self-esteem. Stressing the angular houses for 9–11 years suggests identifying with the conception of ideas, pioneering projects, risk-taking and developing new avenues of interest. When the Sun begins to stress the succedent houses, an individual may acknowledge the importance of settling down, seeing things through to completion, stabilizing their life and being more focused on projects that are already underway. With the cycle of the Sun in cadent houses there is more innovation and change. The individual may feel more inclined to change their lifestyle and reinvent their identity.

Each year a different quadrant of the horoscope is in higher focus. Since Mercury and Venus are always close to the Sun, their positions may emphasize the same quadrant. When the trinity of the Sun, Mercury and Venus are in the same quadrant this is an area of personal interest for the coming year. We might reflect on the quadrants of the solar return horoscope in this way:

Quadrant/Houses	What the Sun Focuses On
1 Houses 1, 2 and 3	These houses represent fundamental images of self-development and identity: our personality, what we value and our communication style. This quadrant focuses on individuality, independence and self-awareness; therefore, the Sun shines its light on being self-motivated, resourceful and optimistic in the coming year.
2 Houses 4, 5 and 6	In these houses a deeper sense of personal security, self-care, self-expression and creative endeavours is forged. This quadrant focuses on developing attachments and rituals; therefore, the coming year identifies the need to honour the private self, develop security, become more self-disciplined and explore the imaginative and playful sides of the self.
3 Houses 7, 8 and 9	These houses explore developing relationships with 'other': that is, peers, equals and partners, as well as aspects of our intimate self and different ways of being in the world. In this quadrant we encounter relationship, whether that is with a partner, another aspect or quality of our self or a foreign culture. Educational experiences, our beliefs and ethics are featured. In the coming year an encounter with an unfamiliar aspect of the self is discovered through others.
4 Houses 10, 11 and 12	The experience of the self in the world is forged in this trinity of houses through our career, our society and our inner life. In this quadrant the focus is on the social self, experienced in the spheres of work, communal activities, spiritual and human values; therefore, the year ahead focuses on ways to enhance our role at work and in the community.

Transits of the Outer Planets to the Sun

Outer planet transits to the Sun are embodied in the solar return chart during the course of the transit. Because the outer planets move slowly through the zodiac, these major transits to the Sun continue to be solar aspects in subsequent solar returns. Imagine a major transit of Uranus conjoining the Sun. Using an orb of 5° for their solar return conjunction, the transit first appears in the solar return when Uranus and the Sun are together within an orb of 5°. Because Uranus will move approximately 4° during the year, the next solar return will have Uranus close to the Sun. In this year, they appear together within a degree or two. The next year the two planets will be together again, within 3° or 4°; therefore, three successive solar returns have Uranus conjunct the Sun within a close orb of 5°.

Neptune's movement of 2° a year elongates the Sun–Neptune transit. Using a 5° orb, the Neptune transit occurs over six solar returns. This may be even more pronounced for Pluto's transit, dependent on its speed through the zodiac. During six years of our life the transit of Neptune or Pluto to the Sun is highlighted. When using a 1° orb for transits, the time frame might be 18 months to 2 years; however, the solar return harnesses these transits for a longer period, specifying important areas each year according to the house the Sun occupies.

Let's use John F. Kennedy Jr as an example of how transits to the Sun become captured in the solar return horoscope. John Jr was born on 25 November 1960 in Washington, DC. The solar returns

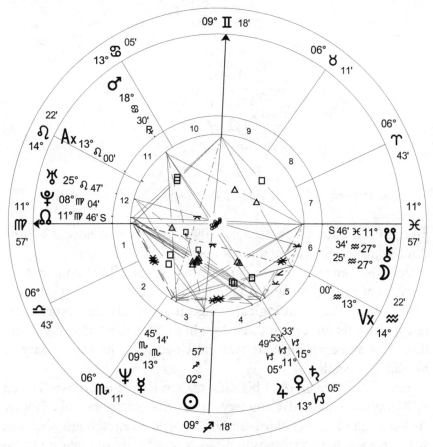

John F. Kennedy Jr
25 November 1960, 12.22 a.m. EST, Washington, DC, USA

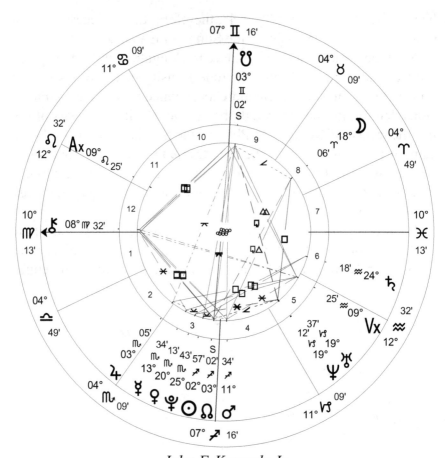

John F. Kennedy Jr
Solar Return: 25 November 1993, 00:13:20, Washington, DC

preceding his death on 16 July 1999 demonstrate how the Sun–
Pluto transits recurred in these horoscopes for five years.

John F. Kennedy Jr was born with Pluto at 8♏04 conjunct his
Ascendant at 11♍57, and square his Sun at 2♐57, which rules the
12th house. This astrological image mirrors his life experience,
having lost his father just three days before his third birthday. From
this early age each birthday was entwined with the anniversary of
his father's death.

On 25 November 1963 his father, John Kennedy, Sr, was buried
at Arlington National Cemetery. Later that same day his mother
Jackie organized his third birthday party, even though she was
still engaged with visiting dignitaries and heads of state after the
funeral. The famous picture of the young boy saluting at his father's

grave was taken on John Jr's third birthday, a few hours before his 3rd solar return.

John Kennedy Jr experienced his solar return on the day of his father's funeral, 25 November 1963, at 5.54 p.m. The solar return for the previous year of 1962 had the Sun conjunct the MC widely squaring Pluto at 12♍03. This chart was still in effect during the time when his father was assassinated three days earlier and buried. The burial occurred only a few hours before his 1963 solar return. The solar return for 1963 places Pluto in the 4th house.

Pluto rising natally captures the entwined experiences of life and loss, images forever woven together through the anniversary of John's father's death and his birthday. In 1993, when John Jr turned 33, the solar return chart returned to its natal angles. Mercury, the chart ruler, was also returning. Positioned at 13♏34, Mercury repeated its natal position of 13♏14 in the 3rd house. Pluto was at 25♏43 Scorpio in the 3rd house within a 7° orb to the angular Sun.[97]

Over the next few years Pluto would remain conjunct the Sun. Three of these conjunctions are angular in the five returns of the series, as follows:

Year	Sun is 02♐57 ☌ Pluto at:	House Position	Quadrant	Notes
1994	28♏10	1	1	Ascendant is 22♏07 – Pluto ☌ Sun is angular conjunct Ascendant
1995	00♐35	10	4	MC is 05♐21 –Pluto ☌ Sun is angular conjunct MC
1996	02♐59	6	3	
1997	05♐22	4	3	IC is 02♐28 – Pluto ☌ Sun in 4th house is angular, conjunct IC
1998	07♐43	1	1	MC is Leo; Ascendant is ♏ so the Pluto–Sun conjunction rules both angles

Pluto has transited from 28♏10 to 7♐43, conjoining the natal Sun of 2♐57 in each horoscope. In 1994 Pluto is angular and rules the Ascendant. In 1995 the Sun and Pluto are both angular; in the 1997 solar return the Sun and Pluto are again angular, this time on the IC. In the 1998 chart Pluto and the Sun rule the Ascendant and the

MC. The angularity of these conjunctions over this five-year period is a strong signal of the Pluto–Sun theme returning and repeating in John Jr's life.

These solar returns suggest the Pluto–Sun theme had been present for these five years and touched each quadrant of his life. Pluto conjunct the Sun moves clockwise through the quadrants each year, focusing on a particular quadrant during this period. John Fitzgerald Kennedy Jr died on 16 July 1999 during his 1998–9 solar return, which had 24♌43 on the MC with the North Node conjunct at 25♌52. Like his Aunt Kathleen and Uncle Joseph, John Jr died in a plane crash. Subsequent investigations timed the plane crash at 9.42 p.m. off the Massachusetts coast, approximately 12 kilometres from Martha's Vineyard.[98] Death occurred on impact. A death horoscope can be generated using this time. This chart represents the transits to both the natal and the current solar return charts. Such a dramatic event would be worth investigating.

Transits of note to the 1998 solar return chart were:

- Transiting Saturn was at 15♉32, having reached the solar return Descendant of 15♉37.

- The transiting South Node at 13♒01 was conjunct the solar return Moon of 13♒49, both of which conjoined John Jr's natal Vertex at 13♒00.

- The Ascendant of the death chart at 24♒43 is exactly conjunct the solar return IC at 24♒43 and the South Node at 25♒52.

- Transiting Pluto was at 8♐01, conjunct John Jr's natal IC at 9♐18, and the solar return Venus was at 9♐29 (conjunct the 7♐43 solar return Pluto).

Although we are using different timepieces, the symbolism of endings echoes throughout the solar return and the event chart, which also link to these themes in his natal chart. In retrospect, the timing is profound, not because it is predictable in any way, but because it reflects the mystery of time and renewal.

Planetary Patterns in the Solar Return Horoscope
Each year the zodiacal position of the Sun in a solar return is fixed
by its birth position. Therefore, every planet tracks its own unique
relationship pattern to the Sun over the lifetime course of solar
return horoscopes. To appreciate the continuity of solar returns it
is essential to understand each planet's cycle in relationship to the
Sun. The synodic cycles of the Moon, Mercury and Venus form
return cycles that accentuate certain years when the planet returns
to its natal position, emphasizing its archetypal nature during that
year. Let's begin by emphasizing the highlights of each planet's
relationship with the Sun before we place it in the context of the
solar return.

☽ *The Moon*
Every year the solar return Moon follows an elemental sequence.
The Moon's forward movement fluctuates between 125° and 145°,
and in successive solar returns it remains in the same element for
2–3 years before it progresses onto the next one. Infrequently, it
may remain in an element for only one year. It takes 8–11 years to
sequentially complete all the elements before it repeats its elemental
sequence. If the solar returns always use the same location, the
Moon advances counterclockwise through the chart for 8–11 years.
This occurs twice before the Moon returns to its natal position after
19 years.

This lunar design embedded in solar return horoscopes is due
to its synodic cycle, which limits its solar return positions to 19,
although an orb of difference occurs throughout the cycle. For
instance, Carl Jung's natal Moon is 15♉32. At age 19 it returned to
9♉26; at age 38 it came back to 9♉35; at age 57 it was at 14♉08 and
at age 76 it returned to 14♉40. Every 19 years since birth his Moon
returned to the natal 3rd house. In the subsequent years between
these ages, the 19-year pattern continues its 19-year synodic cycle.

The Moon's cyclical relationship to the Sun also repeats its
lunation phase every 19 years. Similar to the 19 approximate
positions of the Moon, a sequence of lunations will replicate
themselves. This sequence alters slightly if the lunation phase is
close to the cusp of another phase. Below are the first 19 lunation
phases for Carl Jung's solar returns, which form the template for the
sequencing of his lifetime phases. The solar return lunation phase at

age 19 is Last Quarter; at age 20 it is Crescent, and so on, repeating the 19-year pattern. Like the lunar nodes, this pattern reiterates the importance of 19 and multiples of 19. Each year is coloured by the solar return's lunation phase.

Solar Return	Moon	Zodiacal Forward Movement	Elemental Sequence	Lunation Phase Sun is 03♌18
Birth	15♉32		Earth	Last Quarter
Age 1	08♎04	143°	Air	Crescent
Age 2	13♒50	126°	Air	Full Moon
Age 3	19♊34	126°	Air	Balsamic
Age 4	07♏18	138°	Water	First Quarter
Age 5	27♓51	141°	Water	Disseminating
Age 6	03♌24	126°	Fire	New Moon
Age 7	08♐56	126°	Fire	First Quarter
Age 8	29♈26	140°	Fire	Disseminating
Age 9	17♍40	134°	Earth	New Moon
Age 10	23♑33	126°	Earth	Gibbous
Age 11	29♉00	125°	Earth	Last Quarter
Age 12	21♎11	142°	Air	Crescent
Age 13	07♓10	136°	Water	Full Moon
Age 14	13♋15	126°	Water	Balsamic
Age 15	19♏09	126°	Water	First Quarter
Age 16	13♈10	144°	Fire	Disseminating
Age 17	26♌48	134°	Fire	New Moon
Age 18	02♑46	126°	Earth	Gibbous
Age 19	09♉26	127°	Earth	Last Quarter
Average Forward Movement		132°		

☿ Mercury

From our geocentric standpoint, Mercury is never more than 28° away from the Sun. Therefore, Mercury has a limited zodiacal position in each solar return. There is a possibility of it being in only three signs, unless the Sun is within the first or last degrees of the sign, when the possibility is only two signs. One of these signs is the same as the Sun, but the other two will be elementally incompatible. Take note of the years when solar return Mercury is in an element psychologically distant or contradictory to natal Mercury, as these are years when new modes of learning and communicating may present themselves.

Mercury has a grand cycle with the Sun of 33 years; therefore, its position in the solar return chart will repeat every 33 years, highlighting the ages of 33 and 66 as a homecoming to the natal Mercury. For many at this age the solar return angles may also be repeating. As in the following table for Carl Jung's solar returns, at the ages of 33 and 66, Mercury replicates the natal placement, which continues the pattern for other ages every 33 years throughout his life.

Age at Solar Return	Mercury	Age at Solar Return	Mercury	Age at Solar Return	Mercury
Birth	13♋46	33	13♋35	66	13♋39
1	22♋09	34	23♋45	67	25♋32
2	10♌04	35	11♌41	68	13♌15

Due to the three synodic cycles between Mercury and the Sun each year there are also other ages when Mercury may return closer to its natal position, such as ages 13, 20, 46 and 53; however, the pattern may not always be repeated in these zodiacal degrees in later years. It is important to be aware of the solar return years when Mercury is near its natal position as there is a natural affinity with the Mercurial archetype that year. Here is an example of other ages when Carl Jung's Mercury is close to its natal position and when it repeats itself in this sequence.

Age at Solar Return	Mercury	Age at Solar Return	Mercury	Age at Solar Return	Mercury
Birth	13♋46	33	13♋35	66	13♋39
13	14♋37	26	16♋15	39	18♋52 R
20	13♋54	40	15♋38	60	18♋38
46	13♋58				
53	14♋21				

Mercury is retrograde 18–20% of the time. This proportion is also repeated in solar return horoscopes. Generally, Mercury will be retrograde once every 6 years, sometimes for 2 years in a row, with slight variances for each series of solar returns. When Mercury is retrograde the archetype is emphasized that year as a completion of plans or a recommencement of projects. For individuals with Mercury retrograde natally, the atmosphere for learning, planning, budgeting, taking in information, finishing assignments and making changes in these years feels more natural. Below are the 17 positions of Mercury retrograde in the solar returns for Carl Jung's lifetime; 20% of his solar returns had Mercury retrograde. Note the repetitions in the 33-year cycle; for instance, the retrograde position at age 5 repeats at ages 38 and 71; the retrograde position at age 6 repeats at age 39 within 2 to 3 zodiacal degrees.

Age at Solar Return	Mercury	Age at Solar Return	Mercury	Age at Solar Return	Mercury
5	19♌37 ℞	38	17♌04 ℞	71	14♌18 ℞
6	20♋54 ℞	39	18♋52 ℞		
18	23♌05 ℞	51	21♌00 ℞	84	18♌38 ℞
19	24♋49 ℞	52	22♋17 ℞	85	20♋03 ℞
25	12♌32 ℞	58	09♌28 ℞		
32	29♋23 ℞	65	26♋29 ℞		
45	04♌23 ℞	78	01♌16 ℞		

♀ Venus

Geocentrically, Venus is also close to the Sun, never more than 48° away, which confines its zodiacal position in each solar return to a possibility of 4 or 5 signs. Venus has a grand cycle with the Sun of 8 years; therefore, its position in the solar return chart repeats every 8 years, highlighting the ages of 8, 16, 24, 32, 40, 48, 56, 64, 72, 80 and 88, many of which are already significant due to simultaneous generic planetary patterns. The following table demonstrates the replicated zodiacal position of Venus in Carl Jung's solar returns. The positions of Venus will also be repeated in the successive 8-year sequences for the in-between years (ages 16–23; ages 24–31 and ages 32–39) not shown in the table. Each year there is a variance of almost 1°, except in the years when Venus is retrograde (shown in bold).

Solar Return from Birth to Age 7	Solar Return Venus	Solar Return from Ages 8 to 15	Solar Return Venus	Solar Return from Ages 40 to 47	Solar Return Venus
Birth (0–1)	17♋30	8 (8–9)	18♋04	40 (40–41)	20♋25
1 (1–2)	**15♋55 ℞**	9 (9–10)	**12♋59 ℞**	41 (41–42)	03♋14
2 (2–3)	24♌58	10 (10–11)	25♌32	42 (42–43)	27♌47
3 (3–4)	00♋15	11 (11–12)	00♋46	43 (43–44)	02♋51
4 (4–5)	18♍25	12 (12–13)	18♍09	44 (44–45)	16♍26
5 (5–6)	06♌37	13 (13–14)	07♌13	45 (45–46)	09♌37
6 (6–7)	18♊14	14 (14–15)	18♊26	46 (46–47)	19♊23
7 (7–8)	11♍44	15 (15–16)	12♍11	47 (47–48)	13♍52

If you are born with Venus direct and it is not in proximity to either stationary point, there are 8 consistent positions for your solar return Venus over your lifetime. Venus is generally retrograde for 1 year during this 8-year period, which then is repeated every 8 years, slipping back 2°–3° each year. If Venus is retrograde at birth or near its stationary points the pattern is not as precise, but it will still repeat its retrograde position every 8 years. There is also the possibility that Venus may change direction or signs in one of the sequences in the 8-year pattern. If this is the case the year is highlighted and points to significant changes in personal values, resources and relationships.

For instance, at age 41 in the solar return sequence for Carl Jung, Venus is no longer retrograde. It was retrograde for the first time in the solar return sequence at age 1, repeating every 8 years with an orb of 2°–3°. At age 41 in the sequence Venus was now direct and for the rest of Jung's life it would not retrograde in any future solar return. This year his inner turmoil due to his break with his former colleague Freud became more able to be expressed through significant publications on the concept of the unconscious. There were only five instances, or 6%, of Venus retrograde in Carl Jung's solar returns for his lifetime. Note the eight-year pattern.

Age at Solar Return	Venus
Age 1	15♋55 ℞
Age 9	12♋59 ℞
Age 17	10♋14 ℞
Age 25	07♋42 ℞
Age 33	05♋21 ℞
Age 41	03♋14 Venus is no longer retrograde in this sequence

♂ Mars

The Mars cycle of 780 days is the longest of all planetary synodic cycles, being twice as long as the outer planets' cycles with the Sun. This slower pulse of Mars and the Sun means its cycles do not repeat symmetrically. Mars's nature is to beat its own drum. While Mars's patterning is not always consistent in solar return horoscopes, it generally follows the elements through the zodiac, spending three or four years in each element before it progresses into the next, following the sequence of Fire, Earth, Air and Water. Some years may diverge from this procession. This uniformity of the elemental patterning is disturbed in the years before and after Mars is retrograde in the solar return chart. Mars retrograde is infrequent; therefore, the years when Mars is retrograde are important to note. Mars will be retrograde when in the zodiacal sector opposite the Sun, which includes the sesquisquare and the quincunx aspects.

The great cycle of Mars and the Sun is 32 years; therefore, Mars returns at age 32 within an orb of its natal position if it is not retrograde. This is the case in Carl Jung's solar return sequence as Mars was retrograde at age 32. Being retrograde, it did not return to its natal position in Sagittarius. This was the year that Jung met Freud. Like Freud, Jung had Mars in the 11th house and their collegial rivalry and competition contributed to the severance of their friendship. The Mars pattern was ruptured at age 32 due to it being retrograde, and highlights a change of direction or a turning point in Jung's life. It was his rivalry and differences with Freud that eventually encouraged him to champion his own way forward.[99]

The following table shows how Mars recurs through the elements, stressing a particular quality during the years in question. This also demonstrates the 32-year repetitive pattern of Mars, not always within orb, but reflective of its synodic cycle return.

Age at Solar Return	Mars	Element	Age at Solar Return	Mars
32	08♑04 ℞		64	28♑30 ℞
33	11♌51	Fire	65	14♌38
34	02♈00		66	12♈52
35	23♌49		67	26♌37
36	07♉40		68	12♉59
37	05♍51	Earth	69	08♍48
38	28♉19		70	02♊17
39	18♍32		71	21♍34
40	14♊43	Air	72	18♊08

Mars does not always repeat its natal position after 32 years due to its retrograde sub-cycle; nonetheless, the 32nd year is an important one in relationship to Venus. At age 32 solar return Venus also returns to its natal position; therefore, this age of 32 replicates the natal Venus–Mars synergy – the synodic cycle between Mars and Venus. For instance, on 22 February 2024, Venus and Mars conjunct at 6♒57, a renewal of their cycle that occurred 32 years earlier on 19 February 1992 at 1♒00. It is as if Venus and Mars exchange vows once again, suggesting this timeframe is important in the life cycle of relationships. At age 64 this pattern will repeat.

Let's revisit our four public figures to demonstrate the simultaneous returns of Venus and Mars at age 32 in their solar returns (see the table on the next page). In Marilyn Monroe's case her natal Venus is in late Aries and has now entered Taurus within orb. John F. Kennedy Jr's natal Mars is retrograde; therefore the pattern is altered. At 32 the retrograde does not repeat.

	Marilyn Monroe	Princess Diana	Prince Charles	John F. Kennedy Jr.
Natal Venus	28♈45	24♉43	16♎23	11♑53
Solar Return Venus at Age 32	00♉19	25♉10	18♎28	13♑42
Natal Mars	20♓43	01♍38	20♐56	18♋30 ℞
Solar Return Mars at Age 32	25♓49	04♍45	24♐24	27♋30

♃ Jupiter

Jupiter's movement through the zodiac is consistent, being retrograde once a year for four months. When Jupiter is direct it traverses approximately 40° of the zodiac in nine months before it retrogrades back 10° over the next four months. Therefore, each year Jupiter moves forward by 30° in total, advancing by one sign every solar return. Since its cycle is twelve years, it occupies each sign of the zodiac in twelve successive solar returns. It moves through the solar return in a clockwise direction, averaging two houses per year. Three or four of Jupiter's positions over the twelve years will be retrograde, usually in a sequence.

♄ Saturn

Each year Saturn moves clockwise by two or three houses. Predictably, Saturn follows the quadrants through the chart. It moves forward by about 12°–13° each solar return, remaining in one sign for two or three returns before it proceeds to the next sign. If Saturn is retrograde, it will remain retrograde over subsequent returns. It is important to note the year when Saturn changes direction in the succession of solar returns, as this might signal a shift in attitude towards hierarchy, responsibility and commitment.

⚷ Chiron

Chiron travels through the zodiac at different rates of speed depending on its sign. It travels through Libra in under two years and Aries in nearly eight years. Therefore, in an average lifetime there are about two solar returns with Chiron in Libra, but seven or eight returns with Chiron in Aries. Chiron is retrograde each year and, like the outer planets, remains retrograde in a succession of solar return charts; therefore, it is important to note the years when

Chiron changes direction in the sequence. Just as with the outer planets, the sign position is not as important as the house position since every individual will share the same solar return sign position for the coming year. However, if Chiron changes direction in the sequence this might suggest a turning point in a healing process, with a different attitude towards feelings of marginalization and self-acceptance.

♅♆♇ *Uranus, Neptune and Pluto*

Uranus's annual movement is 4°–5°; Neptune is 2° while, at the time of writing (2020), Pluto averages 2° per year. The minimal movement of these planets suggests that they will rotate in the same way as the Sun; hence they generally move clockwise by about three houses each year through the quadrants of the horoscope.

As with the Sun, their pattern of movement focuses on the angular houses, then the succedent houses and then the cadent houses. However, this will need to be confirmed in each case. If an outer planet is transiting the Sun then the aspect will repeat itself in successive solar return charts, thereby emphasizing the transit, as previously mentioned. Since the outer planets go retrograde and direct in proximity of the same zodiac degrees every year, they will remain retrograde in solar return charts over extended periods. Note the year when an outer planet changes direction in the chain of solar returns. This year signals a change in the experience and focus of this outer planet.

Each planet in the solar return adds its own flavour to the menu of the year. Therefore, it is helpful to familiarize yourself with the annual movement of each one. Let's review their yearly movement and affect.

Summary of the Cycles in the Solar Return
The following précis recapitulates the information we have studied:

The Midheaven
The MC will advance by about 3 signs each year. At the age of either 29 or 33 the solar return mirrors the natal angles.

The Lunar Nodes
The lunar nodes will retrograde by approximately 18°–20° between each solar return.

☉ *The Sun*
In successive solar returns the Sun moves about three houses clockwise, highlighting one quadrant each year. On average, the Sun spends 9–11 years in angular houses, and then slips back to the succedent houses for another 9–11 years.

☽ *The Moon*
The Moon moves forward by approximately 125°–145° every year, sequentially following the elements. It spends on average 2 to 3 solar returns in one element and takes approximately 8–11 years to complete one full elemental round. There are 19 positions of the solar return Moon; therefore, at the age of 19, the Moon repeats the sequence of the first 19 years of life. The Moon also travels counterclockwise through solar return horoscopes, progressing anywhere between 0 and 3 houses each year.

☿ *Mercury*
Mercury is always within 28° of the Sun and returns to its natal position at age 33; however, it can also be close to its natal position at ages 13, 20, 46 and 53. It is generally retrograde every sixth solar return.

♀ *Venus*
Venus is always within 48° of the Sun. Due to its patterning with the Sun there are only 8 possible placements of Venus in the solar return. These positions repeat sequentially every 8 years within a 1° orb, except when Venus is retrograde. Venus is generally retrograde for 1 year during this 8-year period.

♂ *Mars*

Mars generally follows the elements through the zodiac, spending about 3–4 years in an element before it moves on. This is altered when the solar return Mars is retrograde.

♃ *Jupiter*

Jupiter moves approximately 1 zodiacal sign each solar return, moving clockwise by about 2 houses a year.

♄ *Saturn*

Saturn moves an average of about 12° each year and will move clockwise throughout the solar return horoscopes by about 2–3 houses each year.

⚷ *Chiron*

The movement of Chiron is dependent on its sign: it moves fastest in Libra and slowest in Aries. It moves in a clockwise direction for each solar return.

♅ *Uranus*

Uranus travels about 4° from one solar return to the next, moving in a clockwise direction by about 3 houses per year. This varies from year to year, but over 14 years Uranus will probably have tenanted in each house.

♆ *Neptune*

Neptune travels about 2° from one Solar return to the next, and clockwise by approximately 3 houses.

♇ *Pluto*

Pluto's speed is not regular through the zodiac. During the early part of the 21st century it will travel about 2° forward in the zodiac annually, moving in a clockwise direction by about 3 houses, although this may vary.

Now that we are familiar with the patterns of the solar return, we can engage more of our right brain to contemplate and imagine what these patterns might suggest or reveal from year to year.

17

WHAT'S IN STORE?
Considering the Year Ahead with Solar Returns

To work with solar returns effectively, become familiar with the cycles within the annual return, as presented in Chapter 16. Each planet highlights a point in its annual cycle, revealing how that planet will serve, support or challenge the developing identity and character in the coming year. In knowing these cycles you can differentiate and prioritize the solar return patterns. Since the solar return represents the time that has elapsed from one birthday to the next, each chart has a use-by date. Therefore, it is essential to contextualize the chart in respect of the stage of the life cycle that it covers. In a sense, the solar return is a supplementary chart that identifies the archetypal patterns that support and challenge the evolving self during the year. As an auxiliary chart it can be delineated like a natal horoscope, acknowledging this time period.

The study of these returns over a lifetime is an informative biographical tool, especially when contemplating the early years when the psychodynamic forces that underpin behaviour and mental states are psychically impressed upon the child. Solar returns for the first few years of life reveal other dimensions in understanding the family atmosphere, early conditions, influences and experiences. Early solar return charts are snapshots of the formative years.

Using the solar return chart in tandem with the natal chart is most revealing, as our perspective becomes more comprehensive and holistic. It is also beneficial to look at the previous and following solar returns to place the current one in the perspective of recurring cycles. When considering the solar return, reflect on what makes this chart unique. Before any interpretation, be aware of any impressions that you have about the shape of the chart, the planetary distribution throughout the houses, any angular planets, etc. First impressions are often very applicable to the 'feeling' of the chart and its potential meaning.

Be aware of the current planetary ambience, because each solar return exists within the context of the outer planets' relationship to each other during that year. Since the outer planets' zodiacal positions and aspects linger over time, every solar return will reflect these conditions. For instance, everyone's solar returns have Pluto in Capricorn from 2008–23. Uranus will start to appear in Gemini in 2025. Neptune will be in Aries in some 2025 solar returns. During certain years the outer planets' inter-aspects stay in orb, so a majority of solar returns will have these planetary arrangements embedded. For instance, Jupiter is square Saturn during 2024–25 and many solar return charts capture this aspect. During this same period Saturn is semi-square Pluto, so solar returns also reflect this aspect. When a personal planet or angle is constellated with this aspect, the individual is challenged to have a more personal relationship with this planetary dynamic during the year.

Delineating a horoscope is personal, and the most effective method will be forged out of your own experience and intuition. Your approach to solar returns will be crafted from your skill of interpreting natal charts. Here are some ways to consider solar return horoscopes that I find effective, and I encourage you to examine these when developing your own methods. Since the chart represents a moment in time, that moment being a year, symbols and images are often more immediate and perceptible as being symbolic of a year, not a lifetime.

Working with Solar Returns
Each solar return chart echoes the unfolding potentialities of the birth chart. Therefore, while the solar return chart can be read separately, it becomes animated when contrasted to the natal chart. Sometimes solar return patterns repeat birth themes, or angular and planetary positions challenge the natal disposition. Each solar return is like a colourful thread woven into the tapestry of life. Sometimes I think of these charts like photographs in an album of my life.

As we explore ways of thinking about these annual horoscopes, I will comment on Carl Jung's solar return horoscope for 1906. During this year he met Sigmund Freud, a turning point in his life, as discussed when we looked at his secondary progressed chart.

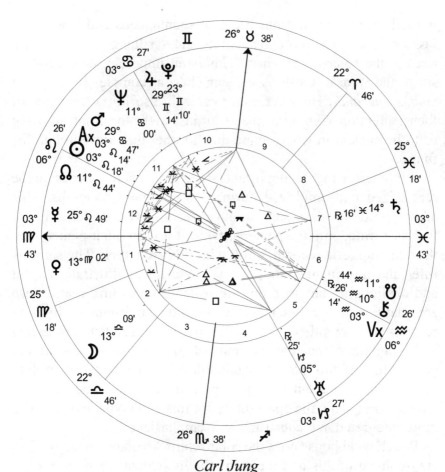

Carl Jung
Solar Return: 27 July 1906, 07:43:51, Kesswil, Switzerland

The Ascendant

The Ascendant of the solar return symbolizes personality attributes that are becoming more apparent and pronounced during the year. The Ascendant is like a costume that might be worn more comfortably during the year, even though it may not be a natural fit. Each year the solar return Ascendant distinguishes a quality that is in focus or being reborn over the course of the year. It is the engine of the personality and the conductor of vitality and energy for that year. If the sign is not compatible with the natal Ascendant, adjustments or compromises in our style of presentation might be necessary. If the element on the Ascendant conflicts with that of the natal rising sign, consider ways that your vitality and energy could be best exercised. For instance, a natal Fire Ascendant, which is used to moving out into life in a spontaneous and headstrong fashion, may feel more restrained and challenged when Earth rises in the solar return chart. This is an important consideration since the year's Earth Ascendant has a completely different *modus operandi*. However, that year will also bring the value of focus, direction, commitment and purpose to the forefront, allowing us to be present in what we are doing rather than rushing into the future.

A planet rising is important since this energy needs to be recognized and employed during the coming 12 months. This archetype demands attention and direction. If the planet is not well integrated into the personality, or if it is an outer planet, then the year suggests reconciliation with this archetype. The sign, its ruler and any planets conjunct the Ascendant illustrate helpful and challenging energies that lie in front of us this year. These are qualities that will be projected onto the environment, inviting responses from others. The ruler of the Ascendant represents a driving force that can be applied to start the engine of the personality. If this planet is underdeveloped or uncomfortable, then it challenges our ability to be self-motivated and directed. On the other hand, the opportunity for this archetypal energy to be more integrated and constructive is emphasized.

Which natal house does the solar return Ascendant occupy? The environment of this house colours the individual's horizon for the next 12 months. In a way, this natal house rises to the Ascendant for the year, bringing its experiences, issues and concerns to the forefront. Individuals represented by this natal house, such as siblings (the 3rd house), parents (the 4th house), children (the 5th house), workmates (the 6th house), equal others and partners (the 7th house), friends (the 11th house), etc., may be more visible during the year. There are opportunities to cultivate a more conscious relationship with these individuals.

The Ascendant is the most prominent and visible aspect of the solar return horoscope. Often an event or an individual symbolizing the rising sign or planets near the Ascendant reveals itself shortly after the Sun returns. The Ascendant represents birth and the solar return Ascendant indicates the prevailing conditions and atmosphere near the time that the year dawns. It is of interest to note your local time for each year's solar return to be aware of the conditions, moods, experiences and events that occur near the time the Sun returns.

In Carl Jung's 1906 solar return, the Ascendant of 3♏43 falls in his natal 7th house, conjoining his natal Vertex at 4♏52. This is a mirror image of the solar return Vertex at 3≈14 conjunct his natal Ascendant at 2≈26. The interconnection between angles and nodes is a recurring image that I have often noticed when significant encounters occur.[100] With the Ascendant–Vertex interchanges I would be alert to the possibility of encounters with significant others, crossroads and karmic relationships. With the Ascendant being in the natal 7th house, significant others and partners are highlighted as this area of life moves to the forefront.

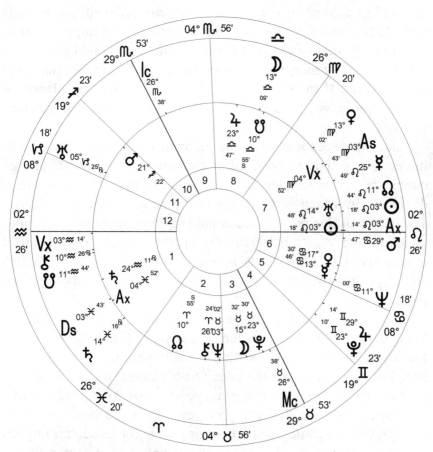

Carl Jung Natal Chart (Inner Wheel)
Carl Jung 1906 Solar Return (Outer Wheel)

The Midheaven

The MC in the solar return suggests the goalposts for the coming year: what is important to achieve, what considerations do I need to be mindful of in my career and what might I do to augment my life path? As the spinal column of the horoscope, the meridian axis structures and supports the ability to be successful and fulfilled. The MC represents conditions in our world, evoking themes of autonomy, influence and self-maturation in relation to our vocational path; therefore it also symbolizes our relationship with authority. In the early solar returns from the first year to adolescence, the MC signifies the rules, expectations, directions and goals of the parental and societal authorities. In adult solar returns it represents the striving for personal authority and excellence, as well as the personification of powerful and controlling figures in our professional environment. As an axis which also symbolizes the familial atmosphere, it is important to be alert to shifts in the familial hierarchy if the MC is highlighted. The MC for the year suggests the need to consider career options and opportunities. If the solar return MC is emphasized by planets or strong aspects, vocational issues will be an important theme during the year.

Like the Ascendant, note the element of the solar return MC in contrast to that of the natal chart. When an incompatible sign culminates, new elements challenge you to diversify your career direction. In which natal house is the solar return MC placed? The nature of this natal house could play a prominent role in your direction and vocational goals during the year. If a natal planet is near the degree of the solar return MC, contemplate how this archetype may be employed through your career goals or in the public arena.

Planets near the MC in the solar return characterize what is brought to public attention during the year. These planets try to find expression through vocational goals, seeking to achieve and be acknowledged during the year. Outer planets, including Saturn, conjunct the MC indicate important years in terms of an individual's direction in the world. For a younger person this could manifest through their education and schooling, while for an adult it implies career opportunities, challenges and changes. A planet conjunct the solar return MC demands to be utilized vocationally during the coming year; therefore, it needs conscious attention directed towards it.

If there is a major transit or progression to the natal MC, then the solar return MC can help to amplify this development. The solar return MC will add perspective and detail to what has already been implied through the natal horoscope's transits or directions. The sign on the solar return MC will suggest a quality while a planet will suggest an important energy arising during the year.

In Carl Jung's 1906 solar return, the MC is 26♉38 which is conjunct his natal 3rd house Pluto at 23♉30 and the IC at 29♉53. This speaks to me of a year when powerful ideas and connections transform his worldview. His vocation impacts his deeply private self and the foundations on which he builds his life.

Angular Planets
A planet becomes emphasized on an angle since it focuses its archetypal nature on a particular life direction. Consider an angular planet like a red flag demanding our attention, alerting us to be more conscious of its nature and impact upon our lives. In the solar return an angular planet has top priority when considering the atmosphere or 'feeling' of the year. An outer planet has immediate impact because it represents something beyond familiar boundaries that now exerts its influence over this sphere of life. This may be experienced as feeling out of control, overwhelmed or inspired. An outer planet suggests the need to let go of preconceptions and control mechanisms, to simply go with it. Something outside our peripheral awareness is potentially able to manifest during the year. With an angular outer planet, the repercussions can reverberate for many years; in other words, this year may only be the opening or beginning of experiencing a new aspect of ourselves.

With Jupiter or Saturn angular, consciousness of social and educational developments is emphasized. An impetus to reach outside familial and social limits arises. An angular inner planet suggests a more personal encounter with the psyche during the year. For instance, an angular Moon might present itself through the impulse to be settled, to change or renovate the home, through feelings and desires for emotional connection or perhaps bodily changes, such as shifts in weight or physical reactions.

All lunar manifestations are a personal striving for security and nurturance.

The specific angle suggests where this energy is focused. Differentiate each angle separately. A planet on the IC concentrates its archetypal nature on the deepest realms of inner security, the family of origin, the home, domestic concerns and living conditions. The IC is our foundation stone, the touchstone of early conditioning and familial patterns. Therefore, a solar return planet, and especially an outer planet, on the IC signals revelations and changes in the way we feel about our family of origin or shifts in the way we experience our family during the year. For younger people, this suggests security, the nature of the current relationships within the familial circle and also how to separate and form alliances outside the family. For adults, the solar return IC includes our family of choice and the repetition of childhood patterns that influence our own parenting. Planets on the IC need to ground and familiarize their energies so they can be more centred and grounded for the coming year. With planets on the meridian both the private and public self need to be acknowledged. When this axis is tenanted, the awareness of balancing the need for privacy and solitude with the urge to be fulfilled and successful in the world is emphasized. The spheres of home and career jointly need attention and our task is to manage to fulfil them both.

Planets on the solar return Descendant focus their archetypal nature on the arena of relationships, especially equal relationships, whether personal or professional. Psychologically, we are becoming more aware of this planetary energy within ourselves through our contact with others in areas outside our normal routines. Planets on the Descendant suggest a growing awareness of relational patterns and how we unconsciously contribute to their repetition through adult relationships. When on the horizon of the solar return, planets suggest that themes of self and other are important during the year. The planet's nature gives us the clue as to how this might manifest.

☉ Transits to the Natal Sun

As the solar return Sun replicates its natal zodiacal position, major transits to the Sun will be set into the landscape of the solar return. In the previous chapter, we witnessed John F. Kennedy Jr's Pluto transit to the Sun being evident over five years of solar returns.

Solar return charts provide another level of insight into outer planet transits to the natal Sun. The solar return shows where important transformations are taking place during any particular year of the transit. As the Sun's house position changes each year, it highlights a different quadrant of experience. This environment is where consciousness is directed and where identity is challenged to develop. The house positions of the Sun and the transiting planet in the solar return can help to distinguish areas where the transit may be intensified during the year.

The house positions of the Sun and its transiting planet give clues to important environments and issues that need to be considered. When this aspect reappears in the following solar return, the house positions will have changed, focusing the transit on other areas for that year.

☽ *The Moon*

The Moon gathers the nuances of personal experience and weaves these feelings, innuendos, perceptions, dreams and impressions into memory. The Moon represents feeling memory and is the mechanism through which the felt experience of the environment, especially the familial sphere, is imprinted upon the individual. Therefore, the solar return Moon will most likely manifest in areas of personal and emotional security and safety, such as the home, family, living conditions, domesticity, emotional connections, moves, residency, etc. It highlights emotional relationships, especially familial and close personal attachments, as well as feelings, moods and a sense of contentment. Like the progressed Moon, the solar return Moon reflects and records the emotional development and maturation of the individual during the year.

We have already noted the repetitive and ordered cycle of the Moon in solar return charts. Its movement through the houses and the elements expresses its annual progress and its 19-year pattern identifies the repetition of its cycles. Take note of the individual's age and the previous ages when the Moon would have been in the same sector. For instance, if the individual is 39 years old then the solar return Moon was in the same sector 19 years previously, at age 20, and 19 years before that, at age 1. This allows you to immediately connect the emotional developments of the year with previous years that may be impacting the feelings this year. Remember to contextualize this 19-year pattern when addressing the solar return Moon, as a trinity of images is repeating, including the lunation phase and the lunar nodes.

The Moon also follows the elements in succession through solar returns; therefore, notice which element the solar return Moon occupies this year. Is the element compatible with the natal Moon? If not, this could suggest being more aware emotionally during the year. Has the element shifted since the last solar return? If the sequence of the elements has changed, contemplate the possibility of new emotional developments. The Moon gathers emotional experiences; therefore, its continuity from one return to the next is important to recognize in terms of memory.

The house position of the solar return Moon indicates the emotional terrain during the year, and it may also indicate the area of life where:

- We are responsive to impressions, dreams and feelings
- We discover a reservoir of feelings and memories
- We are more emotionally engaged
- We are able to be more conscious of our attitudes, instincts, feelings, motives and responses
- We recognize habitual behaviour and emotional patterns

Aspects to the Moon delineate the emotional climate of the year. Years when outer planets are aspecting the Moon, especially by conjunction, opposition or square, are years when habitual routines and emotional security are confronted. Compare the solar return Moon to the natal Moon. What natal house does the solar return Moon occupy? Does it make any aspects to natal planets? If so, it is important to recognize the influence these planets are exerting on our emotional well-being and safety in the coming year.

In Carl Jung's 1906 solar return, the Moon is 13♎09, quincunx Saturn, widely square Uranus and square to Neptune. It occupies his natal 8th house, conjunct his South Node. Being in Air it is incompatible with his natal Taurus Moon. Both Moons are quincunx each other; however, both are ruled by Venus. The solar return Moon squares his natal Mercury–Venus conjunction in the 6th house. With the solar return Moon conjunct the natal South Node, a legacy of past feelings is ready to be released. Its square to the 6th house Mercury and Venus suggests psychological readjustments in work, health and well-being, or quite literally with workmates. Nineteen years earlier (at 12 years old) was a traumatic year. At school Jung was forcefully pushed to the ground, resulting in his confinement at home for several months. It would be interesting to have discussed how these two periods may have been connected in his experience.

Lunation Phase
The lunation phase symbolizes the overall mood of the year and suggests an individual's frame of mind and disposition for the year in question. Each phase suggests a different atmosphere for the overall climate of the year. The lunation cycle can be used effectively in solar returns to illustrate an overall perspective on the year and to question the motives, goals and values of this year. In a way of thinking, the lunation phase considers the resolutions that are needed for the year: being conscious of what the larger issues of life are during the course of the year.

It is revealing to consider the solar return lunation phase in context of the progressed lunation phase. Each progressed lunation phase lasts between three and four years, whereas the solar return lunation phase changes annually. Therefore, the solar return lunation phase is different each year from the current progressed phase.

The lunation phase for Carl Jung's 1906 solar return is Crescent. In his progressed lunation cycle he is at the final few degrees of the Last Quarter Moon. Both phases feel transitional, with the current year's phase revealing that images from the past are arising to challenge and shape the way forward.

Over the page is an exploration of the lunation phases in the context of the annual solar return.

Solar Return Lunation Phase	Prevailing Climate of the Year
New Moon	Is this a year of beginnings? Do you sense that there is a subtle change of direction? A New Moon suggests following your hunches, trusting your instincts and spontaneously responding to the opportunities that are presented.
Crescent	Is this a year of adjustments? Do you need to recognize attitudes and values from the past which are no longer appropriate? Is this a year to change past patterns that hold you back? The Crescent Moon recommends a year of exorcizing past ghosts that still haunt the present.
First Quarter	Is this a year of change and a year to take risks? Do you feel the necessity to act even though you are not clear on your goals? Do you feel restless and yearn to act impulsively? The First Quarter lunation phase implies that this is a year of action and change. Even though the goalposts may not be in sight or your plans may not have been well thought through, it is a year to trust your instincts and your hunches.
Gibbous	Is this a year to plan and concentrate on the tasks at hand? Do you need to be more restrained and committed to the processes that involve you? Do you need to be more prepared and educated? The Gibbous phase advocates being prepared by accumulating the appropriate information, techniques and tools to ensure the success of your projects.
Full Moon	Is this a year of realization and reflection? Do you feel the need to be more in touch with yourself, to understand and reflect on the nature of who you are? The Full Moon phase suggests a culmination of what you have been working towards as well as a clearer reflection of who you are and where you are heading.
Disseminating	Is this a year to put yourself forward, spread your innovative ideas and be more confident about your creativity? Do you need to be more socially active or influential? The Disseminating phase is a time to express your talents and share what you are working on. It is a highly creative year when you can exert influence on the individuals and the environment surrounding you.
Last Quarter	Is this a year when you need to re-examine your values? Reassess your goals? Re-address your lifestyle? Do you feel more inner-motivated rather than outer-focused? Is it important for you to take stock of what is happening in your life and re-examine where you are? The Last Quarter phase is a time of reorientation and questioning, a year of introspection and assessment, a time of stock-taking.

Balsamic	Is this a year of endings? Do you feel it is time to let go of what is not working? Do you feel the need to retreat in order to be in touch with deeper aspects of yourself? Is it a time of dreams and visions? The Balsamic phase evokes an ending of some attachments in your life and brings with it the necessity to find quality time to gestate new potentials that can be seeded in the new cycle. It is a time when deeper levels of the psyche are encountered through dreams and impressions.

The Planets and Lunar Nodes

Each solar return planet needs to be considered on its own merit – its sign and house position, aspects, cycle and any other important considerations – retrograde, intercepted, rulership, etc. The signs of the social and outer planets are not important personally, as most people will have those sign placements in their solar returns for that year. These planets represent collective energies for the year. Similarly, any major aspects between outer planets will be part of the landscape of the year. What is important to note is each planet's house position, as this personalizes the archetypal experience and points to where its energies may be focused during the year. Since there is so much to consider I would prioritize angular planets first, then planets having multiple aspects.

I suggest comparing the solar return planet to the natal horoscope in the following fashion:

- Which natal house does the solar return planet fall in?
  This house may indicate the area where some of the issues
  pertaining to this planet may arise.

- Compare the element of each inner planet to its element in the
  natal chart. Is this a compatible or incompatible element? If
  the element is incompatible then the function of this energy
  may be more challenged during the year.

- Does the solar return planet make any powerful aspects to
  natal planets? I only consider stronger aspects here. If so,
  recognize that these energies may need to cooperate with each
  other during the year to be effective. Be especially aware if
  the solar return planet falls on a natal angle, as this highlights
  the need to address its archetypal nature.

In considering each of the planetary energies it is helpful to address each one's needs for the coming year. Once you have examined the nature of the planet in the solar return, as well as how it affects the natal chart, question its role during the coming year. The inner planets reflect personal and more intimate questions:

- Sun: What do I need to identify and become conscious and mindful of in the coming year?

- Moon: Where do I need to find shelter and nurturing? How can I feel more secure with those I am attached to?

- Mercury: What do I need to communicate and learn this year?

- Venus: What is important for me to value and appreciate? Which patterns of relating do I need to become more conscious of during the coming year?

- Mars: What do I need to explore and aim for during the year? Where could I be more independent and adventurous?

Of interest in Carl Jung's 1906 solar return are the lunar nodes aspecting natal Uranus. The North Node conjunct the 7th house Uranus points to being engaged with independent and equal others in the community, while the South Node draws on the resources of Jung's self-awareness. Solar return Mars is conjunct the Sun which conjoins the natal Descendant, also bringing the themes of independence and others into focus; however, this might also suggest some rivalry, confrontation and competition arising in the environment of communal others.

Aspects and Aspect Patterns
First consider the orbs that you will use for solar return aspects. Often these are smaller than those used in natal charts. It is important to ascertain the closest aspects and prioritize which of these are the most important. To begin your study of solar return horoscopes, I suggest that you consider using tighter orbs than you do in a natal chart analysis: for instance:

Conjunction:	6 degrees	Opposition:	6 degrees
Square:	5 degrees	Trine:	4 degrees
Sextile:	3 degrees	Quincunx:	3 degrees

In a solar return horoscope, any major aspect pattern is a prominent feature of the yearly horoscope and suggests important developments over the upcoming year. Consider the nature of the planets involved and the houses they occupy and rule. Apply the same procedure as you would in delineating aspect patterns in a natal chart, being mindful that the aspect is operative only in the upcoming year. If two or more outer planets are in aspect, nearly all solar returns for that year will have the same aspect. If these outer planets are in aspect to one of the inner planets, this suggests how the individual deals with these collective energies personally during the year. Consider a major aspect pattern a priority in the solar return delineation.

Chart Shapes

The chart shape is a visual snapshot of the way an individual's energy during the year could be expressed, channelled or dispersed; therefore, take note of the shape and distribution of these planetary energies. If the majority of planets is above the horizon then the year is influenced by the outer world and its events. In contrast, if the majority of the planets is below the horizon, the year might be more subjective and introspective, more inner-orientated than outer-directed. If most of the planetary energies are focused on the eastern hemisphere then the individual may want to act more independently, making choices and taking action on their own. If most of the planets are on the western side of the chart, this presents the opposite perspective: choices, actions and experiences are entwined with others.

The visual shape of the chart is a dynamic clue to imagining how the planetary energies are distributed and expressed during the coming year. Using Marc Edmund Jones's seven horoscope shapes, which he described in his book *The Guide to Horoscope Interpretation*,[101] we could speculate how we might experience our energies during the year. If the chart shape is not clear, it is best not to try to fit this into one of the categories. Again, this is only a way of thinking, not a definite delineation:

- The Splash occurs when the planets are evenly distributed around the horoscope, generally with one planet in each house; therefore, there are two empty houses. During the year there may be a wide horizon with many varied experiences, different interests and a potential ability to relate to many things. Caution is needed so the individual does not scatter their resources all over the place by rushing off in many directions without firm goals or commitments.

- The Bundle contains all the planets within a trine; therefore, one third of the horoscope is emphasized while two thirds of the horoscope have no planets. In some cases, this stresses a specific quadrant of the chart and generally there is a stellium within the Bundle. The energetic level of the year is focused and concentrated. During the year there may be an opportunity to make something successful out of a difficult beginning by using the raw materials at hand. A cautionary note is to be aware of the potential for obsession, a high level of self-interest or narrowness of vision.

- The Locomotive is the reverse of the Bundle because one third of the horoscope is unoccupied. Jones termed the planet that was fronting the other planets in a clockwise direction the 'leading planet', suggesting it initiated psychic energy and encouraged movement, motivating the other planetary energies. During the year the individual could become self-motivated and be a driving force when they get started. Once the energy moves there is a dynamic drive and power. Take note of the 'leading planet' as an indication of what may initiate drive and willpower.

- In the Bowl all the planets are contained within 180°, or one half of the horoscope. This concentrates the planetary energies on one or two hemispheres. The year may feel more contained and focused. Some aspects of the individual's experience may feel empty or lacking in energy. The year contrasts the ability to hold and contain experiences with what is left uncontained and difficult to deal with. A cautionary note is to recognize that during the year the individual may need to accept feelings of division between two distinct sides of themselves or a separation between themselves and others.

- The Bucket is either a Bundle or Bowl pattern, but with one planet or tight conjunction of planets on the opposite side of the horoscope. The opposing planet or 'handle' acts as a spokesperson or a release for the conflagration of energies represented by the other planets. During the year the singular planet may be the driving force, becoming the guide or vehicle of expression, or inspiration for the other energies. The stress of the intense focus could weaken the planet's energy, which might collapse under the pressure. It may be difficult to project this energy, creating a sense of agitation. It is important to be conscious of the role the opposing planet/s plays in expressing the self during the year.

- The Seesaw has two or more planets opposing the rest of the planets across two sides of the horoscope, with ideally two empty squares that separate the planetary groups. The chart has two symmetrical groups of planets opposing one another. The year has less definition than for other patterns, and the urge to balance and reconcile opposing parts of the life is a priority. The ability to move back and forth between two opposing views or beliefs could become a preoccupation. At times this could lead to a sense of ambivalence or uncertainty, but when used constructively there is a sense of considering both points of view before moving ahead into action. During the year the theme may be one of conflict resolution and reconciliation.

- The Splay is the most difficult pattern to recognize. It is characterized by the tripod: three corners seem to anchor the chart. The chart is not as evenly spaced as the Splash and has 'spokes' that act to ground the scattered energy. The year may be noted for the ability to ground and harness disparate energies. During the year the energy needs to be focused and directed so the individual does not feel confused or misguided.

Although there is no clear shape to Jung's 1906 solar return, the majority of planets are in the eastern hemisphere, reiterating the theme of independent action.

Elements and Modes

As with natal chart interpretation, notice the balance of elements and modalities in the solar return. An imbalance of elements or modes, or any element that lacks planets, is important to consider. The missing element is often projected onto an object or someone in our environment, endowing events and others in our lives with the qualities that we feel are lacking. The missing element can be persistent, demanding that we relate to it, if not in ourselves, then through others. This missing function often appears in our partners, our bosses, our parents, our children or in other significant relationships. Note the missing element that you need to be conscious of during the year and be aware of the myriad ways this might manifest.

Retrograde Planets

Retrograde planets are naturally subjective as well as reflective. They act instinctively, responding to what appears to be taking place in the environment. Retrograde planets are in a defined relationship to the Sun, so each retrograde planet in the solar return has an important role in the shaping of personal identity, the formation of ego strength and self-discovery. With the planet in the sector opposite the Sun, it is able to be more reflective and conscious of its role. When retrograde it can rebel against customs and traditions, because it is intensified, subjective and instinctive.

Be mindful of the cycle of the retrograde planet as well as its frequency. For instance, in solar returns, Mercury is generally retrograde once in six years; Venus once in eight years; Mars is sporadic but some retrogrades occur successively. The social and outer planets are retrograde over a succession of solar returns. Therefore, for the social and outer planets it is important to recognize in which year the change of planetary direction occurred.

The frequency of the planet's retrograde cycle helps to prioritize its importance. For instance, years when Mercury is retrograde are significant because this only occurs every six years. A pattern of communicating, learning and processing information is different during this year. The Mercurial function is redirected and potentially deeper insights and revelation are available. Years when Venus is retrograde bring a different perspective or approach to relating, perhaps an intense scrutiny of one's values. When the inner planets are retrograde, personal issues represented by the planet become intensified.

In Jung's 1906 solar return there are three retrograde planets: Saturn, Chiron and Uranus. Saturn is the only natal planet that is retrograde; therefore, Chiron and Uranus have turned retrograde since birth. In the sequence of solar returns Uranus turned retrograde in 1896 when Jung was 21 and Chiron became retrograde in 1899 when Jung was 24. Saturn turned direct in the solar return series in 1909, when Jung was 34.

Intercepted Signs
If an intercepted polarity occurs we are alerted to a quality that may be blocked or difficult to access during the year. The house polarity where the interception occurs represents where the blockage might occur. Be aware of the houses where the intercepted energies seek expression, yet feel inhibited or denied. Note the rulers of these intercepted signs and their placement in the solar return horoscope. How could they contribute to an expression of these energies? An interception in a solar return is an important consideration when recognizing areas that demand attention and need more conscious focus. Likewise, it is important to recognize the two (or more) house polarities in which duplicated signs occur. Be aware that these areas are where confusion or enmeshment might occur due to the same sign being on the cusp. During the year it may be difficult to clearly differentiate the concerns of the houses that share the same sign on the cusp.

In Jung's 1906 solar return, Gemini is intercepted in the 10th house with Sagittarius intercepted in the 4th house. Perhaps Jung's career and domestic life were under review during this year. Virgo is duplicated on the 1st and 2nd house cusps, with Pisces on the 7th and 8th house cusps, once again highlighting the self–other axis, as well as emphasizing the theme of sharing Jung's resources with others.

Keys to Considering the Solar Return

To reconsider how we might begin to read or get a feel for solar return charts, let's review the planets to understand what role they play in the coming year. Remember that the astrological arrangements of the planets are time-sensitive. In the solar return the planets can embody a different flavour from the one they have in the natal chart. Consider each planet from the perspective of its cycle in the solar return, as well as in comparison to the natal chart. Taking into account these ideas let's reflect on the planetary energies as we do with the natal chart; however, in the solar return they are more transient symbols, characterizing a year, not a lifetime.

The Sun is the heart of this annual horoscope. From its point of view the year focuses on learning more about the self, identifying what supports conscious development and what challenges the emergent individuality. Being our vitality and life spirit, the Sun indicates the vibrancy, vigour, dynamism and heartiness throughout the year; hence it is a good measure of how to pace oneself, buoy up the spirits and feel acknowledged and recognized for who we truly are.

In any chart, **the Moon** is a barometer for measuring levels of emotional security, the feeling life, as well as our sense of belonging and well-being. Therefore, during any year it is vital to address the needs of the Moon. The Moon will reveal where we need to be vigilant about nurturing ourselves, where we need to attend to our inner life and feelings, how we need to psychologically pace ourselves, the emotional and familial environment as well as our domestic situation and living conditions.

Mercury is never far from the Sun but its aspects will change from year to year, gauging the emerging ideas, the communication style and also important initiatives and plans. Therefore, look to Mercury to help delineate what needs to be communicated this year, which ideas need supporting and which ways of thinking are significant. Mercury makes links and also represents an exchange of ideas and interactions with peers, friends and siblings.

Venus symbolizes our worth, as well as our natural style and values; therefore, it is an indicator of where we place our investments, whether monetarily or emotionally. It is a key to relational developments and growth during the year; hence its aspects might alert us to changes or incidents within important relationships and/or in what we value.

Mars is our internal warrior and its constellation in the solar return reveals how we need to assert our intentions, take action, stand up for ourselves and focus and direct our energy. How should we motivate ourselves during the year and where do we need to be single-minded and applied to the tasks at hand?

Jupiter indicates outreach; therefore, it suggests where we might develop opportunities, reach beyond our comfort zone and expand our possibilities. It is the archetype that suggests innovative learning, so it speaks about education, travel, cross-cultural experiences and exploration. Jupiter embodies authentic beliefs and during the year points to where we can learn and understand more of ourselves and develop faith and optimism in the world we inhabit.

Saturn represents the appropriate limits and boundaries that help to contain and secure what is important and meaningful to us. Saturn reflects what needs to be acknowledged, where to focus our efforts and where we need to be hard-working, conscientious and reliable. Traditionally, Saturn is equated with testing; however, in the solar return we might identify this as prioritizing what is important, taking authority, maturing and being accountable. Boundaries are not barriers and the archetype of Saturn identifies what needs to be respected and where we need to be responsible.

Chiron suggests where we feel off-centre or on the margins during the year. It focuses on where we need to be more accepting and embracing of our weaknesses. As a guide on our healing journey, Chiron identifies areas where wounding and healing are more prevalent during the year.

Each outer planet moves slowly; therefore, we integrate these energies into our lives gradually and with respect. Bit by bit, we become more aware of these energies that are greater than ourselves; therefore, each year the solar return gives us a new opportunity to assimilate these planetary archetypes.

Uranus represents our individuation process, symbolizing the changes, the challenges, the unexpected and the sudden shifts that alert us to becoming more independent. Uranus is the spirit force that calls us to our own individuality and exploration during the year.

Neptune is the muse that inspires our soul and lifts our spirits. But it also determines the levels of uncertainty, doubt and ambiguity that are on this year's horizon. By house and aspect, it helps to orient us to where ambiguities and confusion arise during the year, but it also assists in finding creative outlets that help to ease our tension and insecurity.

Pluto digs beneath the surface to find the treasure. Pluto and its aspects symbolize what might be decaying and in need of letting go, what mourning processes are necessary and where we are confronted with the truth, especially the truth we don't want to face. As the archetype of transformation, it becomes a powerful ally during the year if we can cede control when necessary.

The solar return is an extremely useful addition to working with transits and progressions when ascertaining upcoming trends, or the emotional and psychological landscape of the upcoming year. It is an important chart on its own. And when used in context of the whole life, it reveals an individual's lifetime maturation and development year after year. The cycles that renew themselves in the solar return charts are reminders of the majesty and awe of cosmic order. These cycles remind us to celebrate the rebirth of our solar hero/ine each year and to renew our commitment to the development of the Self on that special day once a year.

You will develop your own approach to working with solar returns; however, to begin your explorations you might want to use a checklist to help generate some ideas and feelings about what the chart may be representing for the year and also what it may be telling you. In the following chapter are some pointers, summarizing what we have covered.

Many Happy Returns.

PART V

TIMING

Cycles, Passages and Returns

People like us who believe in physics,
know that the distinction between past, present and future
is only a stubbornly persistent illusion[102]

Albert Einstein

18

ASTROLOGICAL TIMING
Reading the Cosmic Clock

Planetary cycles carry the horoscope through time. They are the heart of astrological timing; therefore, knowing these cycles and their impact upon the horoscope is essential to becoming proficient in working with astrological time. Our first step is to become fluent with the planetary rhythms, differentiating their cycles as they time travel through the heavens.

Tradition has bequeathed a variety of techniques that have imagined how the gods of time might clothe themselves in human experience. Each technique may serve a different purpose depending on the nature of the time under analysis and the quality of the question. Not all techniques can be used simultaneously nor used for the same outcome. With practice and application you will discern which methods suit your style and which ones support your beliefs. While many branches of astrology deal with timing, the following checklist summarizes the techniques and processes we have considered. I recommend using the techniques that you feel comfortable with and ascertaining in which situations you feel these techniques can be maximized. Over time you will craft your own approach as to how and when you employ these techniques.

Cycles, Passages and Returns Checklist

These are reflections on how you might begin to find your own way of working with timing techniques. I begin with transits, as these are metaphors that eloquently deal with the complexity of transition. Each planet has its own patterns and tells its own time; therefore, become familiar with the timing of each cycle by reflecting on its physical, emotional, psychological and spiritual affects.

Transits

Consider the nature of the time that you are examining and the questions that might arise during this passage. What are the influences as indicated by the transits? How might you consider these symbols in the context of this time as well as considering them in an overview of the life? What is the essence of the transition with respect to the symbolism of the transit? What do you feel is being demanded of this person?

Review how you analyse transits. Assess the following points and incorporate these into your practice. Find your own method for prioritizing the importance of each transit and develop procedures for recording and synthesizing the data:

☑ List the transits in order of priority. The slower-moving planets, especially their transiting aspects to the inner planets or angles, take precedence in defining the larger passages of time.

☑ When examining a particular transit, bear in mind the temperament and character of the transiting planet, the nature and quality of the planet being transited and the landscape of the house it is transiting.
  ✓ What is nature of the *transiting planet* in the natal chart? Which house/s does it rule in the natal chart? How is this energy expressed in the individual's life
  ✓ What is the character of the *planet receiving the transit*? Is it well integrated into the gestalt of the chart? Is this planet in a major aspect pattern and, if so, are there any other accompanying transits taking place to other planets in the pattern? Which house/s are ruled by the planet that is being transited?
  ✓ Consider the *house position of the transiting planet*. Which planet rules the house where the transit is taking place? What is this planet's character in the horoscope?

☑ Take note of any major planet changing houses.
  ✓ Chiron, Uranus, Neptune and Pluto move slowly through the chart, so their movement across a new house cusp may be significant in terms of changes in the individual's psychic environment. One of the ways of thinking about the outer planet transits through the houses is that each house is a sub-cycle or chapter in

the full life cycle. Chiron and Uranus may fully transit the horoscope in a lifetime, while Neptune and Pluto may cover only half the chart.

   ✓ Jupiter and Saturn create a cyclical pattern throughout the chart, so their transits through the houses can be seen as part of their developmental cycle. Note their change of house position and how this may be part of the maturation of this archetype.

☑ Take note of the nodal transits and the upcoming eclipses and their patterns.

   ✓ Bear in mind that the nodal transits and eclipses are cyclical. Note any major conjunctions or oppositions by the nodes or eclipses to planets in the horoscope.

☑ List the timing for the main transits. Be aware of the orb of influence you are using and how you correlate the astrological symbols with the individual's experience and process. Keep in mind that this is *astrological timing*; the personal and psychological timing may be quite different.

☑ What are the main statements suggested by the transit? How do you experience the individual handling and responding to these transits?

☑ For the major transits, what strategies would you suggest, given the natal chart and its transits? Do you feel you need to recommend strategies or refer clients to alternative practitioners? If so, reflect on why you made this assessment.

When establishing your work with astrological timing, be mindful of the many levels of transition that are symbolized by planetary cycles. We connect literal events to the transiting planet, but the emotional, psychological and spiritual atmosphere of the times can also be associated with planetary transits. When you feel confident about working with transits, consider using secondary progressions, which are a helpful resource and ally, to amplify the current transits.

Secondary Progressions

How can you conceptualize secondary progressions to feel more confident and comfortable using this technique? How do you consider these progressions in light of the mood of the times you are examining? Do these symbols reveal the internal or external world, or both? Does this technique support, collaborate or deepen your understanding of the transiting influences? Do the transits and progressions work as a team or do you see and experience them separately?

Contemplate your understanding of secondary progressions and how comfortable you feel using them. If you are only using some progressions, assess these in terms of your own understanding. Do the progressions help you to understand how an individual naturally develops or matures? Review these salient points:

☑ Compare the progressed planets that you are using to the natal chart.
  ✓ What are the major progressions that stand out? Make notes on these. How could you best express these using story, myth, metaphor or image, rather than words?

☑ Examine the progressed Moon and how you work with this symbol. How do you understand its usage or value in timing? Concentrating on the secondary progressed Moon:
  ✓ Note when the progressed Moon changes sign or house. Do you feel this is significant in the context of the period of time that you are examining?
  ✓ Are there any aspects for the current period that reflect other themes in the chart?
  ✓ What phase of life is the individual experiencing in terms of the progressed Moon cycle? What other times of life does this connect with?

☑ Examine the progressed Sun and its relationship to the progressed Moon. What is the current progressed phase of the lunation cycle? Can this be of significance or use in illuminating meaning during the current phase of life?

☑ Have any of the planets changed direction since birth? If so, in what year of life did this occur and do you feel this is significant? Does this have any bearing on this moment of time?

☑ Review the other planets, particularly the inner planets. Are any of these noteworthy by aspect, sign, house position or direction? If so, how does the planet's symbolism add or amplify meaning for this time?

Throughout this book we have considered the importance of the planetary cycles when working with astrological time. Every transit and progression is framed by its larger cycle. It is as if these archetypal cycles are the larger picture from which our experience develops. Therefore, the larger cycle of each transit becomes important when placing the current event and experience in context.

Cycles
Reflect on each planetary cycle. How do you conceptualize each one in the framework of the horoscope? How might you prioritize each one separately in terms of its meaning, significance, timing, influence and development?

When working with cycles there is a beginning, middle and end. Each ending of a cycle is a return, which opens the next cycle; therefore, every cycle embodies the ancient idea of return, rebirth and renewal. Using your astrological understanding of the timing of cycles you can link back to previous times when the same cyclical moment occurred – or ahead to future times when the same aspect will recur. In reflecting on this possibility, how might you formalize a way of thinking about and understanding the nature of cycles?

Reflect on the cycle as an archetypal process. Using your understanding of the planetary cycle helps to assess the repetition of psychic patterns. Which patterns may be repeating, given the cycle and its archetypal process? How could you help the individual to achieve more perspective on the period in question, looking at the previous periods within the context of the cycle they are now experiencing? Have these feelings, patterns, anxieties or moods been experienced before? When? What do you feel is the archetypal force underpinning this pattern? In the context of this period of time, does the cycle suggest a revisiting of old ground or a surfacing of repressed material?

In terms of the life cycle, is the individual in a major phase of transition, such as adolescence, midlife, the Chiron return, the second Saturn return, etc.? The following checklist may help in reflecting upon the powerful occurrence of cycles:

☑ Note if there is an important generic transit such as a Jupiter return, Saturn opposition, Uranus square, etc. If so, reflect on the current life phase and what this might present for the individual. Note any cycles that are beginning, such as the Jupiter cycle at age 12, 24, 35, 47 or Saturn at 29–30, 58–59, etc. Distinguish individual transits from generic ones. Note if these are occurring simultaneously. Are there personal cycles such as a social or outer planet transiting the Sun, Moon or Ascendant; for instance, Jupiter conjunct the Sun or Saturn conjunct the Ascendant? When examining a particular transit, link the current period to a similar stage in the previous cycle or to the last critical point in the cycle. For each planet there will be differing techniques and timing:

  ✓ Jupiter: approximately 6 or 12 years ago
  ✓ Saturn: approximately 7–8, 15 or 29–30 years ago
  ✓ Uranus: approximately 21 or 42 years ago (or in its 7-year cycle through the signs)
  ✓ Neptune: approximately 41 years ago (or its 14-year cycle through the signs)
  ✓ Progressed Moon: approximately 7, 14 or 28 years ago
  ✓ Nodes: approximately 9 or 19 years ago
  ✓ Chiron or Pluto: check the personal cycle because the squares and oppositions occur at irregular times due to the eccentricity of the planets' orbits

Our life experience is punctuated by initiations which open doors onto new life stages. Although these times are natural to the human life cycle, they are also deeply personal. Each planetary transition is best considered in terms of its archetypal arrangement in our horoscopes; attitudes and approaches to navigating these passages are driven by our temperament and character. While each life passage may be similar for all, it is unique for every individual; therefore, understanding and honouring the passages of the life cycle is critical to astrological timing.

Passages

The passages of an individual's life are the archetypal transitions such as birth, relationship, death, as well as the life cycle's natural developmental stages of childhood, adolescence, adulthood, midlife, later life, etc. Life passages are reflected in astrological timing by the natural cycles of astrology. Cultivate a way of thinking about the passages of one's own life in the context of the individual's horoscope and their proclivity for initiation, change and transition.

Astrology helps us to reflect on an individual's development in the context of the life cycle. It also allows a way to reflect on the atmosphere of the individual's generation and its spirit and intentions. Which passage is the individual going through and what is the overall nature of this transition in the context of the individual's life? What are the generational aspects that are being stressed at this time? Consider the following:

☑ How old is the individual? What stage of life are they experiencing and is this a particularly important year in the astrological life cycle?

☑ What is the major passage the individual is undergoing and what are the physical, emotional, psychological and spiritual changes that occur during this passage?

☑ Each individual shares the passage of time with others of his or her generation. Is there any astrological configuration that is particularly unique for this individual's generation, such as a Saturn–Pluto conjunction (1947, 1982 and 2020), a Saturn–Neptune conjunction (1952–53 and 1989), a Uranus–Pluto conjunction (1965–66) or a Uranus–Neptune conjunction (1993)?

☑ What was your experience of the passage in the life cycle that this individual is going through? If you have not experienced this, do you remember your parents' or grandparents' experience of this stage of the cycle? Would you have any reflections or suggestions for the individual experiencing this stage of life?

Returns, as we have explored, are archetypical experiences in human transition. Being archetypal, they are part of each planetary signature, so becoming familiar with the profound nature of each planet's return and its initiation of a new cycle of life is very valuable in working with astrological timing. A pending return is a ceremonial passage that needs to be acknowledged.

Returns

A planetary return marks the beginning of a new cycle for this energy and signals an important initiation in the life cycle. Therefore, it is important to consider any planetary return and what this new cycle might mean to the individual. You may consider other techniques which you might use at this time, such as return charts.

☑ Is the individual having any planetary returns, including any inner planet returns? How would you contextualize this in terms of this moment in time? Have you generated a horoscope for this inner planet return?

☑ Are any planets returning to their natal position this year? This may signal an important initiation in the life cycle. Be aware of returns in context of the overview of one's life and the returns of the inner planets for an indication of any personal beginnings, milestones, anniversaries or introductions. Chart the following returns:
   ✓ Lunar nodes (ages 18–19, 37–38, 55–56, 74–75)
   ✓ Progressed Moon (ages 27–28, 54–55, 81–82)
   ✓ Jupiter (ages 12, 24, 36, 47–48, 59–60, 71–72, 83–84)
   ✓ Saturn (ages 29–30, 58–60, 87–88)
   ✓ Chiron (age 49–51)

A very special astrological timing technique is the solar return. This can be used to study the cycles of a lifetime, as a one-off chart to preview the coming year or to consider a special year of the life. Each chart marks the anniversary of the Sun's return and is a call to celebrate and honour the recommitment to life. Once you feel you have mastered the transits and cycles of time then the solar return horoscope becomes a valuable addition to your timing toolbox.

Solar Returns

In developing your own ways of working with the solar return horoscope you first need to have your own opinion about certain particular variances in return charts, due to the question of timing and location. For instance, will you use a chart cast for the natal birthplace or the relocated address?

In solar return horoscopes, the planets have a different time from the natal chart because they are considered in the framework of the year, not the lifetime. We can reflect on the planetary energies in the same way that we do natally; however, in the solar return chart they are more transient, being symbols for that year only. It is also important to consider each planet from the perspective of its annual cycle in the solar return. To begin your explorations you might want to use a checklist to help generate some ideas and feelings about what the chart represents for the year:

☑ The Ascendant. When examining the solar return Ascendant, take note of its sign's element and quality and any planets in aspect to it for the year. Compare this to the natal Ascendant.

   ✓ How does the solar return Ascendant support or challenge the natal Ascendant? What images are highlighted by the year's Ascendant? How can you incorporate these qualities into your outlook and activities for this year?

   ✓ What is rising on the horizon of the year? Which natal house is coming to the Ascendant? Themes indicated by this house may rise to the forefront during the year; perhaps patterns and issues from this area emerge to confront you or are more integrated into your approach to life.

✓ Are any natal planets conjunct the solar return Ascendant? Natal planets that are conjoining the Ascendant–Descendant axis are significant in finding your bearings and a foothold for the year. What might these planets suggest about how to navigate and drive forward in the year? What are the energies you need to be aware of that might be coming to the surface in you (Ascendant) and others (Descendant)?

☑ The Midheaven. Take note of the sign, element, quality and any planets aspecting the MC. What are your goals for the year? What is the MC ruler for the year and how is this archetype situated in your natal and solar return charts?

✓ How does the solar return MC support or challenge the natal MC? Can it be effective in reaching your goals this year? What are some goals, intentions and projects that will be suitable for the solar return MC? How can you incorporate these qualities into your objectives and targets this year? What are your objectives for the year?

✓ Metaphorically, what is culminating on the meridian of the year? Which natal house is coming to the MC? This could symbolize the environment or territory that becomes important in fulfilling and working on your goals. Perhaps this area needs development and improvement during the coming year.

✓ Are any natal planets conjunct the solar return MC? What might these planets suggest about how to find equilibrium between the inner life and the outer demands this year? What are the energies you need to be aware of that might be affecting your inner sense of security (IC) and your outer objectives and aims (MC)?

☑ Angular Planets. These are a priority because they symbolize dominant themes during the year that demand your attention. Look at each angle separately. Planets dominating the IC seek attention in the sphere of home, family of origin and self-care, and they need a place to belong for the year. Planets on the Descendant draw our attention to personal relationships, equality and self-reflection; planets on the MC suggest focus in the outer world of career, goals and authority, while planets on the Ascendant command attention through our personality, desires and actions. Angular planets act as pointers and guides for the year. Differentiate which angle is accentuated by this energy and revere its energy and urge in this place for the coming year.

- ✓ Do any planets come to the angle in this solar return? If so, what might they signify? How are they placed in the natal chart and how are they supported (or not) in the solar return chart?

☑ The Moon. Remember that the Moon's cycle follows the elements – is this element repeated from last year or is there a change of element? Reflect on the 19-year pattern – what was happening emotionally 19 years ago?

- ✓ Note the element cycle of the Moon.
- ✓ What sign is it in? Is this compatible with the natal Moon? Is the elemental position of the Moon compatible with the natal element? What might this suggest about the emotional ballast for the year? How might safety issues and concerns, security and emotions be coloured differently this year?
- ✓ What house is it in? Where is the focus of security and safety this year?
- ✓ Which aspects are being made and how do they change the landscape of domestic and emotional security this year? What is the major aspect to the Moon this year? How does this planetary energy reshape and contribute to new ways of emotional expression, feelings of safety and feeling secure in general? What are the secondary aspects to the Moon? How do they support or challenge the individual's security systems during the year?

☑ The Lunation Phase. This could represent the overall mood for the year, your frame of mind and disposition. The lunation phase in the solar return suggests a sub-theme for this year, an important way to think about the overall moods and energies of the year, a segment of time when this way of being will be helpful in the overall schema of your life.

    ✓ What is the lunation phase and what mood does it symbolize for the year? How different is this to the secondary progressed lunation phase?

☑ Transits to the Natal Sun. Are there major transits to the Sun in the natal horoscope? Transits to the Sun from an outer planet reflect the ongoing transit and will be in effect for a number of solar returns. Take note of the houses that the Sun and its transiting planet are in, as these will be clues to the areas that the transit may be stressing during the year. The Sun is the area we may need to be identified with during the year in order to improve our confidence, vitality and integrity. Note too that the transits of the outer planets to the Sun will be active for a number of years in the solar return charts. This elongation of the transit suggests the enormity of the process when outer planets transit the Sun and awaken us to a more authentic core self. Be aware of other transits to important parts of the horoscope and how they may be confirmed and amplified by the solar return.

What are the transits to the natal Sun? Use the solar return to help differentiate them during the year. Make journal entries about what might be helpful to sustain your health and vitality during the year, which areas of life will help to promote confidence, how you might start to identify what is helpful and what is unhelpful. How can you acknowledge and support yourself in terms of your own creative self-expression?

☑ The Planets. Study each planet individually. Take note of its cycle in the solar return and note if an important cycle is being repeated during the year. Look at the planetary aspects and ascertain the important planetary dialogues for the year. Where does each planet fall in the natal chart? Note any planets returning to their natal positions.

How might you consider the images of each solar return planet and how it supports or challenges the natal planetary archetype? What strategies might help to maximize the planetary energy during the year?

☑ Aspect Patterns. Major aspect patterns will be a priority when delineating solar returns. Determine the major planetary aspects within the solar return to amplify the planetary dialogues for the year. Take note of planetary combinations that also appear in the natal chart. These emphasize the natal aspect and suggest that the natal theme is highlighted during the year. What are the planets involved in the major aspect pattern? Are these planets in aspect in the natal chart? What is the statement constellated around such an important pattern in the solar return?

☑ Chart Shapes. View the chart holistically. What is the shape of the chart? Where are the planetary energies focused: above the horizon, first quadrant, etc.? Which spheres and areas of interest does the chart shape highlight for the year in review? How is the planetary energy directed and disseminated during the year? Use images and metaphors to articulate the shape and first impressions of the solar return chart.

☑ Retrograde Planets. Note if any inner planets are retrograde in the solar return, especially if they are direct natally. Be aware of the pattern of both Mercury and Venus retrograde. Take note when an outer planet changes direction in successive solar return charts or when a retrograde planet disturbs the sequence of elements or patterns.

☑ Intercepted Signs. Be alert for any intercepted polarity in the solar return as an indication of potential blocks to the flow or rhythm of the year. Take note of planets that are intercepted in the solar return. Be aware of the house that the intercepted polarity occupies in the natal chart.

☑ Balance of Elements and Modes. As in any horoscope analysis, the elemental balance is important to consider. Note any lacking or highlighted elements or modes. Does the elemental composition of the solar return chart support or conflict with the elemental make-up of the natal chart? What new elements or modes of being are being introduced during the year? In which areas do they put in an appearance?

As students we may be overwhelmed by the amount of information that the natal and subsequent charts disclose. Overwhelmed because the data provided by the charts is not only cerebral and rational but is also intuitive and imaginative. The horoscope symbols speak in many ways which contribute to astrology being a unique tradition. Over time we learn to trust the symbols and our impressions, not by rote or in a prescribed fashion, but in our own way.

Astrology permits us to travel through time. And time, like astrology, invites us into its mysteries.

– EPILOGUE –
The Circle of Time

We have come full circle. We use this expression 'full circle' to suggest that after a series of events and changes we return to a similar place from where we started. While there is an ending, a beginning also takes place. Each homecoming bears the fruit of our realizations, which can be applied to understand the place to which we have returned. We started our journey together with reflections on time, exploring transits, progressions and planetary returns along the way.

How might we start to work with astrological periods by applying these concepts to assist us to participate with time more consciously?

'Full circle' encompasses the notion of the eternal return, a concept that underpins our astrological work with time. When we liberate time from its linear trajectory by using planetary cycles, we see through time to the periodical recurrence of patterns, events, themes and episodes. Each planetary cycle assists us to experience the wisdom of transitions from the perspective of its archetypal and astrological associations.

Using astrological symbols in the cyclic context of time permits an astrologer to move through chronological time, connecting events and experiences to the current circumstances. From this approach astrological time is complex, layered and multi-dimensional. But with practice we learn to read and discern the archetypal images inherent in astrological cycles, building our confidence and capability.

Over time we grow accustomed to the paradox of ageing and timelessness. Our physical bodies may age, but the soul is ageless. While time may be embodied through ageing, the spirit is lively and the soul is everlasting. Astrology reveals both transitory and eternal time; it invites us to consider the moment, not only from the perspective of what is occurring, but from the outlook of the soul. The present is not what is just happening now, but a way of perceiving, altered by the consciousness we bring to the moment at hand. Astrology teaches us that time is filled with qualities and virtues, memories and visions, fears and anticipations, emotions and feelings. Astrological time returns us to the gods.

Astrological time is cosmic time: symbolic, eternal and enigmatic.

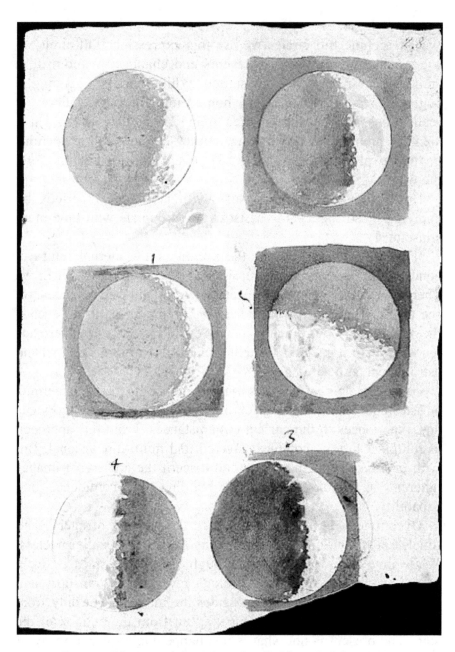

Image: *Phases of the Moon by Galileo Galilei, 1616*

APPENDICES

Appendix 1: The Mercury Cycle

1. Is natal Mercury before or after your Sun in zodiacal longitude?
   a. If before, Mercury is oriental and rising before the Sun – you were born between the inferior conjunction and the superior conjunction. Call yourself Oriental!
   b. If after, Mercury is occidental and setting after the Sun – you were born between the superior conjunction and the inferior conjunction. Call yourself Occidental!

2. Is natal Mercury retrograde or direct?
   a. If retrograde and before the Sun, you were born just after the inferior conjunction and you are Oriental Retrograde. If retrograde and after the Sun then you were born just before the inferior conjunction and you are Occidental Retrograde.
   b. If Mercury is direct then you are either Oriental Direct (1a) or Occidental Direct (1b).

3. What is the zodiacal degree of separation between natal Mercury and your Sun?
   a. From the inferior conjunction to the greatest elongation west (GEW, when Mercury is the morning star), the separation between the planets will range from 0° to a maximum of 28°. When near 20°, Mercury is approaching its GEW.
   b. From the greatest elongation west to the superior conjunction the speed will now increase to its maximum.
   c. From the superior conjunction to the greatest elongation east (GEE, when Mercury is the evening star), the separation between the planets will range from 0° to a maximum of 28°. When near 20°, Mercury is approaching its GEE.
   d. From the greatest elongation east to the inferior conjunction the speed will now decrease from its maximum to 0°.

4. What are the secondary progressed positions of your Sun and Mercury?

   a. Has progressed Mercury changed from oriental to occidental or vice versa? If so, look back to see in which years the Sun–Mercury conjunction occurred.

   b. What is the new phase relationship between progressed Mercury and progressed Sun?

   c. Has progressed Mercury stationed retrograde or direct? If so, when did this happen?

   d. What is the progressed sign relationship now between the Sun and Mercury? Has this changed from your natal configuration?

☿	Inferior Conjunction to Stationary Direct	Stationary Direct to Greatest Elongation	Greatest Elongation to Superior Conjunction	Superior Conjunction to Greatest Elongation	Greatest Elongation to Stationary Retrograde	Stationary Retrograde to Inferior Conjunction
Speed	℞	Slower	Faster	Faster	Slower	℞
Light	Increasing	Increasing	Decreasing	Increasing	Decreasing	Decreasing
Rudhyar phase	Promethean Retrograde	Promethean Direct		Epimethean Direct		Epimethean Retrograde
% of cycle	9.5	40.5		40.5		9.5

Whatever the guise, Mercury is there at turns in the road, as we awaken from the dream, when we forget our way, or in the conversation we are about to have.

Appendix 2: The Astrological Life Cycle
*Please note these ages are approximations and may vary slightly for each
individual due to planetary speed and retrograde periods*

Infancy

First Lunar Return	27.3 days
First Mercury Return	11–13 months
First Venus Return	10–14 months
First Solar Return	1 year
First Mars Return	17–23.5 months

Early Childhood

First Jupiter Opposition	6 years
First Waxing Progressed Moon Square	7 years
First Waxing Saturn Square	7.5 years

Latency Period

First Nodal Opposition	9 years

Early Adolescence

First Jupiter Return	12 years
First Progressed Moon Opposition	14 years
Waxing Uranus Sextile	14 years

Middle Adolescence

First Saturn Opposition	15 years
Second Jupiter Opposition	18 years
First Nodal Return	19 years

Late Adolescence

First Waning Progressed Moon Square	20.5 years
Waxing Neptune Semi-square	20.5 years
Waxing Uranus Square	21 years
First Waning Saturn Square	22 years

Pre-Saturn Return

Second Jupiter Return	24 years
First Progressed Moon Return	27.3 years
Second Nodal Opposition	28 years
Waxing Neptune Sextile	28 years
Waxing Uranus Trine	28 years

Post-Saturn Return

First Saturn Return	29.5 years
First Prog. Lunation Phase Return	29.5 years
Third Jupiter Opposition	30 years
Second Waxing Prog. Moon Square	34 years

Midlife

Third Jupiter Return	36 years
Second Waxing Saturn Square	37 years
Second Nodal Return	37 years
Waxing Pluto Square	36–40 years

*(note: only for the ♇ in ♍ and ♎ generations; other generations
do not experience this aspect so early)*

Uranus Opposition	39–42 years
Second Prog. Moon Opposition	41 years
Waxing Neptune Square	41 years
Fourth Jupiter Opposition	42 years
Second Saturn Opposition	44 years
Third Nodal Opposition	46–7 years
Fourth Jupiter Return	48 years (usually 47)
Second Waning Prog. Moon Square	48 years

The 50s

Chiron Return	50 years
Second Saturn Waning Square	51–2 years
Fifth Jupiter Opposition	53 years
Second Progressed Moon Return	54 years
Waning Uranus Trine	55 years
Third Nodal Return	55 years
Waxing Neptune Trine	56 years
Second Saturn Return	59 years
Fifth Jupiter Return	60 years (usually 59)

Seniority

Third Waxing Progressed Moon Square	61 years
Waning Uranus Square	61–3 years
Fourth Nodal Opposition	65 years
Third Waxing Saturn Square	66 years
Sixth Jupiter Opposition	66 years
Third Prog. Moon Opposition	69 years

Eldership

Sixth Jupiter Return	72 years (usually 71)
Fourth Nodal Return	74 years
Third Saturn Opposition	74 years
Third Waning Progressed Moon Square	75 years
Seventh Jupiter Opposition	77 years
Third Waning Saturn Square	81 years
Third Progressed Moon Return	82 years
Neptune Opposition	82–3 years
Seventh Jupiter Return	83 years
Fifth Nodal Opposition	83–4 years
Uranus Return	84 years

Post-Uranus Return

Pluto opposition	85+ years

(note: those born with ♇ in ♋ will experience this at approx. 85–95; ♇ in ♌ generally between 85 and 87; ♇ in ♍ between 86 and 96, and ♇ in ♎ from 96+ years old.)

Fourth Waxing Progressed Moon Square	88 years
Third Saturn Return	88–9 years
Eighth Jupiter Opposition	89 years
Fifth Nodal Return	93 years
Eighth Jupiter Return	95 years
Fourth Waxing Saturn Square	95–6 years
Fourth Progressed Moon Opposition	96 years
Second Chiron Return	100 years

Appendix 3: Eclipses

There are different types of solar eclipses:

1. A Partial Eclipse is when the Moon does not completely cover the disc of the Sun

2. A Total Eclipse is when the Moon completely covers the disc of the Sun and casts a shadow path or umbra across a partial surface on the Earth

3. An Annular Eclipse is a total eclipse; however, the Moon is too far away from the Earth for its shadow to completely cover the Sun's disc. A halo of light surrounds the darkened Moon

4. An Annular/Total Eclipse is total for part of its path and annular for the rest

There is a minimum of two solar eclipses each year and a maximum of five. Conditions for a solar eclipse to occur are:

1. Occurs at the New Moon (Sun conjunct Moon).

2. The Sun and Moon must be within a certain distance of the nodal axis. If the Sun and Moon are within 15°21' of the nodal axis then a solar eclipse occurs. The types of eclipses, due to the separation from the nodal axis, are:
    - 0°–9°55' from the nodal axis = a total solar eclipse
    - 9°55'–11°15' = a partial or total solar eclipse
    - 11°15'–15°21' = a partial solar eclipse
    - From 15°21'–18°31', a partial solar eclipse may occur

If a lunar eclipse occurs it will always be at the Full Moon preceding or following the solar eclipse. There does not have to be a lunar eclipse in any given year. Conditions for a lunar eclipse to occur are:

1. Occurs at the Full Moon (Sun opposite the Moon)

2. The Sun and Moon must be within a certain distance of the nodal axis. If the Sun and Moon are within 9°30' of the nodal axis, a lunar eclipse will happen. The types of lunar eclipses, due to the separation from the nodal axis, are as follows:
- 0°–3°45' from the nodal axis = a total lunar eclipse
- 3°45'–6° = a partial or total lunar eclipse
- 6°–9°30' = a partial lunar eclipse
- From 9°30'–12°15' = a partial lunar eclipse may occur

Remember:

1. Eclipses occur near the nodal axis and can be predicted because they follow a particular pattern and cycle

2. Two very important cycles are worth noting, which stress 18–19-year patterns in the life cycle:
   a. The Saros Cycle suggests that eclipses will repeat in the same Saros Series every 18 years and 10–11 days
   b. The Metonic Cycle suggests that New Moons follow a 19-year pattern in which eclipses might repeat at the same astrological degree. There is approximately a 75% chance of an eclipse repeating in this cycle

Appendix 4: Using Solar Fire Software
to Calculate Lifetime Secondary Progressions

Using Solar Fire Software to Calculate the Progressed Moon:

The Progressed Moon's Generic Cycle

Calculating your progressed Moon's returns and oppositions

1. Open your chart
2. On the top menu choose Dynamic. Click on Transits & Progressions and make sure your chart is highlighted under Dynamic Radix Chart
3. Under Period of Report choose the Start Date as your birth date and the period as 83 years (to generate the oppositions and returns for three cycles)
4. Under Location choose Natal
5. Under Event Selection choose only Progs to Radix
6. Under Point Selection click on Progs. Another window called Progressing Points will come up. Choose the Moon file – choose Edit to make sure you are only using the Moon and then choose Save and Select. Then click on Radix and again choose the Moon file
7. Under Aspect Selection click on Progs. Another window called Progressing Points will appear. Choose the Harm02 file (this should only include the conjunction and opposition)
8. Then click on Saved Selections. Saved Dynamic Selections will appear. Type in Progressed Moon Opposition and Return and click OK, and this will be saved for other reports
9. Finally, click View and the Dynamic Events Report will generate your progressed Moon's oppositions and returns

The Progressed Moon's Personal Cycle

Calculating your progressed Moon's ingress into the signs and houses

1. Open your chart
2. On the top menu choose Dynamic. Click on Transits &
   Progressions and make sure your chart is highlighted under
   Dynamic Radix Chart
3. Under Period of Report choose the Start Date as your birth
   date and the period as 83 years (three cycles)
4. Under Location choose Natal
5. Under Event Selection choose three boxes: Progs to Radix,
   House Ingress and Sign Ingress
6. Under Point Selection click on Progs. Another window called
   Progressing Points will come up. Choose the Moon file –
   choose Edit to make sure you only are using the Moon and
   then choose Save and Select. Then click on Radix and choose
   None. Choose Edit to make sure no planets or points are
   chosen and then choose Save and Select
7. Under Aspect Selection click on Progs. Another window called
   Progressing Points will appear. Choose the None file – this file
   should have no aspects
8. Then click on Saved Selections and Saved Dynamic Selections
   appears. Type in Progressed Moon through the Houses and
   Signs and click OK and this will then be saved for other
   reports
9. Finally, click view and the Dynamic Events Report will
   generate your progressed Moon's journey through the Houses
   and Signs of your horoscope. Note when the Moon changes
   sign within the house it is progressing through

Using Solar Fire Software to Calculate the Progressed Sun:

The Progressed Sun's aspects for a lifetime

Calculating your progressed Sun's aspects for a lifetime and its ingress into the signs and houses

1. Open your chart
2. On the top menu choose Dynamic. Click on Transits & Progressions and make sure your chart is highlighted under Dynamic Radix Chart
3. Under Period of Report choose the Start Date as your birth date and the period as 90 years
4. Under Location choose Natal
5. Under Event Selection choose three boxes: Progs to Radix, House Ingress and Sign Ingress
6. Under Point Selection click on Progs. Another window called Progressing Points will come up. Choose the Sun file – choose Edit to make sure you only are using the Sun and then choose Save and Select. Then click on Radix and choose Plans&Ch. Choose Edit to make sure this file contains the planets, angles and points you want and then choose Save and Select
7. Under Aspect Selection click on Progs. Another window called Progressing Points will appear. There may not be a 12th harmonic file so you will need to create a file. Call this file Harm12. Enable the aspects you need: the conjunction, opposition, trine, square, sextile, semi-sextile and quincunx. Disable the aspects you do not need. Then click Save and then Select.
8. Then click on Saved Selections. Saved Dynamic Selections will appear. Type in Progressed Sun Lifetime and this will then be saved for other reports
9. Finally, click View and the Dynamic Events Report will generate your Progressed Sun's aspects for your lifetime as well as its ingress into the subsequent houses and signs

Using Solar Fire Software to Calculate the Progressed Lunation Cycle:

Phases of the Progressed Lunation Cycle

Calculating your progressed lunation phases for your lifetime

1. Open your chart
2. On the top menu choose Dynamic. Click on Transits & Progressions and make sure your chart is highlighted under Dynamic Radix Chart
3. Under Period of Report choose the Start Date as your birth date and the period as 90 years (this will encompass three cycles of 29½ years each from your birth)
4. Under Location choose Natal
5. Under Event Selection choose only Progs to Progs
6. Under Point Selection click on Progs. Another window called Progressing Points will come up. Choose the Sunmoon file – choose Edit to make sure you only are using the Sun and Moon and then choose Save and Select
7. Under Aspect Selection click on Progs. Another window called Progressing Points will appear. Choose the Harm08 file – this file will have the 45° aspects only
8. Then click on Saved Selections. Saved Dynamic Selections will appear. Type in Progressed Phases of a Lifetime, click OK and this is saved for other reports
9. Finally, click View and the Dynamic Events Report will generate your life's Progressed Phases

Appendix 5: The Planetary Order Worksheet

Place your planets, nodes and angles (if your time of birth is accurate) on the appropriate line. When all the planets, points, angles and any other points of interest are listed, you will be able to see the years when the progressed Sun aspects other planets as well when it changes sign. Each line is 1°; therefore, each line is approximately one year of movement for the progressed Sun.

Start with the Sun and move to the next line where there is a planet or point. This will be the first aspect the Sun makes. Each space represents 1° or one year. By referencing the natal signs involved, the 12th harmonic aspect will become evident. This exercise shows the ages when the progressed Sun makes its aspects to other planets and points, the order of these aspects and how they will repeat in a 30-year pattern. At a glance this also will show any 12th harmonic transits.

Degrees of a Sign	Planet/ Node/ Angle	Approximate Age Progressed Sun Aspects Planet			Comments on Progression
Planetary Order Worksheet for:					
		1st cycle	2nd cycle	3rd cycle	
00°–00°59'					
01°–01°59'					
02°–02°59'					
03°–03°59'					
04°–04°59'					
05°–05°59'					
06°–06°59'					
07°–07°59'					
08°–08°59'					
09°–09°59'					
10°–10°59'					
11°–11°59'					
12°–12°59'					
13°–13°59'					
14°–14°59'					
15°–15°59'					
16°–16°59'					
17°–17°59'					
18°–18°59'					
19°–19°59'					
20°–20°59'					
21°–21°59'					
22°–22°59'					
23°–23°59'					
24°–24°59'					
25°–25°59'					
26°–26°59'					
27°–27°59'					
28°–28°59'					
29°–29°59'					
Progressed Sun Changes Sign					

Degrees of a Sign	Planet/ Node/ Angle	Approximate Age Progressed Sun Aspects Planet			Comments on Progression See Diary Entry
		1st cycle	**2nd cycle**	**3rd cycle**	
00°–00°59'					
01°–01°59'					
02°–02°59'					
03°–03°59'					
04°–04°59'					
05°–05°59'					
06°–06°59'					
07°–07°59'					
08°–08°59'					
09°–09°59'					
10°–10°59'					
11°–11°59'					
12°–12°59'					
13°–13°59'					

Planetary Order Worksheet for

_____

14°–14°59'				
15°–15°59'				
16°–16°59'				
17°–17°59'				
18°–18°59'				
19°–19°59'				
20°–20°59'				
21°–21°59'				
22°–22°59'				
23°–23°59'				
24°–24°59'				
25°–25°59'				
26°–26°59'				
27°–27°59'				
28°–28°59'				
29°–29°59'				
Progressed Sun Changes Sign				

Appendix 6: The Progressed Lunation Cycle Worksheets

My Progressed Lunation Cycle – My **First** Round

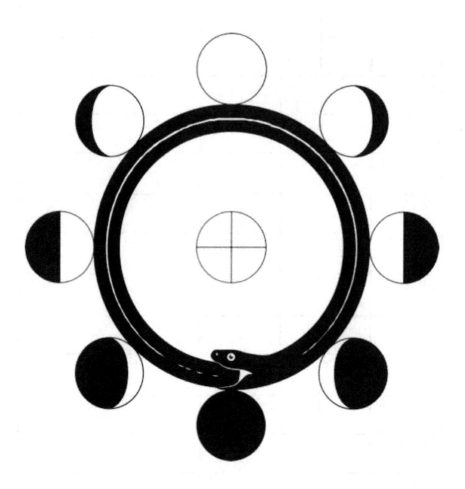

My Next Progressed New Moon is _____

My Progressed Lunation Cycle – My **Second** Round

My Next Progressed New Moon is _____

My Progressed Lunation Cycle – My **Third** Round

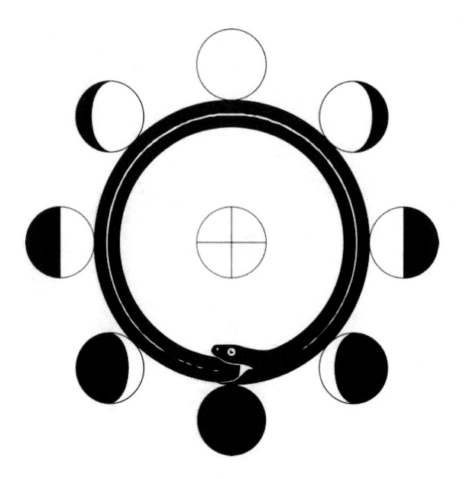

My Next Progressed New Moon is _____

Appendix 7: Using Solar Fire Software
to Calculate the Solar Returns for a Lifetime

The solar return is calculated like any other astrological chart and uses the exact time the Sun returns to its natal position, expressed in degrees, minutes and seconds of zodiacal longitude. The location of the solar return can be the birth place (to view the annual cycles), place of residence (as a relocated chart) or the location at the time of the solar return (as a pilgrimage chart). Each chart is valid in its own right.

Here are instructions on how to generate the solar return charts for your lifetime using your Solar Fire astrological software package.

1. Open the natal chart or the chart for which you wish to generate solar returns for a lifetime
2. Then under Chart on the top menu click on Return & Ingress

- Under Return Search Start Date use the birth date, time and place of the chart being considered
- Under Which One, choose Nearest
- Under Location, choose Natal
- Under Chart Type to Generate, click Advanced & Ingress
- Then click the button marked Options
- In the next box that appears, choose Sun
- In the box Return the Sun to, choose Natal Position and Harmonic 1
- Do not choose any Special Options
- And under Which Returns, choose Nearest Return and then choose the number of returns you want to generate. I suggest at least 50 if you are under 50, or choose the age you are now
- Click OK
- The charts appear immediately; the first one will be the birth chart

– BIBLIOGRAPHY –

This is not designed to be a complete bibliography, but is a list of the books that have been of value when reflecting on astrological time; hence, they are ones I can recommend without reservation.

Arroyo, Stephen. *Astrology, Karma & Transformation*, CRCS Publications, Vancouver, WA: 1978.
    A classic work on considering transits and progressions

Bell, Lynn. *Cycles of Light: Exploring the Mysteries of Solar Returns*, The Centre for Psychological Astrology (CPA), London: 2005.
    This book is one of the most accessible on solar returns

Blaschke, Robert. *Astrology: A Language of Life, Volume I – Progressions*, Earthwalk School of Astrology, Oregon: 1998.
    Includes some creative ways to view progressions

Brady, Bernadette. *Predictive Astrology: The Eagle and the Lark*, Samuel Weiser, Inc., York Beach, ME: 1992.
    Covers many predictive techniques including good work on eclipses and the Saros cycles

Clifford, Frank C. *The Solar Arc Handbook*, Flare Publications, London, UK: 2018.
    An in-depth examination of the technique of solar arc directions with a wealth of case studies and examples of how the technique works

Cornelius, Geoffrey. *The Moment of Astrology: Origins in Divination*, The Wessex Astrologer, UK: 2003.
    A very scholarly and thought-provoking exploration into the history and art of astrological divination

Fallon, Astrid. *Graphic Ephemeris for Forecasts*, Fallon Astro Graphics (www.fallonastro.com), France: 2016.
>   My favoured ephemeris when working with transits and cycles, presented in an overview that honours the cyclic nature of the planets; included are wonderful summaries of the cycles

Forrest, Steven. *The Changing Sky: Learning Predictive Astrology*, Seven Paws Press, Inc., CA: 2015.
>   In the tradition of his classic *The Inner Sky*; an easy and accessible read on transits and progressions

George, Demetra. *Ancient Astrology in Theory and Practice: A Manual of Traditional Techniques*, Rubedo, Auckland, New Zealand: 2019.
>   An exhaustive and rich exploration of traditional timing techniques

Greene, Liz. *The Horoscope in Manifestation: Psychology and Prediction*, Great Britain: 2001.
>   Important reflections on the nature of the psychology of prediction

Hand, Robert. *Planets in Transit: Life Cycles for the Living*, Whitford Press, US: 2002.
>   This is often referred to as 'the bible' of transits, originally written for a computer report – a classic astrological text and the most comprehensive work on the delineation of each transiting combination

Jansky, Robert. *Interpreting the Eclipses*, ACS Publications, San Diego, CA: 1979.
>   An informative approach to eclipses

Martin, Clare. *Mapping the Psyche, Volume 3: Kairos – The Astrology of Time*, The Wessex Astrologer, Ltd, Bournemouth: 2015.
>   An introduction and discussion for students on time and timing techniques from a psychological perspective

Rudhyar, Dane. *The Lunation Cycle*, Shambhala, London: 1971.
    A timeless book which introduces us to the profound technique
    of the progressed lunation cycle

Ruperti, Alexander. *Cycles of Becoming*, CRCS Publications, Davis,
CA: 1978.
    This is a classic, focusing on cycles, written by one of the
    pioneers of humanistic astrology

Sasportas, Howard. *The Gods of Change*, Penguin Arkana, London:
1988.
    Another classic astrological book which I consider a must for all
    astrological students studying astrological timing – it focuses on
    the transits of Uranus, Neptune and Pluto from a psychological
    and mythological perspective

Shea, Mary. *Planets in Solar Returns*, ASC Publications, San Diego:
1992.
    An exploration of the patterns and cycles of solar returns

Tarnas, Richard. *Cosmos and Psyche*, Viking Penguin, New York,
NY: 2006.
    A massive undertaking with an historical base to the cycles of the
    outer planets

– ENDNOTES –

[1] Francis Bacon's book *The Advancement of Learning*, Cassell & Company, Ltd., London: 1893, XI (2) is now available as an E-book at https://www.gutenberg.org/files/5500/5500-h/5500-h.htm [accessed 1 September 2019].

[2] The Indo-European root for the word 'time' – *di* or *dia* – means 'to divide'; see Carlo Rovelli, *The Order of Time*, translated by Erica Segre and Simon Carnell, Penguin Random House, UK: 2019, p. 53.

[3] For more details on the Astro*Synthesis Collection in Applied Astrology, e-workbooks and e-booklets, see www.astrosynthesis. com.au.

[4] From the Grateful Dead, *Walk in the Sun* [https://genius.com/ Grateful-dead-walk-in-the-sun-lyrics – accessed 21/02/2020]. 'Deep-six' suggests 'to dispose of' or 'to destroy'.

[5] Plato, Timaeus, from *Timaeus and Critias*, translated by Desmond Lee, Penguin, 1977, p. 27.

[6] The classic example is *The Odyssey*, which moves back and forth through time as the epic unfolds.

[7] An orb is an allowance of variable degrees either side of a planet, point or angle in which the influence or receptivity to other bodies is considered to operate. There are no agreed-upon standards in astrology regarding the allowance of orbs, but a general rule suggests that aspects to faster-moving planets should have wider orbs. With this directive, the Moon could have an orb up to 10°. Major aspects are often granted wider orbs than minor ones. Astrologers also vary on the orb of influence for transiting planets.

[8] Edward S. Casey, *Spirit and Soul: Essays in Philosophical Psychology*, Spring Publications, Inc., Putnam, CT: 2004, pp. 279–80.

[9] The lecture by James Hillman, called 'Heaven Retains Within its Sphere Half of All Bodies and Maladies', was originally given at the 1997 Return of Soul to the Cosmos conference and repeated at the Alchemical Sky conference in Bath, UK, in May 2005.

[10] Geoffrey Cornelius skilfully demonstrates astrology's susceptibility to becoming mechanistic and literal: 'the Ptolemaic model of astrology has obscured the foundation in participatory significance by treating symbolism as an expression of causes, or as an expression of some objective cosmic order.' See Geoffrey Cornelius, *The Moment of Astrology*, Penguin Arkana, London: 1994, p. 190.

[11] The ancient Greeks saw the planets as wanderers, unlike the other fixed stars. Embedded in the word 'planet' is the Greek notion of wandering. While Edward S. Casey does not refer to astrology, he does associate the irregularity and regularity of the planets with soul, which to me is inspiring: see *Spirit and Soul: Essays in Philosophical Psychology*, p. 279.

[12] Carlo Rovelli, *The Order of Time*, p. 56.

[13] Anyone who has a pet knows they have an internal clock. My dog Winnie knew when I was due home, when it was bedtime and rambunctiously knew when it was mealtime; more part of their circadian rhythms, not necessarily an awareness of time as we know it.

[14] Lord Tennyson, *Tithonus*, The Poetry Foundation, [https://www.poetryfoundation.org/poems/45389/thithonus - accessed 17 September 2019].

[15] See Ginette Paris, *Pagan Grace*, Spring, Woodstock, CT: 1995, p. 121.

[16] 'The Homeric Hymn to Hermes', *The Homeric Hymns*, translated by Michael Crudden, Oxford University Press, Oxford: 2001, lines 429–30, p. 58.

[17] Edward S. Casey, *Spirit and Soul: Essays in Philosophical Psychology*, p. 157.

[18] The underlying theme of Geoffrey Cornelius's *The Moment of Astrology* amplifies and addresses this essential question.

[19] Themis was a Titan, the goddess of divine law and order.

[20] For a discussion on the development of thought around Chronos and time, see John Cohen, 'Subjective Time' from *The Voices of Time*, edited by J.T. Fraser, George Braziller, New York, N.Y.: 1966, pp. 274–75.

[21] Hesiod describes the Golden Age in his *Works and Days*. This quote from the translation by Hugh G. Evelyn-White, Harvard University Press, Cambridge, MA: 2002, p. 11.

[22] James Hillman, 'Notes on Opportunism', from *Puer Papers*, edited by James Hillman, Spring, Dallas, TX: 1994, p. 153.

[23] For a discussion on symbols of time, including time's arrow, see Joost A. M. Meerloo 'The Time Sense in Psychiatry' from *The Voices of Time*, pp. 246–52.

[24] R.B. Onians, *The Origins of European Thought*, Cambridge University Press, Cambridge, MA: 1953, p. 348.

[25] *Astronomy or Astrology*, as Plutarch called it, as well as Hesiod's *Works and Days*, were early Greek epics that related the constellations to timing. See *Hesiod*, The Loeb Classical Library, Harvard University Press, Cambridge: 2002, p. xix.

[26] Gregory Szanto, *Perfect Timing*, The Aquarian Press, Wellingborough, UK: 1989, p. 46.

[27] Synchronicity is another aspect of time that is important in any astrological discourse. This has been widely explored and I would point to two outstanding astrological references for this: 1. Michael Harding, *Hymns to the Ancient Gods*, Penguin Arkana, London: 1992, pp. 23–41 and 2. Richard Tarnas, *Cosmos and Psyche*, Penguin, New York, NY: 2006, pp. 50–60. Maggie Hyde's book *Jung and Astrology*, Aquarian, London: 1992, includes a skilful examination of Jung's experiment into synchronicity.

[28] Manoj Thulasides, The Nature of Time, http://theunrealuniverse.com/2-nature-of-time [accessed 16 July 2013].

[29] Edward S. Casey, *Spirit and Soul: Essays in Philosophical Psychology*, p. 273.

[30] Dane Rudhyar, *A Brief Factual Biography*, James Shore, USA: 1972, p. 3.

[31] Arnold Van Gennep, *The Rites of Passage*, translated by Monika B. Vizedom and Gabrielle L. Caffee, The University of Chicago Press, Chicago, Il: 1960.

[32] Arnold Van Gennep, *The Rites of Passage*, pp. 10–11.

[33] Dane Rudhyar, *Astrological Timing*, Harper and Row, New York, NY: 1972, p. 71.

[34] Our word 'consider' aligns the Latin prefix *con*, meaning 'with', with *sider* or star. Embedded in the word consider is the ancient idea of being with or consulting the stars.

[35] Howard Sasportas, *The Gods of Change*, Penguin Arkana, London: 1989, p 17.

[36] Leyla Rael Rudhyar, Shambala Astrological Calendars 1982 and 1983, Shambala, Boulder, CO.

[37] This time is confirmed from his birth certificate – www.astro.com/astro-databank/Obama,_Barack

[38] This time is confirmed from his birth certificate – https://www.astro.com/astro-databank/Trump,_Donald

[39] 'Liminal' is from the Latin *limen*, meaning the sill of a doorway, threshold or entrance, symbolizing the transitional zone between two separate places or ways of being.

[40] For an excellent book on the psychological approach to transits and progressions, see Liz Greene, *The Horoscope in Manifestation*, CPA, London: 1997.

[41] For an examination of working with astrological symbols, see Brian Clark, *Soul, Symbol and Imagination: The Artistry of Astrology*, Astro*Synthesis, Stanley, Tasmania; 2019.

[42] See Brian Clark, *The Family Legacy*, Astro*Synthesis, Stanley, Tasmania; 2016.

[43] Joseph Campbell, *The Hero with a Thousand Faces*, Princeton University Press, Princeton, N.J.: 1968, p. 30.

[44] An Interview with Richard Tarnas, *The Mountain Astrologer*, Issue #124, Dec 2005/ Jan 2006, p. 49.

[45] Dane Rudhyar, *Person Centered Astrology*, ASI Publishers, New York, NY: 1980, p. 75.

[46] For the ancient tradition of planetary phase, see Demetra George, *Ancient Astrology in Theory and Practice: A Manual of Traditional Techniques*, Rubedo, Auckland, New Zealand: 2019, pp. 285–98.

[47] Dane Rudhyar, *Astrological Timing*, p. 22.

[48] Dane Rudhyar, *The Lunation Cycle*, Shambhala Publications, Inc., Boulder, CO: 1971.

[49] This is an astronomical term, not a judgement.

[50] Plato, *Timaeus*, pp. 28–9.

[51] Life today is more complex; hence we have many more wanderers to consider such as the outer planets, the asteroids, dwarf planets, centaurs and other celestial travellers. Planetary periods have always been part of astrological tradition. In the Vedic system they are known as dashas; the Persians used firdaria; western astrology uses recurring and synodic cycles to delineate its system of time periods.

[52] See Brian Clark, 'Mercury Pi in the Sky', *The Mountain Astrologer*, December 2018/January 2019.

[53] Thomas Moore, *The Planets Within*, Lindisfarne Press, Great Barrington, MA: 1990, p. 153.

[54] There are different schools of thought as to whether the beginning of the synodic cycle of Mercury and Venus begins at the 'inferior' or 'superior' conjunction.

[55] All three Brontë sisters poetically wrote about their observances of Venus. Emily also referred to Venus as 'the glorious star of love'- see http://www.victorianweb.org/authors/bronte/nockholds1.html [accessed 17 September 2019].

[56] In 1769 the best sighting for the Venus transit was on the Pacific Islands. Commissioned by King George III, Captain James Cook set sail for Tahiti to observe the transit. And while the day was ideal for the sighting, the results were not as satisfactory as hoped. However, it was the precursor to Cook's discovery of the great southern land of Australia and its intimate connection with the transit of Venus.

[57] 'Under the Sun's beams' is an ancient expression that captured the planet's obscuration by the Sun.

[58] See Brian Clark, *The Family Legacy*, pp. 264–70, for a discussion of the Jupiter life cycle and all other cycles that recur during each 12-year cycle.

[59] Dr Kübler-Ross defined these as stages in the grieving process.

[60] Mythologically, Chiron is related to each of the namesakes of these three planets, being the son of Saturn, the grandson of Uranus and the half-brother of Jupiter.

[61] As included in *The Standard Edition of the Complete Work of Sigmund Freud*, translated by James Strachey, Vintage: 1999, Volume 9: pp. 236–41.

[62] See Brian Clark, *The Sibling Constellation: the Astrology and Psychology of Sisters and Brothers*, Penguin Arkana, London: 1999. In Chapter 3 there is a full discussion of Freud's chart and especially the Chiron placement in his horoscope.

[63] While life expectancy is not uniform due to national averages and statistics, 84 is the average lifespan in countries like Japan, Italy and Singapore as per the United Nations (2010–15). Female life expectancy is 84 in many other countries. – see https://en.wikipedia. org/wiki/List_of_countries_by_life_expectancy [accessed 9 February 2019].

[64] See Richard Tarnas, *Prometheus the Awakener*, Spring Publications, Thompson, CT: 2018.

[65] See Brian Clark & Kay Steventon, *Celestial Tarot*, US Games Inc, Stamford, CT: 2006.

[66] C.G. Jung, *Psychology and Alchemy*, The Collected Works, translated by R.F.C. Hall, Routledge & Kegan Paul, London: 1953, ¶439.

[67] Carl Jung, *Memories, Dreams, Reflections*, translated by R. & C. Winston, Pantheon Books, New York: 1973, p. 172.

[68] Stanley W. Jackson, *Melancholia and Depression: From Hippocratic Times to Modern Times* quoted in the article 'A Melancholy of Mine Own' by Joshua Wolf Shenk, *Psychotherapy Networker*, July/August 2001.

[69] Hades ventures to Olympus to receive healing from Paeon, the Olympian healer, after he has been wounded – see Homer, *The Iliad*, 5:393–402. Another suggestion is that he may have ventured to Olympus to receive Zeus's approval to abduct Persephone – see Roberto Calasso, *The Marriage of Cadmus and Harmony*, Jonathan Cape, London: 1993.

[70] Latitude is measured north or south of the ecliptic while declination is measured north or south of the celestial equator.

[71] For a delineation of the planet squaring the nodal axis, see Brian Clark, *Vocation*, Astro*Synthesis, Stanley, Australia: 2016.

[72] For further exploration of the nodes and their cycle see *The Dragon's Tale* by Brian Clark, Astro*Synthesis, www.astrosynthesis.com.au.

[73] Brian Clark, *From the Moment We Met: the Astrology of Adult Relationships*, Astro*Synthesis, Stanley, Australia: 2018, pp. 206–8.

[74] See Geoffrey Cornelius, *The Moment of Astrology*, pp. 239–48.

[75] Rumi, Goodreads website, https://www.goodreads.com/quotes/551027-yesterday-i-was-clever-so-i-wanted-to-change-the [accessed 1 July 2019]

[76] See Frank C. Clifford, *The Solar Arc Handbook*, Flare Publications, London: 2018 for an up-to-date exploration of solar arc directions with many excellent examples and case studies.

[77] For a fuller amplification of soul in astrology, see Brian Clark, *Soul, Symbol and Imagination*, pp. 15–24.

[78] The primary movement of the Earth is the revolution on its axis.

[79] The word 'sect' comes from the Latin, suggesting cutting or making a division. In Hellenistic astrology, the term proposed a system whereby traditional planets were grouped into a day or

diurnal sect led by the Sun, or a night or nocturnal sect led by the Moon. The day team consists of the Sun, Jupiter, Saturn and Mercury when it rises before the Sun. The night team consists of the Moon, Venus, Mars and Mercury when it sets after the Sun. When Mercury is conjunct the Sun it changes its membership; therefore, when the progressed Sun and progressed Mercury are conjunct, Mercury will change sect in the progressed chart. As a symbol it is noteworthy, because it speaks about a differing orientation in our Mercurial development of ideas, language and communication.

[80] Nine is a lunar number and one third of the lunar cycle. The lunar cycle can be broken down into three cycles of nine years each, which also creates nine sub-cycles in the three cycles of the progressed Moon.

[81] See Brian Clark, *The Family Legacy*.

[82] Gret Baumann, Carl Jung's daughter, was an astrologer. She used a time of 7.32 p.m. with LMT or -0.37.20 as the time zone. However, when Jung was born, parts of Switzerland including Kesswil, used a time zone set for Bern, called BMT (Bern Mean Time) or -0.29.44. Baumann's chart for her father yields the last degrees of Scorpio on the MC; however, using BMT with this time moves the MC into Sagittarius. Other times have been used over the years, but most place the Sun near the Descendant. It is curious that Jung's MC wavers on the cusp of Scorpio and Sagittarius, as his worldly work highlighted the psychological motifs of descent and rebirth, unconsciousness and knowing. To continue the tradition of the 29° Scorpio MC, I am using the chart Liz Greene proposes for Carl Jung in her book *The Astrological World of Jung's Liber Novus*, Routledge, London; 2018, p. 164.

[83] C.G. Jung, *Memories, Dreams, Reflections*, translated by Richard and Clara Winston, Pantheon Books, New York, NY: 1963, p. 30.

[84] C.G. Jung, *Memories, Dreams, Reflections*, p. 199.

[85] Ibid.

[86] Ibid, p. 175.

[87] Ibid, p. 179.

[88] Barbara Hannah, *Jung: His Life and Work*, Michael Joseph, London: 1977, p. 236.

[89] Brian Clark, *From the Moment We Met*, pp. 202–3.

[90] Ibid, pp. 208–15.

[91] Aristotle, *Meteorologica*, translated by H.D.P. Lee. Loeb Classical Library, Harvard University Press, Cambridge, MA: 1989, Book I, p. 30.

[92] This phrase is credited to Joseph Addison, an English essayist, dramatist, politician and publisher. He suggested that this birthday salutation was used by the ancient Romans.

[93] The word was coined in the 17th century to describe the anxiety and pain of Swiss mercenaries who were fighting away from home.

[94] This method was popularized by James Eshelman, a sidereal astrologer who promoted the sidereal zodiac. While he suggests that the solar return can be in error by one day at age 72, this would depend upon how one interpreted 'error'. Embedded within the tropical degree is the notion of movement; hence I would not necessarily see this as an error. His ideas are expressed in his book *Interpreting Solar Returns*, ACS Publications, San Diego, CA: 1986.

[95] Ray Merriman supports the method of choosing a location in which to experience your birthday and consciously co-create the horoscope. See Ray Merriman, *The Solar Return Book of Prediction*, Seek It Publications, Birmingham, MI: 1977.

[96] The symbolism of the late Scorpio and early Sagittarius MC is again highlighted.

[97] Chiron was rising in this chart at 8♍32, transiting his natal Pluto.

[98] See https://en.wikipedia.org/wiki/John_F._Kennedy_Jr._plane_ crash [accessed 1 December 2019].

[99] See Brian Clark, *The Sibling Constellation*, pp. 64–89.

[100] See Brian Clark, *From the Moment We Met*, pp. 201–22.

[101] Marc Edmund Jones, *The Guide to Horoscope Interpretation*, Theosophical Publishing House, Wheaton, IL: 1974.

[102] Albert Einstein and Michele Besso, *Correspondences*, 1903–1955, Hermann, Paris: 1972, letter dated 21 March 1955.

Praise for Brian Clark's recent publication

Soul, Symbol and Imagination: the Artistry of Astrology

In *Soul, Symbol and Imagination* Brian Clark shows the inestimable riches that lie in the intersection of astrology and depth psychology. Like jewels waiting to catch the light, each theme he treats reveals the value of the creative imagination in the art of astrology. Steeped in myths and metaphors, this book shows the depth of his craft and the fertile fields of his imagination. This is a book I will return to often so to discover a new gem.

– Safron Rossi, editor of *Jung on Astrology*

Soul, Symbol, and Imagination is a rare offering in the world of astrology: reflective and thoughtful, full of the kind of wisdom that accumulates over years of immersion in myth and imagination alongside patient and empathic relating to human beings and their dilemmas and difficulties. Each chapter explores a symbol or theme, to which Brian brings to bear rich stories and images that allow the symbol to lead us into encounter with soul. By turns moving, humorous, and wise, this book returns us again and again to the reservoir of imagination that continuously feeds and refreshes our art. It is my first recommendation to anyone who wants to practice a humane, relational, imaginative form of astrology.

– Jason Holley, psychotherapist and astrologer

When one is willing to dive deeply, the treasures to be found in astrology are vast, yet easily resist language that would do them proper justice. Nonetheless, this art that we are so privileged to practise at this time in history needs voices that reverence the soul poetically while providing both mythic and quotidian guidance for its incarnational trajectory. The subtitle for Brian Clark's *Soul, Symbol and Imagination* is *The Artistry of Astrology*, and the author is an artist at the core of his being. There's an eloquent, grace-full alchemist in his bones, and that comes through in this deep and magnificent contribution to the field.

– Hadley Fitzgerald, co-author of
Images of Soul: Reimagining Astrology

My friend, Brian Clark, has written the best book on astrology that I have ever read. He shows himself a deep master of this quiet and enchanting art. Astrology's value is hidden to the modern mind, but if you can grant yourself the favour of leaving that hard world behind and open to a realm of love and magic, you will be rewarded beyond imagining by reading this book. It now goes on my special shelf of books to live by.

– Thomas Moore, author of *Care of the Soul*

There are few contemporary astrologers who can match Brian Clark's range and depth of experience as professional consultant and as teacher, and this work is a precious distillation of his life-vocation. This is not a how-to manual, although the innovative use of dream-work is certain to inspire a new generation of teachers, while the case studies are insightful and moving. The light of astrological imagination is traced through thought-provoking allusions and references to myth, archetypes and poetry. Brian Clark plumbs the creative depth of the mystery within the art of astrology, which is the mystery of Symbol and Soul.

– Geoffrey Cornelius, author of *The Moment of Astrology*

This book is an immense achievement, a uniquely contemplative, evocative and mature exposition of the embodied and ensouled practice of astrology. Beautifully written and crafted, Brian writes from the depth of his own experience, amply demonstrating the mystery, magic and power of the psychic encounter which can occur in astrological work, when the imagination is released and the archetypal myths come alive.

– Clare Martin, author of *Alchemy: the Soul of Astrology*

Soul, Symbol and Imagination is a must read for any modern astrologer. The book is brimming over with lucid, inspiring insights grounded in a kind of depth and wisdom which can only be attained after a lifetime of rich engagement and reflection. Clark is sharing this finely-honed gift with us as he ruminates mindfully on the big topics that infuse our work as astrologers: time, symbol, imagination, fate and many more. If you're like me, you'll find yourself underlining passage after passage to return to and reflect on for years to come.

– Tony Howard, Astrology University

Astro*Synthesis

Astro*Synthesis was founded in Melbourne in 1986 as an astrological education programme. Since that time Astro*Synthesis has consistently offered an in-depth training programme into the application of astrology from a psychological perspective. The foundation of the course has been constructed to utilize astrology as a tool for greater awareness of the self, others and the world at large.

From 1986 to 2010, Astro*Synthesis offered its dynamic four-year teaching program in the classroom. Astro*Synthesis now offers the complete program of 12 modules through distance learning.

For a detailed syllabus or more information on Astro*Synthesis E-Workbooks, E- Booklets or reports please visit our website:

www.astrosynthesis.com.au

CPSIA information can be obtained
at www.ICGtesting.com
Printed in the USA
BVHW031424140722
642159BV00006B/147